Latin Legal Phrases, Terms and Maxims as Applied by the Malaysian Courts

Latin Legal Phrases, Terms and Maxims as Applied by the Malaysian Courts

Compiled and Edited
By

Hunud Abia Kadouf
&
Kafayat Motilewa Quadri

PARTRIDGE

To order additional copies of this book, contact
Toll Free 800 101 2657 (Singapore)
Toll Free 1 800 81 7340 (Malaysia)
orders.singapore@partridgepublishing.com

www.partridgepublishing.com/singapore

A

A COMMUNI OBSERVANTIA NON EST RECCDENDUM ET MINI-ME MUTANDA SUNT QUA CERTAM, INTERPRETATIONEM common observance is not to be departed from, and things which have a certain meaning are to be changed as little as possible.

A CONSILIIS of counsel; a counsellor. The term is used in the civil law by some writers instead of a responsis.

A DATO from the date.

A FORTIORI 'from stronger reasoning.' It means something can happen with much greater probability. For instance, if a pound of gunpowder can blow up a house, *afortiori* a hundredweight must be able to do it. It is an epithet for any conclusion or inference, which is much stronger than another. *In Re Maria Huberdina Hertogh; Adrianus Petrus Hertogh and Anor v. Amina Binte Mohamed and ORS. [1951] 17 MLJ at pg. 17; Re Kana Moona Syed Abubakar Deceased. Khatijah Nachiar v. Sultan Alauddin and the Assistant Official Assignee, Penang & Others [1940] 9 MLJ 4 at pg. 8; S. Seethainayagee Ammal v. M.R.M. Ramasamy Chettiar [1940] 9 MLJ 289 at pg. 290; Abdul Rahman Talib v. Seenivasagam & Anor [1966] 2 MLJ 66 at pg. 73*

A LATERE from the side. In connection with the succession to property the term means 'collateral'. Collateral. Used in this sense in speaking of the succession to property from, on, or at the side collaterally. A latere as-cendit (jus). The right ascends collaterally. Justices of the Curia Regis are described as a latere regis residentes, sitting at the side of the King. In the civil law, a synonym for a transverso, across. Applied also to a process or proceeding, meaning out of the regular or lawful course; incidentally or casually. From the side of ; denoting closeness of intimacy or connection, as a court held before auditors specialiter a latere regis dstinatis.

A MENSA ET THORO 'From bed and board'. This Latin phrase is usually used in family law. A divorce *a mensa et thoro* is a separation of the parties by act of law, rather than a dissolution of the marriage. It may be granted for the causes of extreme cruelty or desertion of the wife by the husband. *Koh Teng Lam v. Elsie Koh Chen Chee & Anor [1976] 1 MLJ 103 =PG 105*

A MORTE death; after death.

A NON POSSE AD NON ESSE SEQUITUR ARGUMENTUM NECESSARIE NEGATIVE, LICET NON AFFIRMATIVE from impossibility to non-existence, the inference follows necessarily in the negative, though not in the affirmative it also means from the fact that a thing cannot be done, you necessarily draw the conclusion that it is not done ; but from the fact that a thing has not been done, you are not justified in concluding that it cannot be done. An argument flows necessarily in the negative from 'It cannot be' to 'It is not', though not in the affirmative. If a thing is impossible, an argument in the negative may be deduced--viz that it has no existence, but an argument in the affirmative cannot be deduced--viz that if a thing is possible, it is in existence.

A POSTERIORI 'from later', It is an argument derived from subsequent event; an argument founded on experiment or observation; a method of reasoning 'from the consequence to the antecedent; a Baconian method of reasoning.

A PRIORI 'from earlier'. It describes an argument derived from previous event.

A QUO from which. A court a quo (also written 'a qua') is a court from which a cause has been removed. The judge a quo is the judge in such court. A term used, with the correlative ad quem (to which) in expressing the computation of time, and also of distance in space. Thus, dies a quo, the day from which and dies ad quern, the day to which, a period of time is computed. So, terminus a quo, the point or limit from which, and terminus and quem, the point or limit to which, a distance or passage in space is reckoned.

A RETRO in arrears; behind.

A VINCULO MATRIMONII It is a type of divorce. A *vinculo matrimonii* means to be freed from the bonds of matrimony. It is an absolute and final divorce. Such a divorce generally enables the parties to marry again. *Attorney-General of Ceylon v. Reid [1965] 2 MLJ* 34 = Pg. 35

AB ACTIS an officer of the court who records the proceedings.

AB AGENDO unable to act; incapacitated for business transactions; disabled from transacting business; A person becomes ab agendo if he is incapacitated to transact any business through old age, mental incapacity or for any other reason.

AB ANTE in advance; before.

AB ANTECENDENTE in advance; before hand.

AB ANTIQUO from ancient times; from old times.

AB ASSUETIS if a person neglects to insist on his right, he is deemed to have abandoned it.

AB EPISTOLIS an officer having charge of correspondence.

AB EXTRA beyond, without, from without.

AB EXTRA 'from outside'; it can be oncerning a case whereby a person may have received some funding from a 3rd party. This funding may have been considered ab extra.

AB INCONVENIENTE 'From hardship, from what is inconvenient'. *Madhavan Nair v. Government of Malaysia [1975] 2 MLJ 286=Pg. 288*

AB INCONVENIENTI from inconvenience, from hardship. An argument based upon the hardship of the case and the inconvenience to which a different course of reasoning would lead.

AB INITIO 'from the beginning'. It is used generally to indicate that a document or an event — e.g., a contract, statute, deed, marriage, etc. — was effective from and relates back to its inception or creation. The term *void ab initio* establishes that an act or document never had any valid or effective existence. *Ahmad Bin Udon & Anor v. Ng Aik Chong [1970] 1MLJ 82, at 82, 83, 84 Contract V.oid), Goh Yew & Anor v. Soh Kian Tee [1970] 1 MLJ 138, at 139, 140,141, 142, Hassan v. Ismail [1970] 1 MLJ 210, at 210, 211, 213 Kian Hin & Co.Ltd. v. Kan Yeow Weng [1970] 1 MLJ 273, at 274*

AB INTESTATO succession to the properties of a person who has not made a will; from an intestate meaning that property of a person dying without leaving a will is distributed by the Administrators within the legal framework. Any person entitled to such property is said to have acquired such property ab intesto.

AB INTRA from within.

AB INVITO against one's will; unwillingly; against one's wishes.

ABALIENATO transfer of property, alienation.

ABATAMENTUM an abatement of freehold; an entry upon lands by way of interposition between the death of the ancestor and the entry of the heir.

ABDICARE to renounce; relinquish formally; as, to abdicate leadership.

ABESSE in the civil law, to be absent ; to be away from a place. Said of a person who was extra continentia urbis (beyond the suburbs of the city).

ABIGERE to drive out, to expel by force ; to produce abortion.

ABSIT INVIDE let there be no ill will or bad feelings.

ABSIT God forbid, let it be far from the hearts of the faithful.

ABSOLUTE SENTENTIA plain language.

ABSQUE HOC without this; the negative part of a plea. It is a way of presenting the negative portion of a plea.

ABSQUE damage without injury and absque impetitione vasti (without impeachment of waste).

ABUNDANS CAUTELA NON extreme caution does no harm. The maxim is used generally in cases where additional or descriptive words are used out of great caution in deeds, legal documents or Acts. Such superfluous words do no harm in the case of a deed or document as it may be read and construed without the superfluous wordings. Nonetheless such a practice may not be encouraged in conveyancing documents and may be an exception to the generality expounded in the maxim. *Lee Chin Hock v Public Prosecutor [1972] 2 MLJ 30 at 33 Per Ong Hock Sim FJ*

ABUNDANS CAUTELA NON NOCET 'excess of precaution can do no harm' *Re Abdul Razak Bin Rouse [1974] 2 MLJ 164, Pg.166*

AC ETIAM and also.

ACCESSORIUM NON DUCIT, SED SEQUITUR SUUM PRINCIPALE that which is the accessory or incident does not lead, but follows its principal. The incident does not draw, but follows, its principal. The accessory right does not lead, but follows its principal. Rent is incident to the reversion, and by a grant of the reversion thereat will pass Law of Property Act 1925, s 141(1). The law relative to contracts and mercantile transactions likewise presents many examples of the rule. Thus the obligations of the surety is accessory to that of the principal, and is extinguished by the release or discharge of the latter; but the converse does not hold. So, likewise, interest of money is accessory to the principal, and must, in legal language, follow its nature.

ACCESSORIUM SEQUITURE PRINCIPALE the accessory follows its principal. It also means where there is no principal there can be no accessory. The accessory does not carry the principal. The accessory right does not lead, but follows its principal.

ACCESSORIUS SEQUITUR NATURAM SUI PRINCIPALIS an accessory follows the nature of his principal. An application of the maxim results in the proposition that an accessary cannot be guilty of a higher crime than his principal. An accessory follows the nature of its principal.

ACCIDERE to fall, fall in, come to hand, happen. Judgment is sometimes given against an executor or administrator to be satisfied out of assets quando acciderint ; ie why they shall come to hand.

ACCOMORNODATUM in the law of Bailments, a loan for use without pay where the thing is to be returned in specie.

ACCOMPLICE VEL NON 'or not' and on its own is used by the courts in reference to the existence or nonexistence of an issue for determination. So in the instance of '*accomplice vel non*', it means the determination of whether a person is an accomplice to a crime or not. *Tan Kheng Ann & ors. v. The Public Prosecutor [1965] 2 MLJ 108 = Pg. 121*

ACCUMULATIO ACTIONUM accumulation of actions ie the person who has a joint interest or has been aggrieved may com-mence an action jointly. A widow and her children may under this maxim, commence a dependency claim against the negligent party for the death of the husband and father.

ACCUMULO to add to a heap, accumulate, amass.

ACCUSARE NEMO SE DEBET NISI CORAM DEO no one is bound to accuse himself except before God. It also means no one is compelled to accuse himself, except before God.

ACCUSATOR accusor, plaintiff.

ACIO UT FACIAS 'i do, that you may do' or a type of contract wherein one party agrees to do work for the other, in order that the second party can then perform some work for the first in exchange.

ACTA EXTERIORA INDICANT INTERIORA SECRETA acts indicates the intention, where a general license is given by the law, the law judges by the subsequent act with what intent the original act was done. Or external actions show internal secrets. The law, in some cases, judges of a man's previous intentions by his subsequent acts. On this principle, if a man abuse an authority given him by the law, he becomes a trespasser ab initio. Or external acts indicate undisclosed thoughts. Therefore, where a criminal act is done by several persons in furtherance of a common intention, each of such persons is liable for the criminal act as if it were done by him alone. Common intention is usually inferred, since direct evidence is almost an impossibility, from act and conduct

acta exteriora indicant interiora secreta if the inference is a necessary inference deducible from the circumstances of the case, but not, as was suggested by the trial court, by evidence of an identical act or deed.

ACTA PUBLICS things of general knowledge and concern; matters transacted before certain public officers.

ACTIO ARBITRARIA action depending on the discretion of the judge.

ACTIO CALUMNIAE an action for malicious prosecution.

ACTIO CIVILIV a civil action.

ACTIO COMMODATI an action arising from a commodati contract. The person who has commenced such an action seeks the return of the goods gratuitously lent to another and for the recovery of any expenses required for the re-delivery and preservation of the goods.

ACTIO CONTRARIO a counter or cross action.

ACTIO CRIMINALIS a criminal action.

ACTIO DIRECTA a direct action.

ACTIO EMPTI an action to compel a seller to perform his obligations; under a contract of sale, for example, the purchaser may commence an actio empti for the delivery of goods in accordance with the terms of the contract.

ACTIO EXLOCATO an action by a hirer or against a hirer.

ACTIO FURTI an action of theft.

ACTIO HONORATIA an honorary action.

ACTIO in the civil law, an action or suit, a right or cause of action. Term means both the proceeding to enforce a right in a court and the right itself, which is sought to be enforced. It also means an action through which a person commences proceedings in a legally constituted court for an order against another person or party requiring him to fulfill some obligations. Arising from four sources, (contracts, quasi contracts, delicts and quasi delicts) some are either private or personal actions.

ACTIO MANDATI an action to enforce contracts of mandate or obligations.

ACTIO MIXTA a mixed action.

ACTIO NON ACCREVIT INFRA SEX ANNOS the action has not accrued within six years.

ACTIO PERPETUA an action without limitation period.

ACTIO PERSONALIS MORITOR CUM PERSONA 'a personal action dies with the person'. An action for a purely personal right (as for a bodily injury, or injury to the reputation), which must be brought, if at all, by the party injured, and is not transmissible to his representatives; according to this maxim, a personal action dies with the person. But this maxim must not be understood to apply in cases of breach of contract causing damage to a man's estate through the medium of a personal injury, as by incapacitating him from work, or depriving his family of his support. *Karupanan v. Empire Theatre [1941] MLJ 81, Riyna Anak Kassi v. Wong Sie King [1970] 2 MLJ82, at 84 (Action Against the Estate of a Deceased Person)*

ACTIO PIGNORATITIA an action founded on the contract of pledge.

ACTIO POPULARIS means popular or public actions arise out of circumstances affecting the public interest or welfare and such action may be commenced by a citizen as a matter of right.

ACTIO REALIS a real action.

ACTIO TEMPORALIS an action, which must be brought within a limited time.

ACTIO TUTELAE action founded on the duties or obligations of a guardian or ward.

ACTIO UTILIS a beneficial or equitable action; an action founded on analogical imitations of defined legal obligations; an action founded equity rather than strict law.

ACTIO VENDITI an action against the seller to fulfill the obligations of the contract of sale.

ACTIO VULGARIS a legal action.

ACTIONARE to bring an action; to prosecute; or sue. (From actio an action)

ACTIONES DIRECTOE an action founded on accurately defined legal obligations.

ACTIONES PENALES an action to the end of which penal sanctions are attached.

ACTIONUM GENERA MAXIME SUNT SERVANDA the varieties of actions are especially, to be preserved. It also means every action must be in its proper form. Or the correct form of action should be followed. The forms of action were abolished by the Common Law Procedure Act 1852.

ACTOR DOMINAE manager of his master's farm.

ACTOR a pleader or advocate, one who acts for another in case (as) Actor ecclesiae an advocate for a Church; one who protects the temporal interests of a Church. It also means a plaintiff contrasted with defendant. The term is also used of a party who for the time being, sustains the burden of proof or has the initiative in the suit or one who has to commence in the suit.

ACTOR SEQUITUR FORUM the plaintiff follows the forum of the thing'. The plaintiff follows the Court of the Defendant. The plaintiff follows the Court of the property.

ACTORI INCUMBIT PROBATIO 'On the plaintiff rests the proving'. The burden of proof, Roman law

ACTUM something done or a deed.

ACTUS CURIAE NEMINEM GRAVABIT This maxim is founded upon justice and good sense and affords a safe and certain guide for the administration of the law and accommodation. 'The recitals demonstrate the nature and statute of the Inns at the time and the words 'being desirous of perpetuating, as far as in us lies, the welfare of this Realm of England' are in indication of the purpose of the gift. At the top of 234 the property is described, and the words 'Halls, Houses, Edifices, Cloisters, Buildings, Chambers, Gardens, Court's, and further down, on 235, the words 'Church, Edifices and Buildings of the Church ... commonly called the Temple Church, present a picture which is familiar today. The Habendum clause on 237 after the words appropriate to convey the fee simple proceeds as follows in the translation, 'Which said inns, Messuages, Houses, Edifices, Chambers and other premises we will, and by these presents for ourselves, our heirs and successors, strictly (10) command, shall serve for the Entertainment and Education of the students and Professors of the Laws aforesaid, residing in the same Inns for ever'. The Latin words from 'strictly command' onwards are 'mandamus pro hospitacione & educacione studencium & professorum legum preditarum in eisdem hospitiis perpetuis temporibus futuris commorantium deservire'. It has been suggested by counsel on both sides that the word 'hospitacione' would be better translated as 'accomodation', using that word in its widest sense, rather than 'entertainment', and the words 'professorum legum' would be better translated as 'those who profess the Laws' rather than 'Professors of the Laws'; while the word 'commorantium' would be better translated as 'abiding rather than 'residing'. It appears to me, though I make no pretence of Latin scholarship, that these suggestions are correct and I accept them.

ACTUS DEI an act of God.

ACTUS DEI NEMINI NOCET the act of God does injury to no one. The general rule must be applied with due caution. (Ld Raym 433) Thus where, after the indictment and arraignment, the jury charged, and evidence given on a trial for a capital offence, one of the jurymen be-came incapable through illness of proceeding to verdict, the Court of oyer and terminer discharged the jury, charged a fresh jury with the prisoner, and convicted him, although it was argued that actus Dei nemini nocet, and that the sudden illness was a Godsend, of which the prisoner ought to have the benefit.

ACTUS LEGITIMI NON RECIPIUNT MODUM a maxim meaning 'legal actions do not admit a limitation. Lawful actions do not admit a limitation. For a case in which an unsuccessful attempt was made to limit the motives for which a man could lawfully extract from under his land water percolating through undefined channels.

ACTUS an act or action.

ACTUS REUS a criminal act; the "guilty act" or the "deed of crime"; the objective act, which defines or constitutes a crime; e.g., the killing of another is the actus reus of murder or manslaughter. *Public Prosecutor v. Datuk Haji Harun Bin Haji Idris & ors [1977] 1 MLJ 180=Pg. 180*

AD AE QUAE FREQUENTIUS ACCIDUNT 'the laws are adapted to those cases which occur more frequently'. *Singer Sewing Machine Co. v. Low Kam & Others [1949] 15 MLJ 136 pg.137*

AD AUDIENDUM to hear.

AD BARRAM to the bar, at the bar.

AD CERTUM EST QUOD CERTUM REDDI POTEST 'if something is capable of being made certain, it should be treated as certain'. *Tasir Bin Itam Dris v. Jamila & Others [1939] 8 MLJ 190 at Pg. 191*

AD COELUM 'to the sky'. Abbreviated from Cuius est solum eius est usque ad coelum et ad infernos which translates to "[for] whoev.er owns [the] soil, [it] is his all the way [up] to Heaven and [down] to Hell." The principle that the owner of a parcel of land also owns the air abov.e and the ground below the parcel.

AD COLLIGENDA BONA 'to collect the goods'.

AD COLLIGENDUM or collecting as an administrator.

AD COMPARENDUM to appear.

AD CULPAM until misbehavior.

AD CURIAM to court; at a court.

AD CUSTAGIA at the costs.

AD DAMNUM to the damage.

AD DEFENDENDUM to defend.

AD DEPOSITUM for (safe)keeping.

AD DIEM at the day; on the appointed day.

AD EA QUAE FREQUENTIUS ACCIDUNT JURA ADAPTANTUR the laws are adapted to those cases, which most frequently occur. The laws are adapted to those cases, which more frequently occur. Laws cannot be so worded as to include every case, which may arise, but it is sufficient if they apply to those things which most frequently happen.

AD EFFECTUM to the effect, to the end.

AD EXCAMBIUM for exchange.

AD EXITUM at the end of the pleadings; at issue

AD FACIENDUM to do.

AD FIDEM subjects born in allegiance are said to be born ad fidem

AD FILUM at the center.

AD FINEM to the finish; to the end; at or near the end.

AD FORTIORI with stronger reason.

AD HOC 'for this; for this particular purpose only'. It is something created or done for a particular purpose as necessary. It. Someone or something selected or designated for a special purpose, as an ad hoc committee; also used to describe an act done at the spur of the moment, as an ad hoc solution or an ad hoc demonstration. *Malayawata Steel Berhad v. Government of Malaysia & Anor [1977] 2 MLJ 215=Pg. 215, Malayawata Steel bhd v. Government of Malaysia & Anor[1975] 1 MLJ 22=Pg. 22, Melayu Raya Press Limited v. W.L.Blythe The Colonial Secretary [1951] 17 MLJ at Pg. 90; (Certiotari), Chan Fook Wah v. Board of Architects [1965] 2 MLJ 7 = Pg. 8*

AD HOC for particular purpose. Made, established, acting or concerned with a particular and or purpose.

AD HOMINEM 'at the person' or (Relating) to the (particular) person; to the person (with reference to personal argument); to the man, personal. It may involve attacking an opponent's character rather than answering his argument.

AD HONOREM for the sake of glory.

AD IDEM 'to the same end or effect'. Having the same idea or understanding; being on the same wavelength. (e.g., the parties were never ad idem — the parties never had the same understanding.) *The Pangkalan Susu/Permina 3001[1977] 1 MLJ 141=Pg. 144, Acme Canning SDN BHD v. Lee Kim Seng [1975] 2 MLJ 32=Pg. 33, Alice Wee v. Yeo Gek Lang [1978] 1 MLJ 196 =Pg. 198, Jagathesan v.Linggi Plantations Ltd [1969] 2 MLJ 257 (Breach of Contract), Tan Hong Tee v.s. P. & 0. Banking Corporation Ltd [1932] 1 MLJ 68 = Pg.71, 72, Goh Mui Teck v. See Eng Kiat [1967] 2 MLJ 53 Pg. 53*

AD IDEM with a common understanding.

AD INDE thereunto.

AD INFINITUM 'to infinity' i.e. forever and ever, without limit. *Chop Soon Hoe v. Tan Kee [1976] 1 MLJ 172=Pg. 173, Mak Sik Kwong v. Minister of Home Affairs,Malaysia(No. 2)[1975] 2 MLJ175=Pg. 180, Yew Lean Finance Dev.elopment (M) SDN BHD v. Director of Lands and Mines, Penang[1977] 2 MLJ 45=pg. 47*

AD INFINITUM to infinity; endlessly; on and on without end; through an infinite series. Without limit; forever. *Mak Sik Kwong v Minister of Home Affairs, Malaysia (No 2) [1975] 2 MLJ 175 at 180 Per Abdoolcader J*

AD INQUIRENDUM to inquire.

AD INSTANTIAM at the instance.

AD INTERIM in the interval (as) ad interim injunction. In the meantime.

AD LARGUM at large; at liberty.

AD LIB according to pleasure at pleasure. Abbreviation of ad libitum

AD LIBITUM Abbreviated as ad lib; at pleasure.

AD LITEM 'for suit'. It is a phrase used to refer to a person apointed for the purposes of representing another in a suit. Such a person is normally appointed by a court to represent a minor or legally incompetent person in a litigation. *Re Sim Thong Lai [1955] 21 MLJ at Pg. 26; Re Zainab Binte Mat Diah, Deed [1951] 17 MLJ at Pg. 145; (Probate and Administration Enactment), Sithambaran Chettyar v. Chong Fatt [1939] 8 MLJ 230 at Pg. 230; Land (Estoppel), Tan Kheng Kuan v. Lim Chein Teik [1965] 1 MLJ 116 = Pg. 116, RE Man Bin Mihat [1965] 2 MLJ 1 =Pg. 2*

AD at; by; for; near; on account of; to; until; upon.

AD LITERAM to the latter.

AD LONGUM at length.

AD MAJOREM CAUTELAM 'with greater security or with more caution'. *Menaka v. Lum Kum Chum [1977] 1 MLJ 91=pg. 94,*

AD MANDATUM by direction.

AD MANUM at hand and ready for use.

AD MODUM in the same way as.

AD MORTEM to the death.

AD NAUSEAM so far as to nauseate; disgusting; to nausea (to an excessive degree.

AD NOCUMENTUM to the nuisance hurt or injury.

AD OFFICIUM JUSTICIARIORUM SPECTAT, UNICUQUE CORAM EIS PLACITANTI JUSTIAM EXHIBERE it is the duty of justices to administer justice to everyone seeking it from them.

AD OPUS to the work.

AD OSTIUM ECCLESIAE 'at the church door'. It used to be one of the five species of dower recognized at the common law. *In The Estate of Yeow Kian Kee (Deceased) [1949] 15 MLJ 171 Pg.172*

AD PERSONAM to the person; personal.

AD PROMISOR a surety, guarantor, one who binds himself for another; one who adds his own promise to the promise given by the principal debtor.

AD PROSEQUENDUM an administrator appointed to prosecute or defend a certain action.

AD PROTOCOLLUM to the record.

AD QUAESTIONEM JURIS RESPONDENT JUDICES, AD QUESTIONEM FACTI RESPONDENT JURATORES as regards cases tried by a Judge and jury, the Judge does not decide questions of fact and the jury do not decide questions of Law. It also means that it is the office of the Judge to instruct the jury in points of law--of the Jury to decide on matters of fact. To questions of fact judges do not answer ; to questions of law the jury do not answer. Two instances must suffice to show the application of this maxim. Thus, there are two requisites to the validity of deed. (1) that it be sufficient in law, on which the Court decides; (2) that certain matters of fact, as sealing and delivery, be duly proved, on which it is the province of the jury (or, if the judge is sitting without a jury, for the judge acting as a juryman would act) to determine.

AD QUEM computation of time or distance.

AD QUESTIONEM LEGIS RESPONDENT JUDICES to questions of law the judges answer.

AD QUOD DAMNUM 'according to the harm'. Used in tort law. Implies that the reward or penalty ought to correspond to the damage suffered or inflicted.

AD RECOGNOSCENDUM to recognise.

AD RECTUM to do right.

AD REFERENDUM for further consideration.

AD REM 'to the matter or to the purpose'. It is something that is relevant to what is being done or discussed at the time. *Peninsular Land Development Sdn. Bhd. v. K. Ahmad [1970] 1 MLJ 129, at 150, 151, Director-General of Inland Rev.enue v. T.M. SDN BHD [1973] 1 MLJ71=Pg.73, Kersah La'usin v. Sikin Menan [1966] 2 MLJ 20 at Pg. 22, Temenggong Securities Ltd& Anor v. Registrar of Titles & ors [1974] 2 MLJ 45=Pg.47*

AD REM to the matter; to the point.

AD RESPONDENDUM for answering, to answer.

AD SECTAM at the suit of. Commonly abbreviated as ads. Ad terminum annorum: For a term of years. Ad tune et ibidem: at the time and in the same place.

AD TESTIFICANDUM 'to testify' or 'for testifying'. It means to give evidence, bear witness to, It is used to describe the process by which witnesses are compelled to testify; e.g., by a subpoena ad testificandum. Under the law of evidence, it is a process to cause a witness to appear and give testimony, commanding him to lay aside all pretences and excuses, and appear before a court or magistrate therein named, at a time therein mentioned, to testify for the party named, under a penalty therein mentioned. *Law Society of Singapore v. Chan Chow Wang [1975] 1 MLJ 59=Pg. 65*

AD VALOREM 'in proportion to its value'. It is a term used in the law of taxation to describe a tax assessed according to the value of the item or property, as in property taxes or sales taxes. Also, in commercial law in general, it is used to describe certain duties, called ad v.alorem duties, which are lev.ied on commodities at certain rates per centum on their value. *Cheah Choon Gan & ors V. Registrar of Titles, Kedah [1973] 1 MLJ 107=Pg.10, Chin Choy & ORS V. The Collector OF Stamp Duties [1978] 1 MLJ 46 =Pg.46, Gold Clause and Containerisation [1970] 2 MLJ XLIII, at XLIV., Pernas Securities SDN BHD v. The Collector of Stamp Duties [1976] 2 MLJ 188=Pg. 188,190, Tay Geok Yap & Anor v. Commissioner of Stamps, Singapore [1966] 2 MLJ 255 at Pg. 256, Lim Ker v. Chew Seok Tee [1967] 2 MLJ 253 Pg.254*

AD VALOREM according to the value. According to the valuation. Ad valorem duties are always estimated at a certain per cent on the valuation of the property, as opposed to fixed or specific duties. Cheah Choon Gan & Ors v Registrar of Titles, Kedah [1973] 1 MLJ 107 at 108 Per Azmi LP, Allied Signal Inc & Anor The commisioner of Stamp Duties [1988] 1 MLJ 506 at 508 Per Grimberg JC

ADDENDA additions.

ADDICERE in the civil law, to adjudge or condemn; to assign, allot, or deliver; to sell. In the Roman law, addico was one of the three words used to express the extent of the civil jurisdiction of the practors.

ADEMPTIO revocation of a legacy. 'ADEMPTIO' 'Ademption' defined, Act 10, 1865, s 139 ; Act 39, 1925, s 152. A taking away or revocation (applied to legacies). Recalling or cancellation of a legacy; where there is a specific legacy, and the subject-matter does not remain the property of the testator at his death, the legacy is said to/be adeemed; ie, the subject-matter being gone from the testator's estate, the gift also is gone; so, there is an ademption when the purpose for which the specific legacy was given has been otherwise provided for by the testator. (See Tomlin, Stroud) Ademption is complete or partial revocation of a benefit given by will, by a subsequent event in the testator's lifetime, not being a revocation by a testamentary instrument or in a manner authorised by law.

ADHIBERE DILIGENTIAM to use care.

ADJOURNAMENTUM EST AD AD DIEM DICERE SEU DIEM DARE an adjournment is to appoint a day or to give a day. This refers to Parliament, and distinguishes ad-journment from prorogation.

ADJOURNMENT SINE DIE adjournment without a day When an assembly adjourns without setting a date for its next meeting. affidavit he has sworn. It is a formal statement of fact.

ADJUNCTUM ACCESSORIUM an accessory.

ADSCRIPTUS added, annexed, bound by or in writing, enrolled, registered.

ADVENTITIA BONA goods which fall to a man otherwise than by inheritance.

ADVERSUS against.

ADVERTO to turn towards, direct one's attention to, attract.

ADVOCARE to defend; to call one's aid.

ADVOCATI pleaders; speakers.

ADVOCATIA territorial jurisdiction of advocates.

ADVOCATUS DIABOLI devil's advocate.

ADVOCATUS a pleader; a narrator.

ADVOCO to summon / call in an advisor.

AEDES a house; place of habitation.

AEDIFICARE IN TUO PROPRIO SOLO NON LICET QUOD ALTERI NOCEAT it is not lawful to build on one's own land what may injure another. It also means it is not permitted to build upon one's own land what may be injurious to another. So an action lies if, by an erection on his own land, a man causes a nuisance by obstructing another's ancient lights.

AEQUITAS EST CORRECTIO LEGIS GENERALITER LATAE QUA PARTE DEFICIT equity is the correction of that where in the law by reason of its generality, is deficient. It also means equity is a correction of the general law in the part where it is defective.

AEQUITAS EST QUASI AEQUALITAS equity is as it were equality; equity is a species of equality or equalization. Equity favours true equality both of rights and liabilities dividing burdens and benefits in equal shares. On this principle are based the right of contribution between co-sureties; equity's preference of a tenancy in common over a joint tenancy (where the survivor scoops the pool); and the rule that if a power of appointment in the nature of a trust is not exercised the objects of the power take in equal shares. Likewise equality is a 'sort of justice'

AEQUITAS justice, fairness, equity.

AEQUITAS SEQUITUR equity follows the law. Equity generally operates by recognizing the legal rule and adding some further rule, remedy or other machinery of its own. Thus in the case of a trust Equity recognizes the legal title of the trustee but com-pels him to hold it on trust for the beneficiary. The maxim may also understood in the sense that equita-ble interests follow the characteristics of the corresponding legal estates unless this would be inequitable or inconvenient. Equity follows the law. Equity does not claim to override the law. Equity generally operates by recognis-ing the legal rule and adding some further rule, remedy or other machinery of its own. Thus in the case of a trust, equity recognises the legal title of the trustee but compels him to hold it on trust for the beneficiary.

AETAS INFANTILE the age next to infancy.

AETAS LEGITIMA lawful age.

AETAS age.

AETAS PERFECTA complete age.

AETAS PRIMA the first age.

AFFIDATIO swearing of the oath.

AFFINIS DICTUR, CUM DUE COGNATIONES, INTER SE DIVISE, PER NUPTIAS COPULANTUR, ET ALTERA AD ALTERIUS FINES ACCIDIT persons are said to be bound by affinity when two families, divided from one another, are united by marriage, and each approaches the confines of the other.

AFFINITAS AFFINITATIS remote relationship by marriage.

AFFINITAS relationship by marriage.

AFFIRMANTI, NON NEGANTI INCUMBIT PROBATIO the burden of proof rests upon him who affirms, not upon him who denies. It also means The reason for this rule is not that it is impossible to prove a negative, but that a negative does not admit of the simple and direct proof of which an affirmative is capable.

AGGREGATIO MENTIUM the moment a contract is complete; the meeting of minds of the contracting parties. It is the essence of every contract that there should be aggregatio mentium.

AGNATIO relationships through males.

ALBUS LIBER the White Book; a compilation of the law and customs of the City of London.

ALIA ENORMIA other wrongs; a declaration in trespass normally concluded as follows: 'and other wrongs to the Plaintiff then did'.

ALIA other things.

ALIAS A term used to indicate that a named person is also known or more familiar under another specified name. *Puran Singh v. Kehar Singh & Anor [1939] 8 MLJ 57 at Pg 58, 59; (Land), Jagathesan v. Linggi Plantations Ltd [1969] 2 MLJ 257; (Breach Of Contract), Re Chop Kwong Fook Seng [1934] 3 MLJ 34 at Pg. 37, 38, Lee Mion Alias Lee Miow v. Public Prosecutor Of Johore [1934] 3 MLJ 124 at Pg.124*

ALIAS DICTUS other dictus : Otherwise called. Alias writ: A second writ.

ALIAS 'otherwise called or otherwise. A term used to denote a second or further description of a person who has gone by two or more names. at another time ; in another place ; in other circumstances ; otherwise. It is used chiefly in judicial proceedings to connect the different names assumed by a person who attempts to conceal his true name and pass under a fictitious one ; thus, Simpson alias Smith means a person calling himself at one time or one place Smith, and at another Simpson.

ALIAS WRIT a second writ.

ALIBI An explanation or excuse offered to avert blame or guilt by an accused who claims that he was not present at the time or place alleged, or that other circumstances prove his innocence. *T'ng Ban Yick v. Rex [1940] 9 MLJ 153 at Pg. 154*

ALIEN AMI An alien born in, or the subject of, a friendly state. Hendrik Christiaan V.an Hoogstraten v. Low Lum Seng [1940] 9 MLJ 138 at Pg 142, 147

ALIENI FORI *In Re Maria Huberdina Hertogh; Adrianus Petrus Hertogh and Anor v. Amina Binte Mohamed and ors. [1951] 17 MLJ at Pg. 168; (Guardianship of Infants, Marriage Law)*

ALIENI GENERIS 'Of another kind'.

ALIENI GENERIS of another kind.

ALIENI JURIS under another's authority, under the control.

ALIENO SOLO in the land of another; on other's land.

ALIO INTUITIE with another intent than that alleged, ie not bona fide.

ALIO INTUITU in a different view; under a different aspect, with another view or object; with respect to another case of condition.

ALITER 'otherwise'; this term is frequently used to point out a difference between two decisions; as, a point of law has been decided in a particular way, in such a case, aliter in another case. *S. Muthucumaru v. S. Alkaff & Co. [1933] 2 MLJ 27 Pg. 28*

ALITER otherwise. a term often used in the Law reports.

ALIUNDE From another place; evidence given aliunde, as, when a will contains an ambiguity, in some cases, in order to ascertain the meaning of the testator, evidence aliunde will be receiv.ed. *Arthanarisami Chettiar & 2 Others v. Public Prosecutor [1940] 9 MLJ 67 at Pg 68; (Criminal), Raman Chettiar v. Palaniappa Chettiar & Anor [1939] 8 MLJ 132 at Pg 136; (Civ.il Procedure Code), Dharmaratna v. Dharmaratna [1939] 8 MLJ 238 at Pg 240; (Land Journal), Identification Of Deponents; [1939] 8 MLJ x1 at Pg x1, Lim Say Hun v. Public Prosecutor [1950] 16 MLJ at Pg 116; (Criminal Law), Leong & Anor v. Lim beng chye [1955] 21 MLJ at Pg 154; (Will), Comptroller Of Income Tax v. Harrisons & Crosfield [1954] 20 MLJ at Pg 85; (Income Tax Ordinance 1947),* *Karuthan Chettiar v. Parameswara Iyer [1966] 2 MLJ 151 at Pg. 152, Public Prosecutor v. Ang An An, Public Presecutor v. Eng Hock [1970] 1 MLJ 217, at Pg 219*

ALIUNDE from other sources; from elsewhere. Evidence aliunde (ie from without or outside of the will or other document) may be admitted to explain ambiguity in a will.

ALLEGANS CONTRARIA NON EST AUDIENDUS he is not to be beard who alleges thing contrary to each other. It also means one alleging contradictory things (ie) (whose statements contradict each other) is not to be heard', applied to statements of witnesses (4 Inst. 279). The doctrine of estoppel is mainly based on this maxim. He who alleges contradictory things is not to be heard. A man shall not be permitted to 'blow hot and cold' with reference to the same transaction, or insist, at different times, on the truth of each of two conflicting allegations, according to the promptings of his private interest. The doctrine of estoppel, at any rate by deed and in pais, is in great measure a development of the principle expressed in this maxim. But inconsistent alternative allegations of fact may be made in the same pleading. He who alleges contradictory things is not to be heard. A man shall not be permitted to 'blow hot and cold' with reference to the same transaction or insist, at different times, on the truth of each of two conflicting allegations, to suit his private interest. *Yamamori (Hong Kong) Ltd v **Davidson** [1992] 2 MLJ 410 at 418 Per Ian HC Chin JC*

ALLEGANS SUAM TURPETUDINEM NON EST AUDIENDUS he is not to be heard who alleges his own infamy. A person boasting of his own wrong is not to be heard. It also means that the meaning is that no one shall be heard in a Court of justice to allege his own turpitude as a foundation of a right or claim ; not that a man shall not be heard who testifies to his own turpitude, however much his testimony may be discredited by his character.

ALLEGARI NON DEBUIT QUOD PROBATUM NON that ought not to be alleged which, if proved, is not relevant. It also means that which, if proved, would not be relevant, ought not to be alleged.

ALLEGATIO CONTRA FACTUM NON EST ADMITTENDA where a man has entered into a solemn engagement under his hand and seal as to certain facts he shall not be permitted to deny any matter which he has so asserted'. This is the basis of the doctrine of estoppel by deed. An allegation contrary to a deed is not admissible. The rule of evidence contained in this Maxim is that of estoppel by deed. Parties and privies to a deed are estopped from denying statements in the deed which, on its true construction, are intended to be statements by them.

ALLO INTUITU with another view.

ALLOYNOUR one who conceals or steals.

ALLUVIO MARIS formation of soil or land from the sea.

ALLUVIUM, ALLUVION an imperceptible increase; land is said to be acquired by alluvion when it is acquired so gradually that one cannot say how much is added at any particular moment of time

ALMA MATER a fond mother. An epithet bestowed by students on the university in which they received their education.

ALPHA the first.

ALTA PRODITIO high treason

ALTER EGO 'other self'. It is a person's secondary or alternativ.e personality. *Lam Kee Ying Sdn Bhd v. Lam Shes Tong & Anor [1974] 2 MLJ 83=Pg.85, Lam Shes Tong & ors v. Lam Kee Ying Sdn Bhd[1973] 1 MLJ 203=Pg205*

ALTERNATIM interchangeably.

ALTERNIS VICIBUS by alternate turns, alternately.

ALUMNI students at a college. Alumnus - A pupil, one educated at a school, college or university, specifically a graduate of such institution.

AMANUENSIS one who writes when another dictates

AMBIGUITAS VERBORUM LATENS VERIFICATIONE SUPPLETUR NAM QUOD EX FACTO ORITUR

AMBIGUUM VERIFICATIONE FACTITOLLITUR a latent ambiguity may be removed by parol evidence, for an ambiguity which arises from an extrinsic fact may be removed by proof of such fact. It also means latent ambiguity of words may be explained by evidence; for ambiguity arising upon proof of ex-trancons fact is removed in like manner. A latent ambiguity in a written instrument is where the writing appears on the face of it certain and free from ambiguity, but the ambiguity is introduced by evidence of something extrinsic, or by some collateral matter outside the instrument. Thus a legacy in a will to 'my nephew Arthur Murphy' is on the face of it unambiguous, but if the evidence of the state of the testator's family shows that there are two nephews of that name a latent ambiguity is revealed and extraneous evidence of the testator's intention is let in.

AMBUGUITAS ambiguity; doubtful; uncertainty of meaning

AMICUS CURIAE Literally mean 'a friend of the court'. It is usually a stander who is called upon by the court when a judge is doubtful or mistaken in a matter of law. An amicus curia, may make an application to the court in fav.or of an infant, though he be no relation. Amicus Curiae is anyone who is not a party to the litigation but helps the court to resolv.e an issue or dispute. Amicus curiae applications are often submitted in important cases by strangers to the litigation to argue a particular point or rule in which they hav.e an interest. *Chin Swee Hin Sdn Bhd v. Mohamed Arif Bin Khalid [1977] 2 MLJ 31=PG 31, Ting Ing Kwong v. Lau Kah King [1977] 2 MLJ 80=Pg 80, Lt. Col. Wan Abdul Majid v. Capt. Kamarul Azman [1977] 2 MLJ 256=Pg 257, Deraman & ors v. Mek Yam [1977] 1 MLJ 52=Pg 56, Public Prosecutor v. Lim Woon Chong & Anor [1978] 2 MLJ 204 =Pg 210*

AMICUS CURIAE a friend of the Court; it is one, who voluntarily or on invitation of the Court, instructs the Court on a matter of law concerning which the latter is doubtful or mistaken, or informs him of facts, a knowledge of which is necessary to a proper disposition of the case. It also means a friend of the court. A person, usually a barrister who, with the court's permission, may advise the court on a point of law or on a matter of practice. An amicus curiae (as opposed to an intervener) has no personal interest in the case as a party and does not advocate a point of view in support of one party or another. The court may hear an amicus curiae if it considers it in the interests of justice to do so.

AMINO ATTESTANDI means having the intention to attest.

AMOVEAS MANUS that you remove your hands; a judgment ordering the Crown to relinquish possession of land to the complainant. The judgment is so called from the emphatic words quod manus domini Regis amoveantur (that the hands of the king be removed) The writ issued on the judgment.

ANIMO CANCELLANDI with intention to cancel.

ANIMO ENDORSANDI intention to endorse. It is very true that when a man's name is written on the back of an instrument without the intention to endorse, and so make himself liable upon it, he is not so liable; for though it may be said he has put his name on the back of the cheque, that is a writing on the back, but it is not on endorsement in the legal sense of the term; and so in the case of a bank-note, a party who writes his name on the back is not lia-ble on it if he wrote without intending to endorse. The writing must always be done enimo endorsandi in order to make it effectual to bind the endorser. I do no injustice to counsel for the defendant when I say that his argument would have been of more authority if addressed to this court a hundred years ago than it could be expected to have in these times.

ANIMO FELONICO with felonious intent.

ANIMO FURANDI 'with the intention of stealing'. *Hannah v. Peel [1945] KB 509, Quinn and Howland v. Rex [1949] 15 MLJ 217 Pg.222*

ANIMO FURANDI with an intention of stealing. In order to constitue larceny, the chief must take the property Animo Faran-di; for when the taking of property is lawful, although it may afterwards be converted animo furandi to the taker's use, it is not larceny. It also means with intention to steal; if the act done is not done animo furandi, it will

not amount to theft. *Longman Malaysia Sdn Bhd v Pustaka Delta Pelajaran Sdn Bhd [1987] 2 MLJ 359 at 364 Per Gunn Chit Tuan J*

ANIMO with the intention.

ANIMO LUCRANDI with intention to gain or profit.

ANIMO RECOVANDI the intention of revoking.

ANIMO REPUBLICANDI with intention to republish.

ANIMO REVERTENDI with intention to return.

ANIMO TESTANDI with the intention of making a will. Animus testandi is required to make a valid will. An idiot can make no will, for he can have no intention

ANIMUS ARBITRANDI intention to arbitrate.

ANIMUS BELLIGERENDI the intention to wage war.

ANIMUS CAPIENDI the intention to take or capture.

ANIMUS CONTRAHENDI *M.N. Guha Majumder v. R.E. Donough [1974] 2 MLJ 114 Pg.114*

ANIMUS CONTRAHENDI the intention to make a contract. Not only the terms of such contract but the existence of an animus contrahendi on the part of all the parties to them must be shown.

ANIMUS DEDICANDI the intention of dedicating.

ANIMUS DEFAMANDI the intention of defaming.

ANIMUS DERELINQUENDI the intention of abandoning.

ANIMUS DESERENDI *Lee Yung Kiang v. Ling Yun Tie [1965] 2 MLJ 87 Pg. 88*

ANIMUS DIFFERENDI the intention of obtaining delay.

ANIMUS DOMINI the intention of possession and ownership by entry or user.

ANIMUS DONANDI the intention of giving.

ANIMUS FURANDI the intention of stealing.

ANIMUS HOMINIS EST ANIMA SCRIPTI the intent of a man is the soul of his writing. It also means In order to give life or effect to an instrument, it is necessary to look to the intention of the individual who executed the same. Intention is the soul of an instrument.

ANIMUS IMPONENTIS the intention of the law-maker. The key to the opening of every law, is the reason and spirit of the law - it is the animus imponentis, the intention of the law-maker, expressed in the law itself, taken as a whole. Hence, to arrive at the true meaning of any particular phrase in a statute, that particular phrase is not to be viewed, detached from its context in the statute; it is to be viewed in connection with its whole content - meaning, by this, as well the title and preamble, as the purview, or enacting part of the statute. It is to the preamble, more especially, that we are to look for the reason or spirit of every statute; rehearsing, this, as it ordinarily does, the evils sought to be remedied, or the doubts purported to be removed by the statute, and so evidencing, in the best and most satisfactory manner, the object or intention of the legislature, in making, and passing, the statute itself. *Lai Ah Fatt v Timbalan Menteri Dalam Negeri, Malaysia & Anor [1990] 2 MLJ 312 at 314 Per Edgar Joseph Jr J*

ANIMUS intention; mind; soul; disposition. It also means hostilitity; ill will; hatred; animosity.... The appellant admitted that he had punched the complainant two days before the police report was made. Such being the case, there was good reason for the complainant having an animus against the appellant ...Augustine v Public Prosecutor [1964] MLJ 7 at 7 Per Ong J

ANIMUS MANENDI The intention of remaining. To acquire a domicil, the party must hav.e his abode in one place, with the intention of remaining there; for without such intention no new domicil can be gained, and the old will not be lost. Bates v. Bates [1951]

17 MLJ at Pg 96; (Div.orce), Majumder v. Attorney-General of Sarawak [1966] 2 MLJ 41 at Pg. 47, Jambalingam Saminathan v. A. Saminathan [1941] MLJ 68

ANIMUS NOCENDI 'intention to harm'. The subjective state of mind of the author of a crime, with reference to the exact knowledge of illegal content of his behavior, and of its possible consequences.

ANIMUS POSSIDENDI *Loke Tham Chuan v. Public Prosecutor [1955] 21 MLJ at Pg 5; (Dangerous Damages Ordinance 1952), M.K.Ramasamy Pillai v. O. RM.M.SP.SU.Meyappa Chettiar & Anor [1955] 21 MLJ at Pg 108; (Tenancy), Public Prosecutor V. Lim Peng Seng [1955] 21 MLJ at Pg 187; (Gaming), Jagathesan v. Linggi Plantations Ltd [1969] 2 MLJ 257; (Breach of Contract)*

ANIMUS REV.ERTENDI 'with the intention of returning'. A man retains his domicil, if he leav.es it animo (animus) rev.ertendi. *Goh Gok Hoon v. Abdul Hamid & Anor [1967] 1 MLJ 36 –Pg.38, A.C. Willis v. I.M.N. Willis & E.H. Hudgson [1941] MLJ 169 Pg.140*

ANIMUS TESTANDI the intention to make a will.

ANIMUS The intent; the mind with which a thing is done. *Somasundaram & Anor v. Tong Nam Contractors (PTE) Ltd [1976] 1 MLJ 95 Pg 95*

ANNECTERE to take control or possession of; assume jurisdiction over; as, to annex adjoining territory

ANNO DOMINI in the year of the Lord. The year of the Lord. The computation of time from the incarnation of Christ which is generally inserted in the dates of all public writings, with an addition of the year of the king's reign, etc. The Roman began their era of time from the building of Rome ; the Grecians computed by Olympials, and the Christians reckon from the birth of Jesus Christ.

ANNO HEJIRAE in the year of the hejira, or flight, of Mahomed from Mecca (A.D. 622) from which the Mahomedans reckon their time. Commonly abbreviated A.H.

ANNUM a year which is a period of 365 or 366 days in a leap year covered by 12 months.

ANTE Before. Before in time, order, or position; in front of. *Karam Singh v. Menteri Hal Ehwal Dalam Negeri, Malaysia [1969] 2 MLJ 143; (Internal Security)*

ANTE before. when used in a report or legal text book it refers the reader to a previous part of the book. Usually employed in old pleading as expressive of time, as prae (before) was of place, and cram (before) of person.

ANTE-NATUL happening before birth ; pertaining or relating to terms, occurrence or conditions previous to birth.

ANTE-NATUS a child born before the marriage of its parents.

ANTIQUUM DOMINICUM in old or ancient English Law.

APERTA BREVIA an unsealed writ.

APES SUCCESSIONIS (spes successionis) spes succession is which has been referred to in paragraph 54 of Mulla's "Principles of Mahomedan Law", which categorically indicates that a Muslim is not entitled in law to relinquish an expected share in a property. The concept of transfer of spes successionis which has also been termed as "renunciation of a chance of succession". *In Re Mohd Salleh Eusoof Angullia [1941] MLJ 19 Pg.20, A.C. Willis v. I.M.N. Willis & E.H. Hudgson [1941] MLJ 140*

APEX JURIS the summit of the law ; an extreme point or subtlety of law. A close technicality ; a nice or cunning point of law ; a rule of law carried to an extreme point of refinement.

APEX the summit or highest point of anything ; the top.

APICES JURIS NON MINT JURA mere niceties of law are not law. It also means the extremes of Law make bad Law. Or extreme points of law are not laws.

APPENDED PACTUM DE RETROV. ENDENDO *Ho Ying Chye v. The Cheong Huat [1965] 2 MLJ 261 Pg. 262*

ARBITRIUM BONI judgement by good subjects of the king; Award or decision of an arbitrator according to justice.

ARBITRIUM BONI *Syed Husin Ali V. Sharikat Penchetakan Utusan Melayu Berhad & Anor [1973] 2 MLJ 56 Pg.59*

ARBITRIUM EST JUDICIUM the award of an arbitrator has the same force and effect as a judgment. It also means an award is judgment.

ARGUENDO 'for the sake of argument'.

ARGUENDO in arguing; in the course of the argument. A statement or observation made by a judge as a matter of argument or illustration, but not directly bearing upon the case at the bar, or only incidentally involved in it, is said (in the reports) to be made arguendo, or in the abbreviated form, arg.

ARGUMENTUM AB AUCTORIATATE EST FORTISSUMUM IN LEGE an argument from authority is the strongest in law'. (Burrill L Dict) An argument from authority is most powerful in law. It also means the book cases are the best proof or authority of the law.

ARGUMENTUM AB IMPOSSIBILI VALET IN LEGE an argument from an impossibility is of weight in law. It also means an argument deduced from an impossibility greatly avails in law. Or an argument drawn from an impossibility is forcible in law.

ARGUMENTUM AB INCONVENIENTI PLURIMUM VALET IN LEGE argument from inconvenience avails much in law. Arguments of inconvenience are sometimes of great value upon the question of intention. If there be in any instrument equivocal expressions, and great inconvenience must necessarily follow from one construction, it is strong to show that such construction is not according to the true intention of the grantor ; but where there is no equivocal expression inthe instrument, and the words used admit only of one meaning, arguments of inconvenience prove only want of foresight in the parties.

ARGUMENTUM AD ABSURDUM (Reductio ad absurdum), is a common form of argument which seeks to demonstrate that a statement is true by showing that a false, untenable, or absurd result follows from its denial,[1] or in turn to demonstrate that a statement is false by showing that a false, untenable, or absurd result follows from its acceptance. It is a method employed to disprov.e an argument by illustrating how it leads to an absurd consequence. *Ho Hong Bank Ltd v. Ho Kai Neo & Another [1932] 1 MLJ 76 = Pg.79, Assa Singh v. Mentri Besar, Johor [1969] 2 MLJ 31 (Unlawful Detention); Pegang Mining Co. Ltd v. Choong Sam & ors [1969] 2 MLJ 53 (Specific Performance); Comptroller-General of Inland Rev.enue, Malaysia v. Weng Lok Mining Co. Ltd.*

100 (Practice and Procedure); EY YEE HUA v. Public Prosecutor [1969] 2 MLJ 126

ARMA IN ARMATOS SUMERE JURA SINUNT the laws permit us to take up arms against the armed. It also means the laws permit the taking of arms against armed persons.

ARTICULO MORTIS at the point of agony of death.

ASSENSIO MENTIUM the meeting of minds -- ie mutual consent. Mutual assent, which is the meeting of the minds of both parties to a contract, is vital to the

ASSIGNATUS UTITUR JURE AUCTORIS an assignee is clothed with the rights of his principal. It also means an assignee in clothed with the rights of his assignor. This maxim applies generally to all property, real and personal, and refers to assigns by act of parties, as where the assignment is by deed; and to as-signs by operation of law, as in the case of an executor. All rights of the assignor; in the thing assigned must pass from him to the assignee by virtue of the assignment, for duo non possunt in solido unam rem possidere. It should be observed also, that the thing assigned takes with it all the liabilities attached to it in the hands of the assignor at the time of the assignment, except in cases for the encouragement of commerce, such as sales in market overt, negotiation of promissory notes, bills of exchange, etc, and, in the case of equities, where the assignee is a bona fide purchaser for value without notice.

ASTRARIUS HAERES where the ancestor by conveyance has set his heir apparent and his family in a house in his lifetime.

ATTACHIAMENTA BONORUM a distress action taken upon goods and chattels by bailiffs or distress of a man's goods for debt owed.

ATTEMPTARE attempt. The word 'attempt' derives from the Latin 'attemptare' and generally means to make an effort or endeavor to do or accomplish some action.

ATTORN to turn over.

ATTORNARE REM to turn over money or goods.

AU FAIT *The Malacca Mercantile Cooperativ.e Thrift & Loan Society Ltd. v. The Attorney General [1939] 8 MLJ 157 at Pg 158*

AUDI ALTERAM PARTEM 'hear the other side'. Listen to what each party has to allege, before you give your decision. *Mahadev.an v. Anandarajan & ors. [1970] 1 MLJ 50, at 54 Wong Kwai & Anor v. President Town Council, Johor Bahru [1970] 2 MLJ 164, at 164, Chief Building Superv.eyor v. Makhanlall & Company Ltd [1969] 2 MLJ 118; (Administrativ.e Law), Tan Kheng Ann & ors. v. The Public Prosecutor [1965] 2 MLJ 108 = Pg. 114, Phang Moh Shin v. Commissioner of Police & ors [1967]* *2 MLJ 186 Pg.187, Isman Bin Osman v. Government Of Malaysia[1973] 2 MLJ143=Pg 145, Tan Hee Lock v. Commissioner for Federal Capital & ors [1973] 1 MLJ 238 Pg 238*

AUTRE DROIT (EN AUTEB DROIT) 'in another person's right' as, for instance, an executor holds property and brings actions in right of those entitled to his testator's estate. A man may sue or be sued in another's right; this is the case with executors and administrators. *Hendrik Christiaan V.an Hoogstraten v. Low Lum Seng [1940] 9 MLJ 138 at Pg 147*

AUTREFOIS ACQUIT 'formerly acquitted. A plea by a person indicted for a crime for which he or she had prev. iously been tried and acquitted. [1] *Chu Chee Peng v. Public Prosecutor [1973] 2 MLJ 35 Pg 36, Manager, Fook Heng Rubber Works v. Public Prosecutor [1955] 21 MLJ at Pg 181; (Labour Code), Public Prosecutor v. Surjan Singh & ors [1939] 8 MLJ 88 at Pg 88, 89; (Criminal), Public Prosecutor v. Ong Kok Tan [1969] 1 MLJ 121 (Criminal Law), PP v. Lee Siew Ngock [1966] 1 MLJ 225 at Pg. 225, 226, 227, 228, Public Prosecutor v. Abdul Hamid Bin Jamal [1934] 3 MLJ 93 at Pg. 93; (Criminal Law - Extradition), Mohamed Bin Salleh v. Public Prosecutor [1967] 1 MLJ 184 –Pg.185, Syed Ismail v. Public Prosecutor [1967] 2 MLJ 123 Pg.128, Quinn v. Howland v. Rex [1949] 15 MLJ 217 Pg. 221*

---

[1] See Latin Mozeley Whitely Law Dictionary

AUTREFOIS CONVICT A plea made by a defendant, indicted for a crime or misdemeanor, that he has formerly been tried and convicted of the same. As a man once tried and acquitted of an offence is not again to be placed in jeopardy for the same cause, so, a fortiori, if he has suffered the penalty due to his offence, his conviction ought to be a bar to a second indictment for the same cause, least he should be punished twice for the same crime. The form of this plea is like that of autrefois acquit; (q. v.) it must set out the former record, and show the identity of the offence and of the person by proper av.erments. *Public Prosecutor v. Musa [1970] 1 MLJ 101, at* *101, 102, 103 (Internal Security), Yau Tin Kwong v. Public Prosecutor [1970] 1 MLJ 159, at 162 (Import of Prohibited Goods), Manager, Fook Heng Rubber Works v. Public Prosecutor [1955] 21 MLJ at Pg. 181; (Labour Code), Public Prosecutor v. Ong Kok Tan [1969] 1 MLJ 121 (Criminal Law), Notes [1932] 1 MLJ 151 Pg.153, Syed Ismail v. Public Prosecutor [1967] 2 MLJ 123 Pg.128*

AUTREFOIS 'formerly', 'at another time'; and is usually applied to signify that something was done formerly, as autrefois acquit, autrefois conv.ict. *Syed Ismail v. Public Prosecutor [1967] 2 MLJ 123 Pg.128*

B

BANC (BANCO) 'on the bench'. of appeals courts, before a full court, with all judges present. Federal appeals are typically heard by a panel of three judges, but may be reheard by the full circuit court of appeals sitting en banc. sittings in formerly sittings of one of the superior courts of Westmter, for the purposes of determining matters of law and transacting judicial business other than the trial of actions. Sittings *in banc* are opposed to sittings at *nisi prius*, in which a judge sits to try a case, with or without a jury. the business of the courts sitting *in banco* is transferred to div.isional courts of the high court of justice by ss. 40, 41, of the judicature act, 1873. Theory of Precedent [1940] 9 MLJ v.i at Pg ix

BANCUS a high seat, a seat of judgment. A court.

BANCUS REGINAE the queen's bench.

BANCUS REGIS the king's bench.

BELLUM INTERNACINUM a war of total extinction.

BENAMIDAR Lau Tai Thye, Etc. v. Leong Yin Khean and ors. [1934] 3 MLJ 110 at Pg. 117

BENIGE FACIENDAE SUNT INTERPRETATIONE CHARTARUM, UT RES MAGLS VALEAT QUAM PEREAT: ET QUAE LIBET CONCESIO FORTISSIME CONTRA DO-NATOREM INTERPRETANDA- EST deeds are to be liberally interpreted so that their purpose may stand rather than fall; and every grant is to be construed strictly against the grantor.

BIS V.EXATUS Yau Tin Kwong v. Public Prosecutor [1970] 1 MLJ 159, at 162

BIS VEXATUS annoyed twice. The defendant was no bis vexatus, for I feel sure that those words are not to be understood as meaning that a man is not to be more than once annoyed by the same evidence. I turn to consider the doctorine of issue estoppel. The difference between issue estoppel the autrefois principle is that while the latter prevents the prosecution from impugning the validity of the verdict as a whole, the former pre-vents it from arising again any of the separate issues of fact which the jury have decided, or are pre-sumed to have decided, in reaching their verdict in the accuser's favor. This form of estoppel is of course well known to the civil law where separate issues of fact are frequently decided by a judge or by a jury on a special verdict. There is no trace so far of its application to criminal matters. Per Darling J in Connelly v Director of Public Prosecution [1964] 2 All ER 401 at 422, 435, referred to Yau Tan Kwong v Public Prosecutor [1970] 1 MLJ 162 per Chua J.

BONA FIDE 'in good faith' trust, confidence, belief, innocent, honest. Without fraud or deceit;. The *bona fide* holder of a bill of exchange or other security-one without knowledge of any defect in title. *Han Pit Loh Sdn Bhd v. Chun Heng Tin Mine [1976] 2 MLJ 20 PG 20,21, Public Prosecutor v. Ong Ah Kau & ors [1976] 2 MLJ 31 Pg 31, Registrar Of Titles, Johore v. Temenggong Securities Ltd[1976] 2 MLJ 44 Pg 46, Macon Engineers Sdn Bhd v. Goh Hoon Yin[1976] 2 MLJ 53 Pg. 54, Haji Hamid Bin Ariffin & Anor v. Ahmad Bin Mahmud [1976] 2 MLJ 79 Pg 80, Island & Peninsular Dev.elopment Bhd & Anor v. Legal Adv.iser, Kedah & ors [1973] 2 MLJ 71 Pg73, Isman Bin Osman v. Government Of Malaysia [1973] 2 MLJ 143 Pg.145,149, Karrupiah Pillai v. Kaka Singh [1973] 1 MLJ96 Pg. 97, Yap Eng Thong & Anor v. Faber Union Ltd [1973] 1MLJ 191=Pg192, Sdn. Bhd. v. K. Ahmad [1970] 1 MLJ 129, at 150 (Specific Performance), Gerald Fernandez v. Attorney – General, Malaysia [1970] 1 MLJ 262, at 262, 263,267; Sebastian v. Public Prosecutor [1970] 2 MLJ 76, at 77 ; Lin Ah Moy v. Lee Cheng Hor & ors. [1970] 2 MLJ 99, at 100, 102*

BONA FORISFACTA goods that are forfeited.

BONA GESTURA good behavour.

BONA goods; property possessions. In the Roman law, this term was used to designate all species of property, real, personal, and mixed, but was more strictly applied to real estate. In civil law, it includes both personal property (technically so called) and chattels real, thus corresponding to the French biens (q.v.). In the common law, its use was confined to the description of moveable goods.

BONA MOBILIA moveables; those things which move themselves or can be transported from one place to another, and not permanently attached to a farm, heritage, or building.

BONA NOTABILIA notable goods; property worthy of notice, or of sufficient value to be accounted for.

BONA VACANTIA 'to be empty or void'. Applied to goods which were not disposed of in a decedent's will and were also not covered by any provision in intestacy; assets which cannot be claimed by anyone either in intestacy or under the will. Also, any goods without an identifiable owner. Goods found without any apparent owner. They belong to the first occupant or finder, unless they be royal fish, shipwrecks, treasure trov.e, waifs and estrays which belong to the Crown. *Ng Lit Cheng v. Felixia v. Arnakulasinghe & Anor [1977] 2 MLJ 249 Pg 250*

BONA WAVIATA goods that are thrown away by a thief in his flight for fear of being apprehended.

BONAE FIDEI POSSESSOR IN ID TANTUM QUOD AD SE PERVENERIT TENETUR a person in possession in good faith is answerable only for that which he himself has obtained.

BONAM PARTEM to the proper party. The appointment of the respondent in the first instance must be lawful and made in bonam partem, and when this is impugned by the appellants themselves on the basis of the allegations we have adverted to, then this would surely require evidence and examination of the allegations made in order to determine the lawfulness of the initial appointment and whether the 1rd appellant's judgment was in fact impaired as a result in exercising his discretion in making the appointment. The subsequent purported revocation of the appointment would also raise legal and constitutional issues attracting legal considerations. We are therefore of the view that justiciable issues do in fact arise for judicial determination and the matter falls within the jurisdiction of the Court for adjudication. *Tun Datuk Haji Mohamed Adnan Robert v Tun Datu Haji Mustapha bin Datu Harun [1987] 1 MLJ 471 at 484 Per Tan Chiaw Thong J*

BONUM VACANS property without proprietor; Property without any owner of any sort.

BREVE DE RECTO a writ of right available to one who is dispossessed of an estate to recover the possession thereof.

BREVE INNOMINATUM This is a writ containing a general as opposed to a particular claim.

BREVI MANU 'With a short hand'. Off-hand; in a summary manner. *Attorney General v. Pang Cheng Lian & ors [1975] 1 MLJ 69 Pg. 71*

BREVIA ADVERSARIA adversary writs.

BREVIA AMICABILLIA friendly writs (by mutual consent).

BREVIA DE CURSU writs issued as of course.

BREVIA TESTATA an old form of deed used for conveyance.

BREVIS VIA PER EXEMPLA, LONGA PER PRAECEPTA Literally mean the way by examples is short, by precepts long

BRUTUM FULMEN no cause of action arises, to challenge the provisions in an Act, until the Bill is enacted into the constitution (64th Amendment) Act and its enforcement by notification is made and till such period the Doctrine of brutum fulmen (ie the threat to which effect cannot be given) prevails. A wrongful repudiation by one party cannot, except by the election of the other party, so to treat it, put an end to an obligation; if the other party still insists on performance of the contract the repudiation is what is called 'brutum fulman' that is, the parties are left with their rights and liabilities as before. A wrongful repudiation of a contract by one party does not of itself absolve the other party if he sues on the contract from establishing his right to recover by proving performance by him of conditions precedent. *Ganam d/o Rajamany v Somoo s/o Sinnah [1984] 2 MLJ 290 at 296 Per Seah J, Damodaran v Choe Kuan Him [1979] 2 MLJ 267, Aspatra Sdn. Bhd & 21 Ors v Bank Bumiputra Malaysia Bhd & Anor [1988] 1 MLJ 97 at 109 Per Seah SCJ*

C

CADIT it falls, abetes, fails, ends, ceases.

CADIT QUAESTIO 'the question falls' or 'argument collapses'. This means that there is no further argument or discussion. This term is used to refer to a situation where a legal dispute has been settled. The word "cadit" means to fall and "quaestio" means question. Cadit quaestio is used to indicate that a dispute or an issue is no longer in question. *Paidiah Genganaidu v. The Lower Perak Syndicate Sdn Bhd & ORS [1974] 1 MLJ 220 Pg.220, Re Tan Boon Liat [1976] 2 MLJ 83 Pg 88*

CAETERIS PARIBUS other things being equal.

CAETERIS TACENTIBUS the other judges expressing no opinion.

CAETERORUM of the rest; of the others. A general grant of administration made in cases where a limited grant has al-ready been made to a particular personal representative. For example, if a grant has already been is-sued to a nominated executor limited to dealing with a particular item of estate, a grant caeterorum will be made to the general executor to administer the rest of the estate.

CALUMNIANDI ANIMO with a malicious design.

CAMPI PARTITIO division of the field. Where a person agrees to maintain a suit in which it has no interest, the proceeding is known as maintenance; where he bargains for a share of that result to be ultimately decreed in a suit consideration of assisting in its maintenance, it is styled 'champerty'. Both 'champerty' and maintenance tend to en-courage litigation which is not bona fide but speculative. The English law of maintenance and champerty is not in India. A fair agreement to supply money to carry on a suit, in consideration of the leader's having a share of the property sued for, if recovered, is not opposed to public policy and, therefore, not void. Two circumstances must exist: (1) The agreement should not be extortionate and unconscionable so as to be inequitable against the borrower. (2) It should have been made with the bona fide object of assisting a claim and not for the purpose of gambling in litigation for injuring others.

CANCEL to blot out or obliterate; to cross and deface the lines of a writing; to annul or destroy; doing away with.'The Latin verb, from which the term 'cancel' is derived, means to make lattice work, and the corre-sponding noun in Latin, in the plural, cancelli, signifies lattice work; and when applied to marks, means marks made in the forms of lattice work.

CANCELLARII ANGLIAE DIGNITAS EST, UT SECUNDUS A REGE IN REGNO HABE-TUR the dignity of the chancellor is such that he is deemed to be the second after the sovereign.

CAPAX DOLI the condition of one who has sufficient mind and understanding to be made responsible for his actions. It also means capable of deceiving.

CAPE AD VALENTIAM this was a writ of execution, now abolished, whereby a defendant in an action touching lands and tenements, was allowed to recover against a third party the amount of judgment awarded against him. This was in cases where the defendant pleaded that the lands had been warrantied to him by such third party. 'This writ lies where the tenant is impleaded of certain lands, and he vouches to warranty another, against whom the Summons ad warantizandum had been awarded, and the vouchee comes not in at the day given: then if the demandant recover against the tenant, he shall have this writ against the vouchee, and shall recover so much in value of the vouchee' land, if he have not so much, then the tenant shall have execution by this writ of such lands and tenements as descended to him in fee simple; or if he purchase afterwards, the tenant shall have against him a resummons, and if he can say nothing, he shall recover the value.

CAPIAS AD AUDIENDUM JUDICIUM an accused tried in absentia was directed to be brought before the court to hear its judgment by a writ of capias ad audiendum judicium. This writ is awarded and issued, in case of the defendant be found guilty of misdemeanour (the trial of which may happen in his absence), to bring him to the court to receive sentence

CAPIAS AD RESPONDENDUM a form of writ to compel the appearance of a defendant or an accused person to answer the claim of the plaintiff or to defend the charge against him.

CAPIAS IN WITHERNAM DE AVERILS a writ which formerly lay for recovery of cattle wrongfully taken from the owner and driven out of the country.

CAPIAS IN WITHERNAM DE HOMINE a writ which lay for a servant in withernam.

CAPIAS IN WITHERNAM that you take by way of reprisal where pursuant to a writ of replevin, a sheriff is unable to seize the goods replevied by reason of their being concealed, a writ capias in withernam was directed to him to seize goods and chattels belonging to the defendant of an equal value.

CAPIAS you may seize. One of a number of writs authorising the sheriff to arrest a person or seize goods.

CAPIAS PRO FINE a writ authorizing the arrest and detention of an accused who has been found guilty and fined until he has paid the fine.

CAPUT LUPINUM an outlawed felon, a person who is considered a pariah, a friendless man. *Government of Malaysia & Anor v Kong Ee Kim [1965] 31 MLJ 81 at 84 Per Thomson LP*

CARCER AD HOMINES CUSTODIENDOS, NON AD PUNIENDOS, DARI DEBET a prison should be used for keeping or detaining persons, not for punishing or a prison should be assigned to the custody, not the punishment of persons.

CASSETUR BILLA that the bill be quashed. The form of the judgment for the defendant on a plea of abatement, where the action was commenced by bill (billa) 3 BL Comm 303. The form of an entry made by a plaintiff on the record, after a plea of abatement, where he found that the plea could not be confessed and avoided, nor traversed nor demurred to; amounting in fact to a discontinuance of the action.

CASU PROVISO in the case provided for.

CASUS BELLI literlly means 'case of war'. the justification for acts of war.

CASUS FAEDERIS an act or condition invoking the provisions of a treaty.

CASUS FORTUITUS 'fortuitous event'. when h.m.s. bounty was destroyed by hurricane sandy, October 29, 2012, casus fortuitus would describe the H.M.S. bounty being at the wrong place when hurricane sandy came up the coast

CASUS FORTUITUS NON EST SPERANDUS, ET NEMO TENETUR DIVINARE a fortuitous event is not to be expected, and no man is bound to divine it or foresee it. Or a fortuitous event is not to be foreseen; and no person is bound to divine it. This is another way of saying nemo tenure ad impossibile, for to foresee a fortuitous or unlooked for event is impossible, and this the law requires of no one. This maxim, however, would not excuse anyone from liability resulting reasonably from his act, although such liability was not foreseen by the party himself.

CASUS OMISSUS 'A case omitted'. A case for which provision was not made in the statute under consideration, either from neglect, or from the fact of its antecedent improbability. A litigation which arises because a statute has failed to cov.er a particular issue which must then be decided by the courts. An issue or set of circumstances which is not cov. ered by (inadv.ertently omitted from) a statute and is therefore left to be interpreted and decided under common law principles by the court. *Chye Chong & ors V. Public Prosecutor [1975] 1 MLJ 214 Pg. 215*

CASUS OMISSUS ET OBLIVIONI DATUS DISPOSITIONI COMMUNIS JURIS RELIN-QUITUR a case omitted and consigned to oblivion, is left to the disposal of the common law. A casus omissus will not be created by interpretation save where it is inevitable. Where there is a casus omissus in a statute the position is governed by the Common Law.

CASUS OMISSUS a point unprovided for by a statute. A case not provided for (as by a statute) and therefore governed by common law. It also means A case omitted. A circumstance not envisaged by a law or treaty; the omission of a matter in a statute which should have been provided for. *Krishnan Rajan a/l N Krishnan v Bank Negara Malaysia & Ors [2003] 1 MLJ 149 at 164 Per Abdul Malik Ishak J*

CAUSA CAUSANS 'the primary cause' or 'the originator' of an action. It is the foundation of all the causes. It refers to the immediate cause that resulted in the damage. To get the damages the claimant must prov.e that the defendant's breach of duty caused the harm. But the defendant need not prov.e the original cause of the harm. Howev. er while determining the question of harm the court will consider if the defendant has given explanation as to the original cause of the harm. *Ali Anberan v. Tunku Abdullah [1970] 2 MLJ 15, at 17 (Election Law), Lee Fung v. Public Prosecutor [1940] 9 MLJ 115 at Pg. 118*

CAUSA CONSANGUINITATIS by reason of consanguinity.

CAUSA ECCLESIE PUBLICIS CAUSIS EQUIPARATUR; ET SUMMA EST RATIO QUE PRO RELIGIONE FACIT the cause of the Church is equal to public causes; and for the best of reasons - it is the cause of religion.

CAUSA FALSA an untrue cause, reason or motive.

CAUSA HOSPITANDI for the purpose of being entertained as a guest.

CAUSA IMPOTENTIAE by reason of impotence.

CAUSA MATRIMONIALIS a matrimonial cause.

CAUSA MORTIS with reference to or in contemplation of death.

CAUSATOR a litigant; one who takes the part of the plaintiff or defendant in a suit.

CAUSES CELEBRES *a celebrated legal case or an issue arousing widespread controversy or heated public debate. It is a legal case or an ev.ent that a lot of people become interested in. In Re G.G Ponnambalam [1969] 2 MLJ 263; (Advocate And Solicitors)*

CAVEAT EMPTOR 'let the buyer beware'. For he ought not to plead ignorance that he is buying the right of another." he is bound to take all reasonable precautions in such a case, and will be supposed to have seen all patent defects. A maxim implying that the buyer must be cautions, as the risk is his and not that of the seller. The rule of law as to the sale of goods is, that if a person sells them as his own, and the price be paid, and the *title* prove deficient, the seller may be compelled to refund the money. But as to the soundness of the wares, the vendor is not usually bound to answer but there are several exceptions now embodied in the sales of goods act, 1893. *T. Chelliah v. Laxman Singh & Anor [1954] 20 MLJ at Pg. 211; (Estoppel), Tan Ho Cher Trading, ETC v. Yeo Poh, ETC [1932] 1 MLJ 48 Pg. 50, Alsagoff v. Robi & ors. [1965] 1 MLJ 56 Pg. 57, 58, Robin &*

Anor v. Goh Boon Choo [1965] 2 MLJ 215 Pg. 222

CAVEAT 'to beware of, guard against'. A warning or notice alerting the recipient to exercise caution before acting; e.g., notice to a reader to alert her to an important point in the text; to a judge to discourage him from performing certain acts or from proceeding in a litigation; or to the Patent Office by an inventor to prevent issuance of a patent to another applicant. an intimation made to the proper officer of a court of justice to prevent the taking of any step, *e.g.,* grant of probate, without intimation to the party interested (caveator) to appear. *Chin Cheng Hong v. hameed & ors [1954] 20 MLJ at Pg 170; (Land), Dan Sin Wah v. Chan Hai Swee [1951] 17 MLJ at Pg. 195; (Land Code), Haroon Bin Guriaman v. Nik Mat & Anor. [1951] 17 MLJ at Pg. 211; (Land), Lee Eng Teh & ors v. Teh Thiang Seong & Anor [1967] 1 MLJ 45*

CAVEAT VENDITOR let the seller beware. If the seller wishes to secure himself from future responsibility in case the article sold should afterwards be found to be different in kind or quality from what the party supposed it to be, he must take care or provide against such responsibility by a particular agreement with the purchaser. This maxim of the civil law expresses a doctrine the reverse of the rule of caveat emptor of the common law. It applies to executory sale, to contracts for goods to be manufactured or produced or to sales where the buyer has no opportunity to inspect the articles purchased. Let the seller beware. The maxim is reflected in federal, State and Territory sale of goods legislation, which imposes non-excludable strict liability on the supplier or a product that is not of merchantable quality, not fit for its purposes, or that does not correspond with its description or a sample: for example (CTH) Trade Practices Act 1974 Pt V Div 2; (NSW) Sale of Goods Act (1923), Pt 8.

CEPIT ET ASPORTAVIT he took and carried away.

CERTA DEBET ESSE INTENTIO, ET NARRATIO, ET CERTUM FUNDAMENTUM, ET CERTA RES QUAE DEDUCITUR IN JUDICIUM the intention, count, foundation, and thing, brought to judgment ought to be certain. It also means this intention, the count, and the foundation, ought to be certain, and so ought the thing to be which is brought for judgment. The design and narration ought to be certain, and the foundation certain, and the matter certain, which is brought to court.

CERTIORARI 'to be informed of', or 'to be made certain in regard to'. If an appellate court has the power to rev.iew cases at its discretion, certioari is the formal instrument by which that power gets used. A writ of certiorari orders a lower court to deliv.er its record in a case so that the higher court may review it. The U.S. Supreme Court uses certiorari to pick most of the cases that it hears. It is also the name given to certain appellate proceedings for re-examination of actions of a trial court, or inferior appeals court. The U.S. Supreme Court still uses the term certiorari in the context of appeals. *Sim Yan Hoo v. MTU and Daro District Council [1967] 1 MLJ 71 Pg. 73, Munusamy v. Public Services Commission [1967] 1 MLJ 238 Pg.200, Lijah Binte Mahmud v. Commissioner of Lands and Mines, Terengganu & Anor [1967] 1 MLJ 78, Eshah Binti Sa'at v. Meriam Binti Sa'at & ors [1975] 2 MLJ 97 Pg 97, Mak Sik Kwong v. Minister of Home Affairs,Malaysia [1975] 2 MLJ168 Pg. 168, Mak Sik Kwong v. Minister of Home Affairs,Malaysia (NO 2)[1975] 2 MLJ175 Pg 176, Zainab Binti Othman V. Superintendent of Prison,Pulau Jerajak, Penang[1975] 2 MLJ 221 Pg 222, South East Asia Fire Bricks Sdn Bhd v. Neo-Metallic Mineral Products Manufacturing Employees Union & ors [1975] 2 MLJ 250 Pg 251, Yeap Hock Seng v. Minister For Home Affairs,Malaysia [1975] 2 MLJ 279 Pg. 281, Law Society Of Singapore v. Chan Chow Wang [1975] 1 MLJ 59 Pg 66, Sungai Wangi Estate v. UNI [1975] 1 MLJ 136 Pg 136, Deraman Bin Din & ors v. Ibrahim Bin Mamat [1975] 1 MLJ 142 Pg. 142*

CERTIORARI EX DEBITO JUSTITIAE *District Council Central, Province Wellesley V. Yegappan [1966] 2 MLJ 177 at Pg. 177*

CERTUM EST QUOD CERTUM REDDI POTEST 'that is certain which may be rendered certain'. If something is capable of being made certain, it should be treated as certain. For example, a landlord can only distrain for rent (see

distress) if the amount of rent is certain. However, if the amount of the rent is capable of being ascertained, it is treated as certain. *Ooi Phee Cheng v. Kok Yoon San [1950] 16 MLJ at Pg. 189*

CESS an assessment or tax. The word 'Cess' has a definite legal connotation, indicating tax allocated to a particular thing, not forming part of the general fund. The word 'cess' is only tax and not a mere fee. It is not necessary for the purpose of levy of cess, there should be quid pro quo between the service actually rendered and the amount of tax levied, as it is not a fee but a tax. The word 'cess' means a tax and is generally used when the levy is for some special administrative expense which the name (health cess, education cess, road cess, etc) indicates. A 'cess' also means is a tax levied for a specific purpose often with a prefixed word defining the object. A 'licence' on the other hand involves a permission to trade subject co-compliance with certain conditions.

CESSANTE CAUSA, CESSAT EFFECTUS the cause ceasing the effect ceases also.

CESSANTE STATU PRIMITIVO, CESSAT DERIVATIVUS the derived estate ceases on the determination of the original estate. It also means the original estate ceasing, that which is derived from it ceases. Or when the original estate ceases anything derived from it ceases.

CESSIO BONORUM a surrender of relinquishment or an assignment analogous to an assignment in bankruptcy, in civil law. It alos means the yielding up of goods by a debtor to his or her creditors.

CESTUI QUE TRUST 'the one who trusts' or the person who will benefit from the trust and will receiv.e payments or afuture distribution from the trust's assets. It also refers to a beneficiary hav.ing an equitable interest in a trust, with the legal title being v.ested to the trustee. The law looks with suspicion upon transactions between trustees and beneficiaries, and, when the cestui que trust sells trust property to the trustee, the burden is placed upon the grantee or trustee to whom such transfer is made to show that the grantor or cestue que trust was in possession of full information and acted upon her own volition or independent advice, and free from all influence of the grantee or trustee to whom such transfer is made. *Che dah & Anor v. Commissioner of Land Titles [1973] 2 MLJ 29 Pg. 30, Inter-Continental Mining Co. Sdn Bhd v. Societe Des Etains De Bayas Tudjuh [1974] 1 MLJ 145 Pg. 148*

CESTUIS QUE 'a beneficiary' or 'The person for whom a benefit exists'. *Al. Al. Alagappa chettiar v. Ramaratnam Naidu [(1951] 17 MLJ at Pg 163; (Japanese Judgment And Civil Procedure Ordinance-Civil Procedure Code), Re H. Somapah DECD; Rajinder Singh & Anor V. P.R. Naidoo & ors [1955] 21 MLJ at Pg. 87*

CESTUIS QUE TRUSTENT *Liew Siew Yin & Another v. Lee Pak Yin & Another*

[1940] 9 MLJ 135 at Pg 136; (Trust), Lim Eow Thoon & Anor v. Tan Peng Neoh (m.w) [1950] 16 MLJ at Pg 258; (Trust), Dan Sin Wah v. Chan Hai Swee [1951] 17 MLJ at Pg 193; (Land Code), Tan Joo Hern and Anor. V.S. The Sze Hai Tong Banking Insurance Co. Ltd. and ors. [1934] 3 MLJ 127 at Pg. 128; (Trust – Trustees's Power), Chai Sau Yin v. Kok Seng Fatt [1966] 2 MLJ 54 at Pg. 58

CETERIS PARIBUS 'with other things the same'. more commonly rendered in english as "all other things being equal."

CHARTA DE NON ENTE NON VALET a charter or deed concerning a thing not in existence is not valid or a deed relating to a thing not in existence is of no avail. This maxim relates primarily to subject-matter of any grant, or to the person to whom a grant is made of an immediate interest in possession.

CHARTA PARDONATIONIS SE DEFENDENDO a form of pardon for killing another man in his own defence.

CHARTARUM SUPER FIDEM, MORTUIS TESTIBUS, AD PATRIAM DE NECESSI-TUDINE RECURRENDUM EST the witnesses being dead, the truth of charters must of necessity be referred to the country, ie, a jury. The witnesses being dead, it must be referred, as to the truth of charters, out of necessity, to the country - ie a jury.

CHIROGRAPHUM APUD DEBITOREM REPERTUM

PRAESUMITUR SOLUTUM an evidence of debt found in the possession of the debtor is presumed to be paid. It also means a deed or bond found with the debtor is presumed to be paid.

CIRCUTUS EST EVITANDUS; ET BONI JUDICIS EST LITES DIRIMERE NE LIS EX LITE ORIATUR circuity is to be avoided and it is the duty of a good judge to determine litigations, lest one law suit arise out of another.

CLAM DELINQUENTES, MAGIS PUNIUNTUR QUAM PALAM secret offenders are more severely punished than open ones.

CLAUSULA GENERALIS NON REFERTUR AD EXPRESSA a general clause does not refer to things expressed. A general clause of residuum does not comprehend those things which may not be of the same kind with those which have been specially expressed. This is the well-known 'ejusdem generis rule'. The rule is that where a list of particular things of a single genus is followed by general words the latter will be taken as having been intended to fill in any gaps left in the enumeration of the genus and not to extend beyond it.

CLAUSULA QUAE ABROGATIONEM EXCLUDIT AB INITIO NON VALET a clause (in an Act) which precludes it's a brogation, is void from the beginning.

CLAUSULA VEL DISPOSITIO INUTILIS PER

PROESUMPTIONEM REMOTAM, VEL CAUSAM REMOTAM EX POST FACTO FULCITUR a useless clause or disposition (one which expresses no more than the law by intendment would have supplied) is not supported by a remote presumption or by a cause arising afterwards. It also means an unnecessary clause or disposition is not upheld by a remote presumption or a cause arising after the event. Lord Bacon explains clausula vel dispositio inutilis 'when the act or words do work or express no more chan [sic]the law by intendment would have supplied', and such a clause or disposition is not supported by any subsequent matter 'which may induce an operation of those idle words or acts'.

CLAUSULAE INCONSUETAE SEMPER INDUNT SUSPICIONEM unusual clauses (in an instrument) always excite suspicion. It also means an unusual provision in an instrument, whereby the draftsman of the instrument obtains an advantage over the other party, excites a suspicion of a fraudulent motive. This rule was applied in the case to a provision in the release of a cause of action, stating that the party making the release agreed to release deliberately, and of his own free will, and without any undue influence from any one

CLAUSUM close, closed up, sealed. Inclosed, as a parcel of land. A writ was either clausum (close) or apertum (open).

COGITATIONIS POENAM MEMO MERETUR no man deserves punishment for a thought. It is laid down by Lord MANSFIELD that, so long as an act rests in hare intention it is not punishable, yet when an act is done the law judges not only of the act itself but of the intent with which it was done.

COGITATIONIS POENAM NEMO PATITUR 'nobody suffers punishment for mere intent'.

COGNOVIT ACTIONEM he has confessed the action.

COHAEREDES SUNT QUASI UNUM CORPUS OR UNA PERSONA CENSENTUR, PROPTER UNITATEM JURIS QUOD co-heirs are deemed as one body, or one person, on account of the unity of right which they possess.

COLLEGATARIUS colegatee.

COLLEGIUM EST SOCIETAS PLURIUM CORPORUM SIMUL HABITANTIUM a college is an association of several persons dwelling together

COMMANDITUM bailment of goods which are lent to a friend gratis to be used by him. Ng Chye Giat v Rex [1938] MLJ 126 at 128 Per Howes J, Gan Beng v Public Prosecutor [1939] MLJ 314 at 315 Per Murray-Aynsley J

COMMAONDANS the person who lends as commodatum.

COMMISCERE to mix together. Commingle also means to combine; mix; mingle; blend; as, to force ethnically disparate tribes to commingle.

COMMODATARIUS the person who receives the goods as commodatum.

COMMODOTUM A contract, by which one of the parties binds himself to return to the other certain personal chattels which the latter deliv.ersto him, to be used by him, without reward; loan -for use. He who lends to another a tiling for a definite time, to be enjoyed and used under certain conditions, without any pay or reward, is called "commodans;" the person who receiv.es the thing is called "commodatarius," and the contract is called "commodatum." *Gan Beng v. Public Prosecutor [1939] 8 MLJ 242 at Pg 242*

COMMORANTIUM abiding.

COMMORIENTES persons dying together or simultaneously or persons dying together in the same place, or from the same cause. Commorientes are persons who perish at the same time in consequence of the same calamity like shipwrecks, collisions, bomb explosions, conflagrations, earthquakes, fatalities during the war. Japanese Occupation and Ex Post Facto Legislation in Malaya (1959) MLJ xvi at xx

COMMUNIO BONORUM 'a community of goods'. When a person has the management of common property, owned by himself and others, not as partners, he is bound to account for the profits, and is entitled to be reimbursed for the expenses which he has sustained by v.irtue of the quasi-contract which is created by his act, called communio bonorum. *In Re Estate of Abraham Penhas (Deceased) [1949] 15 MLJ 223 Pg.227*

COMMUNIS LEX EST MAGIS DIGNA the common law has the pre-eminence (where jurisdictions conflict.)

COMPENDIA SUNT DISPENDIA, ET MEWUS EST PETERE FONTES QUAM SECTARL RIVULOS time saved in consulting abridgments, is often time lost; and it is better to search the fountain, than follow the rivulets. 'Therefore it is ever good to rely upon the book at large.

COMPENSATIO MORAE 'balance of delay'. This is a situation whereby there is a delay in payment or performance on the part of both the debtor and the creditor.

COMPOS MENTIS 'In the enjoyment of his understanding'. In control of one's mind; sane; mentally competent. of sound mind. *Mahesan v. Public Prosecutor [1970] 1 MLJ 255, at 261*

COMPOS MENTIS 'having command of mind'. of sound mind. It is also used in the negative "non compos mentis", meaning "not of sound mind".

COMPOS MENTIS of sound mind. 'One qualified legally to execute a deed. It was open to the legislature, if minded so to do, to insert in the Law of Property Act, 1925, a saving to the effect that the conversion effected by the statutory trusts should not alter the character or quality of any interest in an undivided share to which a lunatic or defective might have been entitled before the commencement of the Act. No such saving was inserted, and the undivided share of a lunatic or defective suffered the same fate as the share of any person who was fully compos mentis. Had the legislation rested there, the result as regards devolution, would have been quite plain. By force of the conversion, a former undivided share, or rather a share in the proceeds of sale corresponding to the former undivided share whether of a lunatic or defective or of a person of sound mind, instead of passing to the heir, would have passed to the persons entitled to his personal estate under the statutes of distribution in force before the Law of Property Act, 1925, but, in fact, in addition to the Law of Property Act and the other Acts passed at the same time, there was passed the Administration of Estates Act, 1925, which altered the devolution of property on an intestacy.

COMPROMISSARII SUNT JUDICES Arbitrators are judges.

COMPROMISSUM submission to arbitration

COMPTROLLER one who examines and verifies the accounts of collectors of public money.

CONATUS, QUID SIT, NON DEFINITUR IN JURE what an endeavoring is, is not defined in law.

CONDICERE to agree. Conditional, contingent or dependent on something else; limited by conditions; as, a conditional contract.

CONDICIO SINE QUA NON 'a condition without which it could not be'.an indispensable and essential action, condition, or ingredient.

CONDICTIO CAUSA DATA CAUSA NON SECUTA an action ("condictio") for recov.ery of a transfer of property, where the purpose for the transfer had failed (*causa non secuta*). During the recognition of innominate contracts, and their enforcement via the *actio praescriptis verbis. Menaka v. Lum Kum Chum [1977] 1 MLJ 91 Pg 94*

CONDITIO BENEFICIALIS, QUOE STATUM CONSTRUIT, BONIGNE SECUNDUM VERBORUM INTENTIONEM, EST INTERPRETANDI ODIOSA AUTEM QUOE STATUM DESTRUIT, STRICTE SECUNDUM VERBORUM PROPRIETATEM ACCIPIENDA a beneficial condition which creates an estate, ought to be construed favourably, ac-cording to the intention of the words; but a condition which destroys an estate is odious and ought to be construed strictly according to the letter of the words. Further, 'Where a vested estate is to be defeated by a condition on a contingency that is to happen afterwards, that condition must be such that the Court can see from the beginning, precisely and distinctly, upon the happening of what event it was that the preceding vested estate was to determine.

CONDITIO a condition.

CONDITIO PRAECEDENS ADIMPLERI DEBET PRIUSQUAM SEQUATUR EFFECTUS a condition precedent must be fulfilled before the effect can follow. In case of conditional contract the condition precedent must happen before either party becomes bound by the contract.

CONDITIONES QUAELIBET ODISE MAXIME AUTEM CONTRA MATRIMONIUM ET COMMERCIUM any conditions are odious, but especially those which are against in restraint of) marriage and commerce or some conditions are odious, but chiefly those which are against commerce and marriage. a condition precedent must be fulfilled before the effect can follow.

CONFESSIO, FACTA IN JUDICIO, OMNI PROBATIONE MAJOR EST a confession made in court is of greater effect than any proof. It also means a confession made in judicial proceedings if of greater force than all proof.

CONFESSUS IN JUDICIO PRO JUDICATO HABETUR, ET QUO DAMMODO SUA SENTENTIA DAMNATUR a person confessing his guilt when arraigned is deemed to have been found guilty, and is, as it were condemned by his own sentence. It also means a person confessing a judgment a deemed as adjudged, and in a manner is condemned by his own sentence.

CONFIRMARE NEMO POTEST PRIUSQUAM JUS EI ACCIDERIT

no person can confirm a right before the right shall come to him.

CONFIRMATIO EST NULLA UBI DONUM PROECEDENS EST INVALIDUM

confirmation is void where the preceding gift is invalid. It also means an illegal act cannot be rendered valid by a subsequent confirmation. Thus, a lease for twenty years fraudulently executed by a life tenant cannot be confirmed by the remainderman or treversioner.

CONGE 'permission', and is understood in that sense in law. cunn. diet. H. T. in the french maritime law, it is a species of passport or permission to navigate, delivered by public authority. it is also in the nature of a clearance. (Q. V.) bouch. inst. N. 812; repert. de la jurisp. du notoriat, by rolland de v.illargues. conge'. *Criminal Law and Crime; Mr. Abdul Hasanat, J.P., Superintendent of Police, Naokhali, Bengal, India; [1939] 8 MLJ ii-v.ii at Pg v.i*

CONSCIENTLE DICITURE A CON ET SCIO, QUASI SCIRE CUM DEO

conscience is derived from con and scio, to know, as it were, with God.

CONSENSUS AD IDEM 'agreement to the same'. parties must be of one mind and their promises must relate to the subject or object.

CONSENSUS AD IDEM 'consensus / agreement, consent / the same'. a meeting of the minds. Two minds with the same thought. *Indo-Australia Trading Co. Ltd v. Hin Ann Huay & ors [1954] 20 MLJ at Pg 164; (Land Law), Ooi Phee Cheng v. Kok Yoon San (1950) 16 MLJ at Pg 189; (Contract), Sammiyah v. Sakano & Co. [1939] 8 MLJ 16 at Pg 18; (Damages), Haji Abdul Hamid v. M.K. Ramasamy Pillai [1949] 15 MLJ 15 Pg.17*

CONSENSUS AD LITEM *International Trading Co. v. Chan Chow Kian [1970] 1 MLJ 192, at 192 (Agency), Appuhamy v. Dato' Ajit Singh [1970] 1MLJ 194, at 194 (Implied Terms in Contract Of Employment)*

CONSENSUS FACIT LEGEM 'consensus makes the law'. stipulates that when two or more persons arrive at a good faith agreement, the law will insist on that agreement being carried out.

CONSENSUS TOLLIT ERROREM consent removes a mistake or the acquiescence of a party who might take advantage of an error obviates its effect. Or consent takes away error. The acquiescence of a party who might take advantage of an error obviates its effect. On this maxim depends the important doctrine of waiver - that is, the passing by of a thing - a doctrine which is of wide application both in the science of pleading and in those practical proceedings which are to be observed in the progress of a cause from the first issuing of a writ to the ultimate signing of judgment and execution. There is a legal maxim 'the acquiescence of a party who might take advantage of an error obviates its effect.' If the maxim has application to this case and we think it has, it means that a party cannot, itself raise an issue, expressly ask and obtain submission of that direct issue to the jury as a question of fact on the evidence, and then on motion or a new trial complain that there was no evidence to sustain the given issue and the resulting judgment.

CONSENSUS VOLUNTAS MULTORUM AD QUOS RES PERTINET, SIMUL JUNCTA consent is the union of the will of several persons interested m the same subject matter.

CONSENSUS, NON CONCUBITUS, FACIT NUPTIAS VEL MATRIMONIUM consent, and not coition, constitutes marriage; and the parties are not able to consent before marriageable age. The common law conception of marriage knows no distinction of race or nationality.

CONSORTIO MALORUM ME QUOQUE MALUM FACIT evil company makes me evil.

CONSTITUERE to set up, constitute'. Constitutional – Lawful; consistent with the fundamental principles established by the constitution of a state or society; as, a citizen's constitutional rights.

CONSTRUCTIO LEGIS NON FACIT INJURIAM the construction of the law (a construction made by the Law) works no injury. It also means the construction of law does not work any injury.

CONSUETUDO DEBET ESSE CERTA; NAM INCERTA PRO NULLA HABETUR a custom should be certain; for an uncertain custom is considered null. A custom should be certain, for uncertain things are held as nothingit also means a custom should be certain, for uncertain things are held as nothing.

CONSUETUDO a custom or usage.

CONSUETUDO MANERLI ET LOCI OBSERVANDA EST the custom of a manor and place is to be observed. A custom may be defined to be a usage which has obtained the force of law, and is, in truth, the binding law within a particular district or at a particular place, of the persons and things which it concerns. There are several requisites to the validity of a custom: it must be certain, reasonable in itself, have existed from time immemorial, have continued without any interruption, have been peaceably enjoyed and acquiesced in, be compulsory, be consistent with other local customs; while customs in derogation of the common law must be strictly construed; and if it is sought to attach a usage or custom to a written contract it must not be inconsistent therewith.

CONSUETUDO PRO LEGE SERVATUR 'custom is held as law'.

Where no laws apply to a given situation, the customs of the place and time will have the force of law

CONSUETUDO REGNI ANGLIAE EST LEX ANGLIAE the custom of the kingdom of England is the law of England. the custom of England is the law of England.

CONSUETUDO SEMEL REPROBATA NON POTEST AMPLIUS INDUCI a Custom once disallowed cannot be again brought forward: (or relied on). Custom once disallowed cannot be again alleged.

CONTRA 'against; opposed to; on the opposite side; contrary to; in violation of; in defiance of' for example, "the view of the new York court is *contra* the decision of the new jersey court." *Rex v. Abu Kassim Bin Babu [1940] 9 MLJ 243 at Pg 243; (Criminal), Rex V.S. C. Sanmugam & Anor. [1932] 1 MLJ 75 Pg. 75, The Official Assignee Of The Property of Loh Chuk Poh v. The Over Sea Chinese Bank [1934] 3 MLJ 76 at Pg. 78, Yue Sang Cheong Sdn Bhd v. Public Prosecutor [1973] 2 MLJ 80 Pg81*

CONTRA BONOS MORES 'against good morals'. Contracts so made are generally illegal and unenforceable.

CONTRA FORMAM COLLATIONIS an obsolete writ that lay for the recovery of lands and tenements that had been granted to a religious house for specific purposes. It lay where a man had given lands and perpetual alms to any of the houses of religion, 'as to an abbot and his convent; or other sovereign; or to the warden or master of any hospital and his convent, to find certain poor men and to do other divine service; if they alien the lands, then the donor or his heirs had the said writ to recover the land. But this writ had to be brought against the abbot or his successor and not against the alienee, although he be tenant. But in all other actions where a man demanded freehold, the writ had to be brought against the tenant of the land

CONTRA LEGEM 'against the law'. It is used when a court or tribunal hands down a decision that is contrary to the laws of the governing state.

CONTRA NEGANTEM PRINCIPIA NON EST DISPUTANDUM against a man denying principles there is no disputing.

CONTRA NON VALENTEM AGERE NULLA CURRIT PRAESCRIPTIO contrary to one unable to act, no prescription runs or no prescription runs against a person unable to bring an action. Thus the periods of limitation of actions laid down by the Limitation Act, 1939, run from 'the date on which the cause of action occurred'.

CONTRA PROFERENTEM 'against the offeror'. It refers to a standard in contract law which states that if a clause in a contract appears to be ambiguous, it should be interpreted against the interests of the person who insisted that the clause be included. This usually comes up when a contract is challenged in court. If the court reviews a contract and finds that a clause is ambiguous or could have more than one meaning, it determines which party wanted that clause included and interprets in favour of the other party. Howev.er the contra proferentem doctrine has no application when both parties are involved in the wording and the inclusion of the ambiguous clause in the contract. *Chew Soon Tat v. Malaysia National Insurance Sdn Bhd [1977] 1 MLJ 241 Pg 242, Skyline Trading Co. v. Tiow Yoke Lan [1969] 2 MLJ 214 (Lease), Jagathesan v. Linggi Plantations Ltd [1969] 2 MLJ 257 (Breach of Contract), Tiun Eng Jin v. Wong Sie Kong[1975] 2 MLJ 34 Pg 34, Port Swettenham Authority V. T.W. WU & Co. (M) Sdn Bhd [1975] 2 MLJ 73 Pg 79*

CONTRADICTIO IN ADJECTO 'contradiction in itself'. A contradiction in terms.

CONTRATATIO REI ALIENA, ANIMO FURANDI, EST FURTUM the touching of property not one's own, with an intention to steal, is theft.

CONTRECTATIO REI ALIENAE, ANIMO FURANDI, EST FURTUM the touching mother's property with intent to steal is. It also means the touching of property not one's own, with an intention to steal, is theft.

CONTRIBUTIONE FACIENDA formerly, this was a writ whereby a coparcener sought to compel other praceners to make contribution. Such a Writ 'lies where there are diverse parceners and he who had the part of the eldest makes all the suit to the lord, the others ought to make contribution to him, and if they will not, he shall have against them this writ.

CONVENIENS the doctrine of forum non conveniens appears to have originated in Scotland and has finally found full acceptance by the House of Lords in Spiliada Maritime Corp v Cansulax Ltd (The Spiliada) [1987] AC 460 ; [1986] 3 All ER 843 ; [1986] 3 WLR 972 after a series of decisions, as described and set out so well in that very interesting and readable joint article by RH Hickling and Wu Min Aun, 'Stay of Actions and Forum Non Conveniens' [1994] 3 MLJ xcvii. The main judgment in The Spiliada was delivered by Lord Goff, who adopted the dictum of Lord Kinnear in Sim v F Robinow (1892) 19 R (Ct of Sess) 665 at 668 being the fundamental principle in re-gard to this doctrine, ie that 'there is some other tribunal, having competent jurisdiction, in which the case may be tried more suitably for the interests of all the parties and for the ends of justice'. Lord Goff cautioned that the word 'conveniens' in forum non conveniens meant suitability or appropriateness of the relevant jurisdiction and not one of convenience. We are in entire agreement with the fundamental principle so expressed. In our view, where an application by a defendant for stay of proceedings is concerned, in applying the said doctrine, the defendant would have to satisfy the court that 'some other forum is more appropriate' per Lord Templeman in The Spiliada. American

Express Bank Ltd V Mohamed Toufic Al-Ozeir & Anor [1995] 1 MLJ 160 at 167 Per Peh Swee Chin FCJ

CONVENTIO ET MODUS VINCUNT LEGEM a contract and agreement overcome the law.

CONVENTIO PRIVATORUM NON POTEST PUBLICO JURI a private agreement cannot derogate from public law. It also means a convention of private persons cannot detract from public right. (Latin for Lawyers)

CONVICT To find someone guilty after consideration of the evidence. To determine guilt of a criminal offense. A *conv.ict* is a person convicted, or found guilty, of a crime. is he that is found guilty of an offence by the v.erdict of a jury, or else appeareth and confesseth. *Yeap hock seng v. Minister for Home Affairs, Malaysia [1975] 2 MLJ 279 Pg. 285*

CONVICTIUM CONVITIO TEGERE, EST LUTUM LUTO PORRIGERE to cover reproach with reproach, is to lay mud upon mud.

CORAM NON JUDICE 'before one who is not a judge'. Refers to a legal proceeding without a judge, or with a judge who does not have proper jurisdiction.

CORAM NON JUDICE before one who is not the juge. The phrase is particularly applied to a court that lacks jurisdiction in a matter. There has been no hearing of the case, and it must now be heard and tried out. It ought to be tried by the judge with a completely fresh mind, and the previous proceedings, which all took place coram non judice, ought not to be referred to at all. The evidence was not evidence, as it was not coram judice.

CORPUS JURIS SECUNDUM An authoritativ.e legal encyclopedia that prov.ides general background knowledge of the law with footnoted citation to relev.ant case law. Abbreviated C.J.S. *Loh Kooi Choon v. Government of Malaysia [1977] 2 MLJ 187 Pg. 193*

CORPUS DELICTI 'The body of the offence'. The sum and substance of the crime. any object proving that a crime may have been committed. A charred house and an empty gasoline can are the *corpus delicti* of arson. Objective proof that a crime has been committed. The body of the victim of a homicide. Generally, an objective showing that a crime, any crime, has been committed and that there is an identifiable victim. *Ong Kim Piaw v. Public Prosecutor [1949] 15 MLJ 137 pg.139*

CORPUS HUMANUM NON RECEPIT AESTIMATIONEM a human body is not susceptible of appraisement. The human body does not admit of valuation. It also means a human body is not susceptible of appraisement.

CORPUS JURIS CIVILIS 'body of civil law'. The complete collection of civ.il laws of a particular jurisdiction or court. Also sometimes used to refer to the code of justinian.

CORPUS JURIS GENTIUM 'body of the law of nations'. The complete collection of international law.

CORPUS 'the main body', 'mass, or part of something'. a collection of things that, when together, can be considered or regarded as a single thing (such as a collection of writing by an author). The capital or principal sum (as opposed to income or interest). The property or subject matter of a trust. *In Re Wan Eng Kiat Deceased [1940] 9 MLJ 63 at Pg 63; (Succession), Re Alkaff Settlement; Alkaff & Anor V. Alkaff (1955) 21 MLJ at Pg 86, Re Lim Yew Teok, DECD; British and Malayan Trustees Ltd V. Chng Kiat Leng & ors [1966] 2 MLJ 260 at Pg. 262, The Halcyon Isle [1978] 1 MLJ 189 Pg 191*

CORPUS a body; human body; an artificial body created by law, as a corporation; a body or collection of laws; a material substance; something visible and tangible, as the subject of a right; something having local position distinguished from an incorporeal physical substance as distinguished from intellectual conception; the body of an estate, or the capital of an estate.1. In Roman law, the physical aspect of something; the whole of the writings of a jurist. 2. The body of main part of a fund or deceased estate comprising the capital or principle, as opposed to the income, interest, profit or dividends generated by the principal. The corpus of an estate may comprise monetary funds, real property and personal property. It can also mean an abstract collection of body.

CORPUS POSSESSIONIS the thing possessed. The plaintiffs acquired the freehold of 'Quetta' in January, 1959, and in December, 1959, com-menced the present proceedings, whereby they claim possession of the premises. Their claim is founded on an allegation that, the first defendant having left the premises in 1954 and never returned, her possession thereof has accordingly ceased. It is not in dispute that the second defendant has no independent right of her own. The case for the plaintiffs is that the passage of so long a time during which the first defendant has been absent from the premises raises a presumption against her that she has abandoned her possession. This, it is said, she can only rebut by proving affirmatively (a) that she has retained an animus revertendi, and (b) that she has in the meantime maintained what is described as a corpus possessionis. No question arises as to the latter in this case, for it is conceded that the continued occupation of the premises by her daughter, the second defendant, with her furniture would amount to a sufficient corpus possessionis. As to the former, it is contended that, so far from any intention to return being proved, the first defendant, by reason of her mental condition, has been throughout, and still is, incapable of forming any intention at all. In this connexion it is agreed that it is not enough to prove merely a vague, general desire to return.

CORRIGENDUM something which needs to be corrected; a list of corrections to be made in a printed book.

45

COST EX DEBITO JUSTITIAE *Arjan Sigh v. Hashim Anguilla [1941] MLJ 48*

COUP DE GRACE an action or ev.ent that finally ends or destroys something that has been getting weaker or worse. *B.A Rao & ors v. Sapuran Kaur & Anor [1978] 2 MLJ 146 Pg 150*

COUPLATIO VERBORUM INDICAT ACCEPTATIONEM IN EODEM SENSU the coupling of words together shows that they are to be understood in the same sense. It also means the coupling of words shows that they are to be taken in the same sense. The coupling of words shows that they are to be taken in the same sense.

CREAMUS, ERIGIMUS, FUNDAMUS, INCORPRAMUS we create, we erect, we found, we incorporate. According to Blackstone, the king may incorporate by Royal charter a corporation by using these words

CRESCENTE MALITIA CRESCERE DEBEL ET POENA vice (crime) increasing, punishment ought also to increase.

CRI DE COEUR 'a cry from the heart; heartfelt or sincere appeal. A passionate appeal, complaint, or protest. *Hagemeyer v. Trading Co. (M) Sdn Bhd v. Gibson Trading Co. [1978] 2 MLJ 101 Pg 103*

CRIMEN FALSI DICITUR, CUM, CUI NON FUERIT AD HAEC, CARTASVE CON-SIGNAVERIT the crimen falsi, is when a man illicitly and without authority for that purpose, signs writs or charters with the king's seal, which he has either found or stolen. (But, in a larger sense, crimen falsi is taken for forgery of any kind.

CRIMEN FALSI 'crime of falsifying'. forgery.

CUI BONO 'as a benefit to whom'. It suggests that the perpetrator(s) of a crime can often be found by investigating those who would hav.e benefited financially from the crime, ev.en if it is not immediately obvious.

CUI PATER EST POPULUS, PATER EST SIBI NULLUS ET OMNIS whose father is the people, has no father, and yet every man is his father.

CUICUNQUE ALIQUIS QUID CONCEDIT CONCEDERE VIDETUR ET ID SINE QUO RES IPSA ESSE NON POTUIT the Grantor of anything to another grants that also without which the thing granted would be useless. 'Whoever grants a thing is supposed also tacitly to grant that without which the grant itself would be of an effect. The grantor of anything to another grants that also without which the thing granted would be useless. Where a man, having a close surrounded with his land, conveys the close, the grantee has a way of necessity over the retained land as incident to grant. If a man lease his land and all the mines therein, when there are no open mines, the lessee may dig for the minerals. By the grant of the fish in a man's pond is granted power to come upon the banks and fish for them. It trees be excepted in a lease, the lessor has power, as incident to the exception, to enter the land demised at any reasonable times to fell and remove the trees, and the like law holds of a demise by parol. Likewise a grant of a right of way carries with the right to make up the road.

CUILIBET IN SUA ARTE PERITO EST CREDENDUM credence should be given to one skilled in his peculiar profession. It also means Whosoever is skilled in his profession is to be believed.

CUIUS EST SOLUM EIUS EST USQUE AD COELUM ET AD INFEROS 'for whoever owns the soil, it is theirs up to heaven and down to hell'. It is used in reference to the rights of property owners to the air above, and land below, their property.

CUIUS EST SOLUM, CUIUS EST USQUE AD COELUM *Tan Hua Lam V. Public Prosecutor [1966] 1 MLJ 147 at Pg. 149*

CUJUS EST COMMODUM EJUS EST ONUS he who has the benefit has also the burden. Whose is to give, his is to dispose. This maxim sets forth the principle on which the old feudal system of feoffment depended, but it must now be received with considerable caution. In an-other form (Maxim 598) it is still applicable to modern grants; the grantor of an estate may, since the land moves from him, annex such conditions as he pleases to the estate granted, provided that they are not illegal, repugnant, or impossible; so may he, by insertion-of exceptions, reservations or covenants in a conveyance or lease, reserve to himself rights of easement and other privileges in the land so conveyed or demised, and thus surrender the [enjoyment] of it only partially and not absolutely, to the transferee or tenant.

CUJUS EST DOMINIUM EJUS EST PERICU LAM the risk lies upon the owner of the subject.' He that institutes may also abrogate.

CUJUS EST SOLUM EJUS EST USQUE AD COELUM ET AD INFEROS to whomsoever the soil belongs, he owns also to the sky and to the depths. It also means whomsoever has the soil, also owns to the heavens above and to the centre beneath. Land, in its legal signification, has an indefinite extent upwards, so that by a conveyance of land all buildings, growing timber and water, erected and being thereupon, likewise pass. Any interference with the super-incumbent column of air may give rise to an action of trespass or nuisance, save insofar as it is authorized by the Air Navigation Act 1920. In law land extends also downwards, so that whatever is in a direct line between the surface-and the center of the earth belongs to the owner of the surface, unless it has been expressly excepted from a grant or separately conveyed away or severed by custom, or vested in the National Coal Board by statute.

CULLIBET LICET JURI PRO SE INTRODUCTO RENUNTIARE one may waive a legal right existing in his favour. Where two clauses in a will are repugnant one to the other, the last in order shall prevail. The rule was stated thus by Mr. JARMAN in his work on Wills. Doubt is sometimes cast on the intention of a testator by the repugnancy or contradiction between the several parts of his will, though each part taken separately is sufficiently definite and intelligible. In such cases the context (which is so often successfully resorted to for the purpose of throwing light on a doubtful passage) becomes itself a source of obscurity; and unless some principle of construction can be found authorising the adoption of one and the rejection of the other of the contrarviant parts, both are necessarily void, each having the effect of neutralising or frustrating the other. With a view to prevent this most undesirable result it has become an established rule in the construction of wills, that where two clauses or gifts are irreconcilable, so that they cannot possibly stand together, the clause or gift which is posterior in local position shall prevail, the subsequent words being taken to denote a subsequent intention.' Thus an absolute gift may be cut down by subsequently engrafted trusts or a gift over on the death of the donee. But observe that even subsequent words will not prevail over a previous absolute gift if they are inconsistent with it, eg directing the capital to be retained and the income paid to the donee until he is 35. The maxim is in practice often cited but hardly ever followed because the Courts strive to reconcile seemingly inconsistent provisions.

CULPA 'to blame, accuse'. Fault, blame, neglect, as in *culpable negligence*; i.e.,

negligence which goes beyond ordinary negligence; i.e., a conscious disregard of the rights or safety of others. *K. R. Taxi Service Ltd & Anor. v. Zaharah 7 ors. [1969] 1 MLJ (Negligence)*

CULPA CARET QUI SCIT SED PROHIBERE NON POTEST he is clear of blame who knows, but cannot prevent. It also means he is free from fault who knows but cannot prevent.

CULPA an act of neglect causing damage but not implying an intent to injure. Wrongful default. In Roman Law, the liability which arose from failure to observe the standard of care required in the performance of contractual obligations.

CULPA TENET SUOS AUCTORES 'A fault finds its own'. *Keppel Bus Co. Ltd. v. Sa'ad Bin Ahmad [1974] 1 MLJ 191 Pg.193*

CULPABILIS guilty. Culpabalis de instrusione, guilty of instrusion. Non culpabilis (abbreviated to non) the plea of 'not guilty'.

CUM DUE INTER SE PUGNANTIA REPERIUNTUR IN TESTAMENTO ULTIMUM RATURN EST

CUM IN TESTAMENTO AMBIGUE AUT ETIAM PERPERAM SCRIPTUM EST, BE-NIGNE INTERPRETARI DEBET ET SECUNDUM ID QUOD CREDIBLE EST COGITA-TUM CREDENDUM EST where an ambiguous, or even erroneous, expression occurs in a will, it should be construed liberally and in accordance with the testator's probable meaning.

Cupiens v.itare charybdin *Rauf Bin Haji Ahmad v. Public Prosecuter (1950) at Pg. 193; (Contract)*

CURIA the original family unit into which all Roman citizens were divided. Historically, there is no reason why it should be so extended. Summary punishment by attachment for contempt of court owes its origin to the fact that the offence was that of interfering with the King's justice administered in his 'aula', ie courtyard, or 'curia', ie council: see Holdsworth, History of English Law (7rd Edn, 1956, vol 3, at 391-393) and Oswald, Law of Contempt (3rd Edn, 1910, at 13). It was an offence against the judicial power of the sovereign. In the nineteenth century the judicial system was developed so as to include courts established not under the royal prerogative of justice but by statute, notably the county court and the courts of summary jurisdiction. The question arose at the beginning of the twentieth century whether the High Court, which clearly could punish for contempt of its own proceedings, could also punish for contempt of inferior courts. In 1906 in R v Davies, the King's Bench Divisional Court (Alverstone CJ, Wills and Darling JJ) decided that it could. The judgment of the court was delivered by Wills J. He reviewed the law. He cited with approval a dictum of Bowen LJ in Helmore v Smith (No 2) (1886) 35 Ch D 449 at 445 : 'Contempt of court is not to vindicate the dignity of the court ... but to prevent undue interference with the administration of justice.'

CURIA REGIS the king's court.

CURSUS course.

CUSTOS MORUM guardian of morals. In England, the court of king's bench was regarded as the guardians of morals of the nation.

Cy-pres 'as near as possible'. the name of a rule employed in the construction of suchinstruments as trusts and wills, by which the intention of the person who executes the instrument is effectuated as nearly as possible whencircumstances make it impossible or illegal to give literal effect to the document. *Lim Eow Thoon & Anor v. Tan Peng Neoh (m.w) (1950) 16 MLJ at Pg 262; (Trust)*

D

DAMNA damages. Also the fee payable to the clerks of the court of common pleas, king's bench or exchequer upon the amount of damages recovered, before the plaintiff could obtain a writ of execution.

DAMNUM (AD DAMNUM) 'to the loss, damage, injury'. The amount of damages demanded in a pleading; the amount the plaintiff or claimant asserts as his damages. The *ad damnum* clause of a complaint is the formal statement of damage. The amount of money sought as damages by the plaintiff in a civ. il action. *Guan Soon Tin Mining Co. v. Wong Fook Kum [1969] 1 MLJ 101 (Negligence)*

DAMNUM damage; the loss or diminution of what is a man's own, either by fraud, carelessness, or accident; loss, damage, injury/a fine.

DAMNUM SENTIT DOMINUS the owner suffer the damage.

DAMNUM SINE INJURIA 'condemnation without injury' or 'njury with no damages'. Damnum sine injuria refers to a legal situation in which plaintiff's right is not respected by another but where the breach of plaintiff's right does not cause damage, or at least not a calculable or admissible damage. A finding of damnum sine injuria can be the basis for a finding of nominal damages. Thus in cases of damnum sine injuria the injury is de minimis, i.e. too small to be remedied practically at the law. In such cases the plaintiff will hav.e a satisfaction remedy of nominal damages - which are also called symbolic damages. *Raffles Hotel Ltd. v. L. Rayner, Same v. Malaya Banking Ltd. [1965] 1 MLJ 60 Pg. 61, Darjit Singh v. Jinder Pal [1975] 2 MLJ 128 Pg 129*

DAMNUM SINE INJURIA ESSE POTEST there may be damage or injury inflicted without any act of injustice. There may be damage or loss inflicted without any act being done which the law deems an injury. For such damage no action can be maintained. The maxim Ubi jus ibi remedium does not apply, for there is no jus, no legal right to demand that the act which causes the damage shall not be done, and therefore there is no remedium.

DAS *Thurairajah v. The Public Prosecutor [1940] 9 MLJ 58 at Pg 60; (Criminal)*

DATIO IN SOLOTUM Falkland's basic premises is that the former owner of the 'Virgo I', that is VBTRF, by a document dated 16 January 1998 transferred the vessel to Falkland as datio in solutum. The Latin phrase means 'An ac-cord and satisfaction under the civil law, wherein the consideration is in property and not in money'. The document states 'indemnity' as the equivalent of datio in solutum. The vessel was then known as 'Kapitan Voloshin' and belonged to the Port of Vladivostock, which appeared in the transfer document.

DATIO a giving, or act of giving.

DATUM a first principle; a thing given; a date.

DE ARBITRATIONE FACTA of arbitration. A writ for enforcing a judgment of arbitrators

DE BENE ESSE 'As being well done for the present'. Or 'for what it is worth'. A thing is done de bene esse, when it is done conditionally, and is to stand good till some time named, when the question of its being rightly or wrongly done will be determined. Depositions are often taken de bene esse, the question as to whether they shall be used for the benefit of the party so taking them, being reserv.ed for consideration at a future time. *Sheikh Abdullah Bin Sheikh Mohamed v. Kang Kok Seng & ors [1974] 1 MLJ 174 Pg.175, Successors Of Moine & Co. Ltd V. East Asiatic Co. Ltd & Singapore Harbour Board [1954] 20 MLJ at Pg 114; (Estoppel), K.A.R.S.T. Arunasalam Chettiar v. S. Abdul Raman Bin Suleiman & Anor. [1933] 2 MLJ 48 Pg. 50, In Re Estate Of Abraham Penhas (Deceased) [1949] 15 MLJ 223 Pg. 223*

DE BONIS ASPORTATIS'Carrying goods away'.Specifies that larceny was taking place in addition to any other crime named. E.g. "trespass de bonis asportatis".

DE BONIS of goods not administered. It refers to a grant of administration for the unadministered part of a deceased estate and applies when an executor or an administrator has partially completed administering an estate and then dies or becomes otherwise incapable of completing outstanding administration duties, so that the court then appoints a substitute administrator to complete the administration of the estate. Shorthand for administration de bonis non-administratis. The term 'de bonis non' comes from the full Latin title of 'de bonis non administratis', which means 'of goods not administered'. If a person to whom a grant of representation has been made has died leaving part or all of the estate of the deceased un administered then, unless there is a chain of executorship, a grant in respect of the un administered estate may be made to a new personal representative to enable the administration to be completed. Such a grant is described as 'de bonis non. Tristram and Coote's Probate Practice, (28ᵗʰ Ed), at 432 and Re Ramanathan s/o Aranachiappan (Administrator de bonis non with the will annexed, of the Estate of KALRM Kuruppan Chettiar, deceased) [1998] 2 MLJ 90 at 99). As described by Halsbury's Law of England (4ᵗʰ Ed), para 984, at 514: Where a sole or last surviving executor dies intestate without having fully administered the testator's estate, the deceased executor's administrator does not become the representative of the original testator, and it is accordingly necessary to appoint an administrator to administer the goods of the original testator left unadministered. This is a grant of administration cum testamento annexe de bonis non-administrates (that is 'with the will annexed for unadministered estate'). The learned author of 'Probate and Administration in Singapore and Malaysia: Law and Practice', G Raman (at 70), states: Sometimes a person who has taken out probate or letters of administration may die without completing the administration of the estate. Where this happens, the person next entitled to the letters of representative or any other suitable applicant, would be appointed by the court to finalize the administration of the unadministered part of the estate. The administrator in this sort of cases acts under the will of the deceased in the event of testacy, or, if it is an intestate estate, he derives his authority from his appointment as administrator and carries out the functions of his predecessors. The role of an administrator de bonis non is restricted to finalizing the administration of the estate. In Malaysia, matters relating to probate and letters of administration are governed by the Probate and Administration Act 1959 'the Act'. *In the Estate of Ngau Ken Lock (deceased) (Ngau Voon Kiat, petitioner) [2002] 4 MLJ 74 at 78 Per Ramly Ali J*

DE BONIS NON ADMINISTRATES

'Of goods not administered'. It is the assets of an estate remaining after the death (or remov.al) of the designated estate administrator. An "administrator de bonis non administratis" will then be appointed to dispose of these goods.

DE BONIS NON ADMINISTRATIS

relating to goods or assets which have not been administered. Where an executor dies intestate or an administrator dies, without having fully administered the assets of the deceased, a grant of probate or letters of administration de bonis non may be granted.

DE BONIS NON 'administrator of goods not administered'. This phrase is used in cases where the goods of a deceased person hav.e not all been administered. when an executor or administrator has been appointed, and the estate is not fully settled, and the executor or administrator is dead, has absconded, or from any cause has been remov.ed, a second administrator is appointed to to perform the duty remaining to be done, who is called an administrator de bonis non, an administrator of the goods not administered and he becomes by the appointment the only representative of the deceased. *Frank Merrels & Others v. Wee Chin Koon [1940] 9 MLJ 212 at Pg 212; (Probate), Safiah Binte Tohor Deceased [1940] 9 MLJ 285 at Pg. 286; (Succession), Chia Teck Leong & ors v. Estate & Trust Agencies [1927] Ltd [1939] 8 MLJ 96 at Pg 96, 97; (Limitation Ordinance), Re Syed Abdulah Bin Abdulrahman Bin Sahil Decd [1939] 8 MLJ 141 at Pg 141; (Probate), Chia Wan Kiat v. M. Theynappa Ltd [1955] 21 MLJ at Pg 199; (Limitation), Ang Hoi Yin v. Sim Sie Hau [1969] 2 MLJ 3 (Succession)*

DE BONIS PROPRIIS of his own goods. Where an administrator or an executor has been guilty of waste, the judgment ob-tained against him to make good the loss is known as judgment de bonis propriis for waste against the executor or administrator. It also means the first Defendant was no doubt under the impression that he was lending money to the Estate but it is admitted that the executor had no power to borrow on behalf of the Estate and if the first Defendant so lent in ignorance of what his legal rights would be and without ascertaining whether the executor had such power he did so at his own risk. It is thus clear that the first Defendant was not entitled to the judgment which he obtained against the second Defendant as executor. The judgment should have been 'de bonis propriis'and not 'de bonis testatoris'. It should not be allowed to stand and that being so the only question for me to decide is whether the Plaintiffs have adopted the correct procedure to remedy the matter. *Cheah Wong Nyan and Cheah Sin Kee v 1. K.A.L.R.M. Palaniappa, 2. Cheah Lean Guan, 3. Official As-signee of the Property of Cheah Lean Guan (a bankrupt) [1935] MLJ 31 at 32 Per Whitley J*

DE BONIS TESTATORIS ET SI NON DE BONIS PROPRIIS *Arunasalam Chettiar V. Mohamed Abdul Latheef Maricar and Another [1934] 3 MLJ 30 at Pg. 30; (Probate and Administration)*

DE BONIS TESTATORIS 'of the goods of the testator'. Historically, the termed referred to a judgment awarding execution on the property of the testator, rather than the administrator's property. The phrase is mainly seen used under probate law. *Bank Bumiputra Malaysia Bhd V. Yap Kiow Moi & ors [1973] 2 MLJ 104 Pg.105*

DE BONIS TESTATORIS, OR INTESTATI a judgment against the property of a deceased is one de bonis testatoris or intestati, depending on whether he died testate or intestate.

DE DIE IN DIEM 'From day to day'. Generally refers to a type of labor in which the worker is paid fully at the completion of each day's work.

DE FACTO 'to make do' ;In fact; in reality; actually. Anything which exists in fact but not necessarily of right. A body, group, institution, committee, person or entity which exercises, or acts in given circumstances as though it had, the authority to perform a given act, without necessarily hav.ing such authority. A usurpation of authority. Used in conjunction with other words or phrases, as follows: *de facto authority; de facto board of directors; de facto court; de facto incumbent; de facto judge; de facto jury; de facto officer; de facto trustee; de facto segregation.* In all these cases, the sense is of authority claimed or exercised without legal right. A *de facto merger* occurs when one corporation purchases the assets of another and assumes all its debts but fails to call the transaction a merger. An expression iudicating the actual state of circumstances, independently of any remote question of right or title; thus, a king *de facto* is a person acknowledged and acting as king, independently of the question whether someone else has a better title to the crown. *B. H Oon & ors. v. The Government of the State of Penang & ors. [1970] 1 MLJ 244, at 249 (Land Law), Re Balasingam & Parav.Athy, Infants Kannamah v. Palani [1970] 2 MLJ 74, at 74, 75 (Custody and Control of Infant),*

Government of Malaysia v. Selangor Pilot Association [1977] 1 MLJ 133 Pg.141

DE FIDE ET OFFICIO JUDICIS NON RECIPITUR QUAESTIO; SED DE SCIENTIA SIVE SIT ERROR JURIS SIVE FACTI the bona fide and honesty of purpose of a judge cannot be questioned, but his decision may be impugned for error either of law or of fact. It also means of the good faith and intention of a judge a question cannot be entertained but it is otherwise as to his knowledge, whether the error be one of law or fact. It is a general rule that no action will lie against a judge for any act done by him in the exercise of his judicial functions, provided such act, though done mistakenly, were within the scope of his jurisdiction; but his errors may be corrected by appellate tribunals in all cases where the law allows of an appeal.

DE FUTURO *Victoria Hotel V. Ho See Teck [1966] 1 MLJ 29 at Pg. 32*

DE INTEGRO 'Concerning the whole'. Often used to mean "start it all ov.er", in the context of "repeat de integro"

DE JURE 'right, law'. By right, by justice, by force of law. Lawful; legitimate. The v.alid, lawful power to do or perform a given act. Contrasted with *de facto*. *De facto segregation* is segregation which exists as a matter of practice, fact and history; *de jure segration* is segregation imposed or created by a law or statute. A *de jure* corporation is a corporation created by the state after observ.ing and fulfilling all legal requirements. A *de facto* corporation is one which conducts its business as though it had all the requisite authority but which does not in fact have it. *Re Balasingam & Parav. Athy, Infants Kannamah v. Palani [1970] 2 MLJ 74, at 75 (Custody and Control of Infant), United States of America v. Yang Soon Ee & Another [1949] 15 MLJ at Pg. 103; (Public International Law), Stephen Kalong Ningkan V.Tun Abang Haji Openg & Tawi Sli (NO 2) [1967] 1 MLJ 46 Pg.50, Rex V. L. W. Burgess [1941] MLJ 104*

DE LEGE FERENDA 'Of the law as it should be'.Used in the context of "how the law should be", such as for proposed legislation.

DE LEGE LATA 'Of the law as it is'. Concerning the law as it exists, without consideration of how things should be.

DE of, from, about; out of; concerning; among; for.

DE MEDIETATE LINGUAE half of one language and half of another, The phrase referred to juries comprised of six who spoke English and six who spoke the language of the accused who did not understand English. 'Jurors, where aliens are parties, are to be, the one half aliens, the other half citizens or subjects of the country where the fact is tried.

DE MELLORIBUS DAMNIS of or for the better damages. Where a jury returned by error the verdict assessing damages separately against each individual defendant, a plaintiff might take judgment de melioribus damnis against one.

DE MINIMIS 'smallest, the least important'. Insignificant; minute; friv. olous. In law, something so triv.ial the court will not act upon it, as in a *de minimis* crime. *Boon & Cheah Steel Pipes Sdn Bhd V. Asia Insurance Co. Ltd & ors [1973] 1 MLJ 101 Pg.105, K.P Kunchi Raman v. Goh Bros Sdn Bhd [1978] 1 MLJ 89 Pg. 91*

DE MINIMIS NON CURAT LEX The law does not notice or care for trifling matters. *Boon & Cheah Steel Pipes Sdn Bhd V. Asia Insurance Co. Ltd & ors [1973] 1 MLJ 101 Pg.101, Jackson & Co. Ltd v. Seng Seng [1954] 20 MLJ at Pg 229; (Bills of Sale Ordinance), District Council Central, Province Wellesley V. Yegappan [1966] 2 MLJ 177 at Pg. 177*

DE MINIMIS NON CURAT LEX diminutives are not noticed by law. Or The law cares not for small things. It also means the law does not concern itself with trifles. Courts of justice generally do not take trifling and immaterial matters into account, except under peculiar circumstances, such as the trial of a right, or where personal character is invovled; they will not, for instance, take notice of the fraction of a day, except in cases where there are, conflicting rights, for the determination of which it is necessary that they should do so. *Hong Siew Sin & Anor v Menteri Hal Ehwal Dalam Negeri, Malaysia & Anor [1990] 2 MLJ 90 at 91 Per Hashim Yeop A Sani CJ*

DE MORTE HUMINIS NULLA EST CUNCTATIO LONGA when the death of a human being is concerned, no delay is long. (Burrill) Concerning the death of a man no delay is long.

DE MORTUIS NIL NISI BONUM 'Of the dead, [speak] nothing unless good'. Social convention that it is inappropriate to speak ill of the recently deceased, even if they were an enemy.

DE NON APPARENTIBUS, ET NON EXISTENTIBUS EADEM EST RATIO as to things not apparent, and those not existing, the rule is the same. Where the court cannot take judicial notice of a fact, it is the same as if the fact had not existed. It also means of things which do not appear and things which do not exist, the rule in legal proceedings is the same. What is not in evidence is presumed to be non-existent. This maxim applies where a party seeks to rely upon any deeds or writings which are not produced in Court, and the loss of which is not accounted for or supplied in the manner which the law prescribes; for in this case they should be treated, as against such party, as if non-existent. It may also means the rule is the same for those things, which are not apparent as for those which do not exist.

DE NOV.O Literally means 'new, young, fresh'. Renewed, rev.iv.ed. Once again; a second time. Trial *de nov.o*, a new trial; hearing *de nov.o*, a second hearing. When a judgment upon an issue in part is rev.ersed on error, for some mistake made by the court, in the course of the trial, a v.enire de nov.o is awarded in order that the case may again be submitted to the jury. *Chu chee peng v. Public Prosecutor [1973] 2 MLJ 35 Pg.35, Deraman & ors v. Mek Yam [1977] 1 MLJ 52 Pg. 53, Public Prosecutor v. Kulasingam [1974] 2 MLJ 26 Pg. 26, N.Y.F. Realty Sdn Bhd. v. Comptroller of Inland Revenue [1974] 1MLJ 182 Pg.184*

DE NULLO TENEMENTO, QUOD TENETUR AD TERMINUM, FIT HOMAGII, FIT TAMEN INDE FIDELITATIS SACRAMENTUM in no tenement which is held for a term of years is there an avail of homage; but there is the oath of fealty.

DE NULLO, QUOD EST SUA NATURA INDIVISIBILE, ET DIVISIONEM NON PATITUR, NULLAM PARTEM HABEBIT (VIDUA) SED SATISHFACIAT EL AD VALENTIAM the widow shall have no part of that which is in its nature indivisible, and will not undergo division; but let her be satisfied with something of equal value.

DE SIMLLIBUS IDEM EST JUDICIUM in like cases or matters the judgment is to be the same. (Ame Cyc) Decisions of the contemporaneous or superior Courts should be respected. It also means in like cases the judgment is the same.

DE SON TORT 'of his own wrong'. this term is usually applied to a person who, hav.ing no right to meddle with the affairs or estate of a deceased person, yet undertakes to do. so, by acting as

executor of the deceased. vide executor de son tort. *Chia Foon Sian & Anor v. Lam Chew Fah & Anor [1955] 21 MLJ at Pg. 205; (Administration), Ex Parte Public Trustee, Federation of Malaya [1950] 16 MLJ at Pg. 230; (Trust), Re Chop Sin Guan Seng [1934] 3 MLJ 1 at Pg. 1 ; (Bankruptcy)*

DE TEMPORE CUJUS CONTRARIUM MEMORIA HOMINUM NON EXISTIT from time immemorial, from time whereof the memory of man does not exist to the contrary.

DEBELLATIO 'Warring down'. It is the complete annihilation of a warring party, bringing about the end of the conflict.

DEBILE FUNDAMENTUM FALIT OPUS where the foundation fails all goes to the ground. It also means a weak foundation destroys the superstructure.

DEBITA SEQUUNTUR PERSONAM DEBITORIS debts follow the person of the debtor.

DEBITOR NON PRAESUMITUR DONARE a debtor is not presumed to give. This maxim has reference to the equitable doctrine of satisfaction.

DEBITORUM PACIONIBUS CREDITORUM PETITIO NEC TOLLI NEC MINUI POTEST the right of a creditor to sue cannot be taken away or lessened by the contracts of their debtors. It also means the rights of creditors can neither be taken away nor diminished by agreements among the debtors.

DEBITUM ET CONTRACTUS SUNT NULLIUS LOCI debt and contract are of no place.

DEBITUM IN PRESENTI SOLVENDUM IN FUTURO a debt due at present to be paid in future.'

DEBITUM a debt.

DECISION 'a conclusion reached after an evaluation of facts and law'. It is the outcome of a proceeding before a judge, arbitrator, Government agency or other legal tribunal. "decision" is a general term often used interchangeably with the terms judgment or "opinion." to be precise, howev.er, a judgment is the written form of the court's decision in the clerk's minutes or notes, and an opinion is a written document setting out the reasons for reaching the decision. *The Sultan of Johore v. Tungku Abubakar & ors. [1950] 16 MLJ at Pg. 8; (Constitution)*

DECREE 'to decide, determine'. It used to originally be a determination on the merits by a court of chancery or equity. This distinguished a decree from a judgment, which was normally awarded only in courts of law. The distinction is ignored by most modern courts It also means a court judgment, especially in a court of equity, bankruptcy, admiralty, divorce, or probate. Yeap Lean Seng & 4 ors v. Kok Ho Teik & Anor [1951] 17 MLJ at Pg. 235; The Sultan of Johore v. Tungku Abubakar & Ors. [1950] 16

MLJ at Pg. 8; Ban Kok Hotel v. Low Phek Choon [1950] 16 MLJ at Pg. 251

DECREE NISI A provisional decree of divorce, which becomes absolute only upon the passage of a specified interv. al of time, usually six months. Also, a decree which becomes effective at a future date in the absence of an intervening application or order; or a provisional decree which becomes final only on the entry of a final order following a motion. *Ng v. Lim [1969] 1 MLJ 140 (Family Law)*

DECREE NISI a decree to be made final unless a contingency happens. A decree is said to be made nisi when it is to take effect after a specified period or after the person affected by it fails to show cause against it within a certain time. A provisional decree which will be made absolute on motion or otherwise unless cause is shown against it. In family law, a decree granted in the first instance for the dissolution of a marriage:

DECREE-HOLDER any person in whose favour a decree has been passed or an order capable of execution has been made. *Kuna Sockalingam Mudaliar v. Yang Saripah & Anor [1954] 20 MLJ at Pg. 14*

DEDITITI criminals who had been marked in the face or on the body with fire or an iron, so that the mark could not be erased and subsequently manumitted.

DEFALCATION 'Cutting off with a sickle'. The misappropriation of funds by one entrusted with them.

DEFECIENTE UNO NON POTEST ESSE HAERES one blood being wanted, one cannot be heir. It also means one blood being wanting, he cannot be heir.

DEFECTUS POTESTATIS NULLITAS NULLITATEM *Chan Siew Kim v. Woi Fung Sheng Tim Medical Store & Anor [1978] 1 MLJ 144 Pg. 146*

DEFUNCTUS dead.

DEI GRATIA by the grace of God.

DEI JUDICIUM the judgement of God.

DEL CREDERE 'to trust, entrust, commit'. It is an agency built on trust. An agency in which a seller's agent is entrusted with custody of goods and the authority to deliv.er them to a buyer in exchange for payment. Also, a transaction in which one that acts as agent for another in the sale of an item guarantees the credit of the purchaser, usually for an extra sales commission. A *del credere* agent acts as surety for the benefit of his principal in transactions with third parties. Used in connection with agents who guarantee the good faith or financial capability of the persons or entities on whose behalf they act. *Royal Insurance Group v. David [1976] 1 MLJ 128 Pg. 129*

DELEGATA POTESTAS NON POTEST DELEGARI a delegated power cannot be delegated. It also means a delegated power cannot be delegated. This rule applies wherever the authority involves a trust or discretion in the agent for the exercise of which he is selected; but does not apply where it involves no matter of discretion, and it is immaterial whether the act be done by one person or another, and the original agent remains responsible to the principal.

DELEGATUS NON POTEST DELEGARE 'that a delegated authority cannot further delegate'. This is one of the fundamental principles of administrative law. When a higher authority delegates an authority or decision-making power to a person or institution, that person or institution cannot delegate such authority to another unless there is explicit authorization for it in the original delegation. *Tan Seng Tin & ors. v. Public Prosecutor [1970[1 MLJ 100, at 101 (Custom evasion), Johnson Tan Han Seng v. Public Prosecutor [1977] 2 MLJ 66 Pg. 77, Chop Eng Thye Co. v. Malaysia National Insurance Sdn Bhd [1977] 1 MLJ 161 Pg. 163*

DELEGATUS NON POTEST DELEGARE 'That which has been delegated, cannot delegate [further]'.

DELEGATUS NON POTEST DELEGARE delegation cannot be made by a delegate. It also means a delegate cannot delegate; A delegated power cannot be further delegated. *Woon Mooi Hua & Anor v Tan Kay Swee [1971] 1 MLJ 169 at 171 Per Chang Min Tat J* The award must comply with the submission of the parties. The arbitration must not delegate his duties with regard to the award (delegatus non potest delegare) unless the parties authorize him to do so. However, the arbitrator may delegate a purely ministerial act in which nothing is left to discretion. He may, in certain cases, consult other learned persons when there is no requirement for a hearing of evidence and the arbitrator was chosen for his particular skill. *Kuala Ibai Development Sdn Bhd v Kumpulan Perunding Sdn Bhd [1999] 5 MLJ 137 at 148 Per Nik Hashim J*

DELIBERANDUM EST DIU QUOD STATUENDUM EST SEMEL that which is to be resolved once for all should long be deliberated upon.

DELICATUS DEBITOR EST ODIOSUS IN LEGE a luxurious debtor is odious in law.

DELICTUM tort or wrongdoing which gave rise to a private action resulting in a pecuniary penalty being paid to the victim.

DELINQUENS PER IRAM PROVOCATUS, PUNIRI DEBET NITIUS a delinquent provoked by anger ought to be punished with less rigour. This maxim relates to the principles involved in imposing punishment on a convicted person. It is still the law that provocation offered by the victim at the time of commission of the crime is to be considered as a mitigating factor in sentencing the criminal.

DEMENTIA PRAECOX 'early insanity'. This term is applied to a form of mental illness seen in young people that have a split personality. *Angullia v. Rahimaboo [1939] 8 MLJ 80 at Pg. 82;*

DEMISSIO a demise or letting. Chiefly used in the phrase ex demissione (on the demise). Which formed part of the title of the cause in the old actions of ejectment, where it signified that the nominal plaintiff (fictitious person) held the 'estate on the demise' of, that is, by a lease from, the real plaintiff. (Black's Law Dict)

DEMO JUDEX IN CAUSA SUA (NEMO IUDEX IN SUA CAUSA) 'no-one should be a judge in his own cause'. It is a principle of natural justice that no person can judge a case in which they hav.e an interest.[1] The rule is very strictly applied to any appearance of a possible bias, ev.en if there is actually none: «Justice must not only be done, but must be seen to be done. *Isman Bin Osman v. Government of Malaysia [1973] 2 MLJ143 Pg.145*

DEO VOLENTE God willing.

DEORUM INJURIAE DIIS CURAE 'The gods take care of injuries to the gods'. Blasphemy is a crime against the State, rather than against God.

DEPOSITUM traditionally, the simplest form of bailment, being the transfer of possession of goods to the bailee for safe custody for the benefit of the bailor.

DERELICTION 'to forsake, neglect, abandon'. It is a failure or neglect of duty or the abandonment or neglect of property. Also, land created by the gradual withdrawal of waters, such as a new beach created by the withdrawal of the ocean. *B. H Oon & ors. v. The Government of the State of Penang & ors. [1970] 1 MLJ 244, at 248*

DERIVATIA POTESTAS NON POTEST ESSE MAJOR PRIMITIWA derived power cannot be greater than that from which it is derived. The derivative power cannot be greater than the primitive. The power derived cannot be greater than that from which it is derived.

DESIDERATA (DESIRATUM) 'things which are desired'. *Tan Kheng Ann & ors. v. The Public Prosecutor [1965] 2 MLJ 108 Pg. 120*

DESIGNATIO UNIUS EST EXCLUSIO ALTERIUS, ET EXPRESSUM FACIT CESSARE TACITURN the specifying of one is the exclusion of another, and that which is expressed makes that which is understood to cease. It also means the naming of one is the exclusion of another, and that which is expressed makes that implied to cease.

DETENU 'a person held in custody; a detainee'. *Mak Sik Kwong v. Minister Of Home Affairs, Malaysia (No. 2) [1975] 2 MLJ175 Pg. 181, Re Tan Boon Liat [1976] 2 MLJ 83 Pg. 84 DEV.I v. Francis – A Critique [1970] 1 MLJ x, at xii*

DEUS God.

DEVASTAVIT a loss suffered to the state of a deceased person by the negligence of the executor or administrator. (5 Rawle 266, 282; Lamax Exors P 475 Wil Exors) It is the mismanagement of the estate of a deceased person in squandering and misapplying assets contrary to the duty imposed on the executor or administrator. It may result from the improper payment of claims which, by the exercise of due diligence, the administrator might have ascertained to be unjust and illegal. It may also result where an administrator purchases the property of the estate of which he is administrator, for himself. So also, a neglect to collect a debt due on an estate, which might with proper exertion be collected, is a devastavit. It also means a breach of duty or failure by the personal representative of a deceased estate to properly preserve, protect and administer estate assets which causes loss to the estate and renders the personal representative personally liable for any loss to the estate arising from such breach or mismanagement.

DICTA (dictum) in a court's decision, a statement of opinion or of a general rule that is explanatory or suggestive only, and not binding on courts in future cases, because it does not form part of the court's central argument. a statement of opinion or belief considered authoritative because of the dignity of the person making it. The term is generally used to describe a court's discussion of points or questions not raised by the record or its suggestion of rules not applicable in the case at bar. Judicial dictum is an opinion by a court on a question that is not essential to its decision even though it may be directly involved. It also means the opinions of a judge that do not embody the resolution or determination of the specific case before the court. They are the expressions in a court's opinion that go beyond the facts before the court and therefore are individual views of the author of the opinion and not binding in subsequent casesas legal precedent. The part of a judicial opinion which is merely a judge's editorializing and does not directly address the specifics of the case at bar; extraneous material which is merely informative or explanatory. Re Lim Kwang Teik & ors [1954] 20 MLJ at Pg. 160; The Sultan of Johore v. Tungku Abubakar & ors. [1950] 16 MLJ at Pg. 24; (Land, Trust, Constitutional - Sovereign Ruler), Gopal Rajaram v. Public Prosecutor [1940] 9 MLJ 101 at Pg. 103; (Negligence), Murugappa Chettiar v. S. Seeniv. Asagam [1940] 9 MLJ 217 at Pg. 219, 221; Assa Singh v. Mentri Besar, Johore [1969] 2 MLJ 31 (Unlawful Detention), Sim Yan Hoo v. Mtu and Daro District Council [1967] 1 MLJ 71 Pg.73

DIES AMORIS days of love or favour. This was the day appointed by the indulgence of the court to the defendant for his appearance when all parties appeared in court and had their appearance recorded by the proper officer. The term has its origin in the notion that a defendant was allowed to appear in court at all only by the grace of the court.

DIMINUTIO taking away.

DISCRETIO EST DISCERNERE PER LEGEM QUID SIT JUSTUM discretion consists in knowing what is just in law. Where a judge has and exercises a judicial discretion his order is unappeasable unless he did so under a mistake of law or fact or in disregard of principle, or after taking into account irrelevant matters. It will help to show this if it can be shown that there were no materials on which he could exercise his discretion in the way he did.

DISJUNCTIM separately; severally. The opposite of conjunctim (QV).

DISPARATA NON DEBENT JUNGI things unequal ought not to be joined.

DISSENTIENTIBUS dissenting, the dissenting Judge.

DISTINGUENDA SUNT TEMPORA DISTINGUE TEMPORA ET CONCORDABIS LECES times are to be distinguished; distinguish times and you will make laws agree.

DOLI CAPAX capable of crime. Having sufficient understanding to distinguish between right and wrong. Incapable of malice. In Indian Law, this conclusive presumption has been adopted for children under seven years of age. [s 82, IPC]

DOLI INCAPAX 'Incapable of guilt'. Presumption that young children or persons with diminished mental capacity cannot form the intent to commit a crime.

DOLI INCAPAX incapable of crime. Under Common law, no person shall be convicted of an offence in respect of an act or omission on his part while he was uner the age of seven years.

DOLO MALO PACTUM SE NON SERVABIT a pact made with malicious intent will not be upheld

DOLUS CIRCUITU NON PURGATUR fraud is not purged by circuity. Dolus here means a wrongful act contrary to law.

DOLUS DANS LOCUM CONTRACTUL fraud or deceit giving rise for the contract. A false representation or misrepresentation that is not inno-cent, and that is material in the formation of a contract.

DOLUS EST MACHINATIO, CUM ALLUD DISSIMULAT ALLUD AGLT deceit is a trickery for it pretends to one thing and does another.

DOLUS ET FRAUS UNA IN PARTE SANARI DEBENT deceit and fraud should always be remedied.

DOLUS wilful injury, fraud, deceit, trap, ambush or treachery all of which is employed to circumvent, cheat or deceive another party. A distinction may be made between 'dolus malus' which refers to fraud in the civil law and 'dolus bonus' which refers to the craftiness and skill of a person, for example of a seller, describing or overstating the quality of a product. While a 'dolus bonus' may not vitiate a contract of sale, misrepresentation may amount to dolus malus.'dolus incidens' meaning 'incidental fraud' on the other hand may not go to the root or essentials of the contract to make it a void contract' but it will always void what is affected by the 'dolus': see Watt 8 D.529 per Lord Mackenzie.

DOLUS SPECIALIS 'Specific deceit'. Heavily used in the context of genocide in international law.

DOMINIUM A POSSESSION CEPISSE DICITUR right is said to have its beginning from possession.

DOMINIUM NON POTEST ESSE IN PENDENTI a fee or right of property cannot be in suspension, ie it must always be vested in some one. It also means Lordship cannot be in suspense.

DOMINIUM PLENUM full and complete ownership (including possession of the property).

DOMINUS LITIS 'The master of the suit'. It means the person who was really and directly interested in the suit as a party, as distinguished from his attorney or advocate. But the term is also applied to one who, though not originally a party, has made himself such, by interv.ention or otherwise, and has assumed entire control and responsibility for one side, and is treated by the court as liable for costs. *Khoo Chin Inn & Anor v. Reliance*

Enterprise Sdn Bhd & ors [1976] 1 MLJ 35 Pg. 37

DOMINUS LITIS master of the suit. The party who has carriage and control of an action. It also means the party to a proceeding which is conducted by a procurator on his behalf. Or the plaintiff cannot be compelled to fight against a person against whom he does not wish to fight and against whom he does not claim any relief. I find myself unable to subscribe to the view that the English bank as from the transfer date ceased to have any rights in or in respect of this action and locus standi. Admittedly, as from the transfer date, the English bank ceased to have any rights or interest in the defined business as such. But certainly to my mind, the English bank had an interest and a right at all times to protect itself from liability arising from the consequences of such transfer. It seems to me that such a liability could arise in the realm of costs as long as the English bank remained a plaintiff In this action. Having divested itself of its rights including its right in these proceedings in favour of the Malaysian bank, the English bank as long as it remains as plaintiff in this action, would be in jeopardy as to costs, seeing that by reason of the transfer of rights the Malaysian bank is dominus litis; and the English bank is no more in control of the proceedings. It follows therefore, that the English bank has certainly a right and is well advised to take all proper steps immediately to remove itself as plaintiff in the proceedings, thus protecting itself from being mulcted in costs by reason of any possible act or default of the Malaysian bank relative to these proceedings. It follows therefore that the English bank did have locus standi to bring the application, seeking the order that it be substituted in these proceedings by the Malaysian bank. I might add that I could see nothing wrong in the English bank and the Malaysian bank making the application jointly. Standard Chartered *Bank v Asia Transport Service (M) Sdn Bhd & Ors [1996] 1 MLJ 157 at 164 Per Richard Talalla J.*

DOMUS a house or dwelling; a habitation. Domus is a very extensive word, and has different significant according to the subject-matter to which it is applied. In order, therefore, to understand the true meaning of it in this case, we must considered the subject-matter concerning which it is used, and inquire what was the intention of the person who used it. There are a variety of instances in the course of the statutes, in which the word 'domus' is used as synonymous to 'the society', and only means the master and scholars, and in different places the words 'nostra domus scholauim' are used.

DOMUS SUA CUIQUE EST TUTISSIMUM REFUGIUM every man's house is his castle. It also means to everyone his house in his surest refuge; or, every man's house is his own castle. If thieves come to a man's house to rob or murder him, and he or his servants kill any of the thieves in defence of himself and his house, this is not felony. When any house is recovered by action, the sheriff may break the house, and deliver the possession to the plaintiff; for after judgment it is not the house of the defendant. In all cases where the Queen is party (as where a felony or misdemeanour has been committed), the sheriff may break the party's house to execute the Queen's process, if otherwise he may not enter. In all cases when the door is open the sheriff may enter the house and do execution, at the suit of any subject. It may also meanto every one his own house is the safest refuge!

DONA CLANDESTINA SUNT SEMPER SUSPICIOSA calandestine gifts are always suspicious.

DONARI VIDETUR, QUOD NULLO JURE CAGENTE CONCEDITUR that is considered to be given which is granted without the obligation of any law. It also means a thing is said to be given when it is yielded otherwise than by virtue of a right.

DONATIO a gift.

DONATIO MORTIS CAUSA 'Gift caused by death'. "The donor, contemplating imminent death, declares words of present gifting and delivers the gift to the donee or someone who clearly takes possession on behalf of the donee. The gift becomes effective at death but remains revocable until that time.

DONATIO NON PRAESUMITUR a gift is not presumed' i.e. the general presumption is against the gift. A gift is not presumed. The presumption is the other way and accordingly where

a purchaser has the property he has bought transferred into the name of another there is a presumption of a resulting trust for the settlor, which can, however, be rebutted by proving that a gift was intended.

DONATIONUM ALIA PERFECTA, ALIA INCEPTA ET NON PERFECTA, UT SI DONA-TIO LECTA FUIT ET CONCESSA, AC TRADITIO NONDUM FUERIT SUBSECUTA some gifts are perfect, others incipient and not perfect; as if a gift were read and agreed to, but, delivery had not been followed. Some gifts are perfect, others incipient or not perfect; as where a gift is chosen and granted, but delivery has not then followed. This is the position at common law. A gift is revocable until it is completed by delivery or such other form of transfer as the property given requires. And there is no equity to perfect an imperfect gift, which will not be construed as a trust.

DONATOR NUNQUAM DESINIT POSSIDERE ANTEQUAM DONATORIUS INCIPIAT POSSIDERE he who gives never ceases to possess until he that receives begins to possess or he who gives never ceases to possess before the receiver begins to possess or donor never ceases to possess before the donee beings to possess.

DONUM, a gift; a free gift.

DORMIUNT ALIQUANDO LEGES, NUNQUAM MORIUNTUR the law sometimes sleeps and that they never die.

DOS RATIONABILIS VEL LEGITIMA, EST CUJUSLIBET MULLERIS E QUOCUNQUE TENEMENTO TERTIA PARS OMNIUM TERRARUM ET TENEMENTORUM, QUAE VIR SUUS TENUIT IN DOMINICO SUO UT DE reasonable and legitimate dower belongs to every woman, of a third part of all the lands and tenements of which the husband was seized in his demesne, as of fee.

DOTI LEX FAVET; PRAEMIUM PUDORIS EST' IDEO PARCATUR the law, favours dower it is the reward of chastity, therefore let it be preserved.

DRAMATIS PERSONAE the persons of the drama or the performers or the conspicuous actors.

DRAMATIS PERSONAE 'the characters in a play or story'. Re Syed Eidrus Alsagoff; Syed Mohamed Alsagoff v. Poh Kim San & ors. [1966] 1 MLJ 75 at Pg. 77

DUBIA IN MELIOREM PARTEM INTERPRETARI DEBENT 'Doubtful things should be interpreted in the best way'. Often spoken as "to give the benefit of the doubt."

DUBIO in doubt left to wonder.

DUCES TECUM 'Bring with you'. A "subpoena duces tecum" is a summons to produce physical evidence for a trial.

DUCES TECUM 'Bring with you'. A writ which commands a person to appear in court on a certain day, and bring with him certain writings or evidences. The name for a subpeona or writ which requires a party or witness to produce and bring with him documents, papers, records or other evidence relev.ant to a case, trial or controversy. *Law Society of Singapore v. Chan Chow Wang [1975] 1 MLJ 59 Pg. 65*

DUM BENE SE GESSERIT during good behavior; This is the term applicable to an office where the incumbent holds the office during his good behaviour and not merely at the pleasure of a superior. It also means during good conduct; for so long as he or she conducts himself or herself properly. Used of someone who holds office from the Crown during good behavior, but who can be removed (such as a juge, by a decision of the parliament).

DUM CASTA VIXERIT so long as she shall remain chaste. A dum casta clause in a separation agreement is one whereby the husband is required to provide for the support of the wife so long as she remain chaste.

DUM FUIT INFRA AETATEM while he was within age. An ancient writ that lay where an infant alienated his land in fee simple or for a term of life. He could avail of this writ when he came of full age; he must be of full age the day his writ was issued. Also, if an infant alienated his land and died, his issue on attaining full age had the remedy of this writ.

DUM LEGO, ASSENTIOR while I read I assent. I yield to the author's opinions.

DUM While, as long as, until; upon condition that; provided that.

DUM NON FUIT COMPOS MENTIS while he was not of sound mind. This was the name of an ancient writ available when a man of unsound mind alienated his land in fee simple and died; his heirs after his death had the remedy of this writ. The writ, however, was not available to the alienor himself for 'a man shall not be received to disable himself.

DUO NON POSSUNT IN SOLIDO UNAM REM POSSIDERE ownership or possession in entirety cannot be in two persons of the same thing. It also means two persons cannot possess one thing in entirety. Or two cannot possess the whole of one thing in specie.

DUO SUNT INSTRUMENTA AD OMNES RES AUT CONFIRMANDAS AUT IMPUGNANDAS - RATIO ET there are two instruments either to confirm or impugn all things 'reason and authority.

DURANTE BENE PLACITO 'during good pleasure'. It is used in some law phrases. For example, durante absentia means during absence, durante minor cetate means during minority, durante bene placito means during our good pleasure. *Haji Ariffin v. Government Of Pahang [1969} 1 MLJ 9 (Administrative Law), Najar Singh V. Government Of Malaysia & Anor [1973] 2 MLJ191 Pg.194*

E

EA QUAE COMMENDANDI CAUSA IN VENDITIONIBUS DICUNTUR SI PALAM AP-PEREANT VENDITOREM NON OBLIGANT

these things which are said for the sake of commendation in sales, if they are plainly apparent; do not bind the seller. The maxim, caveat emptor, applies as a rule in cases where the seller gives a general warranty against defects, if there is a visible defect and one obvious to the senses.

EADEM EST RATIO, EADEM EST LEX the same reason, the same law.

EADEM MENS PRAESUMITUR REGIS QUAE EST JURIS, ET QUAE ESSE DEBET, PRAESERTIM IN DUBIIS the mind of the Sovereign is presumed to be coincident with that of the law, and with that which it ought to be especially in ambiguous matters. It also means the mind of the king is presumed to be in conformity with the law, and with what it should be, especially in doubtful cases.

EI INCUMBIT PROBATIO QUI DICIT 'proof lies on him who asserts'. It is the concept that one is innocent until proven guilty.

EI INCUMBIT PROBATIO QUI DICIT NON QUI NEGAT the proof lies upon him who affirms, not upon him who denies.

EI QUI AFFIRMAT NON EI QUI NEGAT INCUMBIT PROBATIO
Chen Soon Lee v. Chong v. Oon Pin & ors [1966] 2 MLJ 264 at Pg. 267, Nanyang Development (1966) Sdn Bhd. v. How Swee Poh [1970] 1 MLJ 145, at 145 (Removal of Private Caveat)

EJECTIONE FIRMAE a writ of ejectment which lay for one who was dispossessed of lands and tenements whereof he had been a tenant, by the reversioner, remainder or a stranger. 'A writ of ejectione firmae is in its nature merely an action of trespass, and the plaintiff shall only recover that part of the term which is unexpired, the same as in trespass, a man shall recover no damages for a trespass not committed but to be com-mitted. But to recover his term he must sue by an action of covenant at common law ... where a man is ousted from his term by a stranger, the common law is, that he shall have a writ of ejectione firmae against him who ousted him; and if he be ousted by his lessor, a writ of covenant; and if by the lessee, or grantee of the reversion, a writ of covenant against his lessor, and he shall count a special count etc. it also means This, it will be recollected, was an action of ejectione firmae, and not an ejectment molded and regulated by rules of court as it is at present. The court very properly distinguished there between what operates by way of bar to a future recovery for the same thing and what by way of estoppel. That was the case of a mere recovery in ejectione firmae without title alleged, and the plaintiff might in respect of possession or other varying circumstances of title,

be well entitled to recover at one time, and not be so at another. It is not the recovery, but the matter alleged by the party, and upon which the recovery proceeds, which creates the estoppel. The recovery of itself in an action of trespass is only a bar to the future recovery of damages for the same injury, but the estoppel precludes parties and privies from con-tending to the contrary of that point of matter of fact which, having been once distinctly put in issue by them or by those to whom they are privy in estate or law, has been, on such issue joined, solemnly found against them.

EJUS EST INTERPRETARI CUJUS EST CONDERE it belongs to him to interpret (or explain) who enacts; the right of interpreting belongs to him who enacts. It also means it is for him who made the law to construe it.

EJUS NULLA CULPA EST CUI PARERE NECESSE SIT he is not guilty for fault who necessarily obeys; that is, no non incurs fault or blame through, the performance of an act which he is under the necessity of performing. He who is bound to obey is in no fault. As where the proper officer executes a criminal, or where an officer of justice, in the exercise of a particular duty, kills a person who resists.

EJUSDEM GENERIS 'of the same class'. known as a "canon of construction", it states that when a limited list of specific things also includes a more general class, that the scope of that more general class shall be limited to other items more like the specific items in the list.

EJUSDEM GENERIS 'of the same kind or nature e'.jusdem generic is used to interpret loosely written statutes. Where a law lists specific classes of persons or things and then refers to them in general, the general statements only apply to the same kind of persons or things specifically listed. The general words shall be construed as applicable only to persons or things of the same general nature or kind as those enumerated in the list. for example, if a law refers to automobiles, trucks, tractors and motorcycles, then the term "vehicles" would not include airplanes, since the list was of land-based transportation. *Yeap Lean Seng & 4 ors v. Kok Ho Teik & Anor [1951] 17 MLJ at Pg. 237; (Land, Japanese Judgments and Civil Proceedings Ordinance), Dawoodshah & Co. v. Glas & ors [1939] 8 MLJ 90 at Pg. 90; (Taxation) Public Prosecutor v. Ho Ah Loke [1939] 8 MLJ 231 at Pg. 232; (Nuisance) Haji Ariffin v. Government Of Pahang [1969] 1 MLJ 21 (Administrative Law) Rex v. S. Nadaison [1933] 2 MLJ 41 Pg. 42 Michi (F) and Anoyu (F) v. Rex [1934] 3 MLJ 11 at Pg. 11; The Eastern Shipping Co. Ltd. of Penang v. His Majesty's Attorney General for The S.S. [1934] 3 MLJ 99 at Pg. 106; Hashim v. Public Prosecutor [1967] 1 MLJ 251; Tan Ah Lek v. Rex [1941] MLJ 49*

ELECTIO EST INTERNS LIBERA ET SPONTANEA SEPARATIO UNIUS REI AB ALIA SINE COMPULSIONE CONSISTENS IN ANIMO ET VOLUNTATE election is an internal, free and spontaneous separation of one thing from another without compulsion, consisting in intention and will. It also means election once made cannot be recalled or the right of selecting one of several forms of action for the redress of injury or enforcement of a right.

ELECTIONES FIANT RITE ET LIBERE SINE INTERRUPTIONE ALIQUA let elections be made just and free without interruption.

EMPTOR a buyer or purchaser.

EO NOMINE 'in the name of'. In that name or by that designation or mark. In law and commerce, the name given to a commodity in the marketplace, generally a product name which is in common use and therefore well known. *The Halcyon Isle [1978] 1 MLJ 189 Pg. 191, The Sultan Of Johore v. Tungku Abubakar & ors. [1950] 16 MLJ at Pg. 30: (Constitutional Law - Sovereign Ruler.); Mohindar Singh & Another v. Rex [1950] 16 MLJ at Pg. 98; (Criminal Law); Rex v. Sim Keng Chuan [1933] 2 MLJ 212 Pg. 213*

EODEM LIGAMINE QUOLIGATUM EST a bond is released by the same formalities with which it is contracted. Although the obligor of a bond cannot, at the day appointed, pay a less sum in satisfaction of the whole, yet if the obligee then receive a part and give his acquittance under seal for the whole, this will be a good discharge.

EPISCOPUS ALTERIUS MANDATO QUAM REGIS NON TENETUR

OBTEMPERARE a bishop need not obey any mandate save the kings.

ERCISCUNDUS to be divided.

ERGA OMNES 'towards all'. Refers to rights or obligations that are owed towards all.

ERGO 'therefore'.

ERRATA errors in printing corrected.

ERRATUM 'having been made in error'.

ERRATUM error.

ERROR FUCATUS NUDA VERITATE IN MULTIS EST PROBLILIOR; ET SAEPE-NUMERO RATIONIBUS VINCIT VERI TATEM ERROR varnished error is in many things more probable than naked truth; and frequently error conquers truth by reasoning. It also means painted error appears in many things more probable than naked truth; and again and again conquers truth by reasoning.

ERROR QUI NON RESISTITUR, APPROBATUR an error which is not resisted is approved. Thus, one who enables another to commit a fraud is answerable. a person who has a title to property offered at auction, and, knowing his title, stands by and encourages the sale, or does not forbid it, will be bound by the sale.

ERRORES AD SUA PRINCIPIA REFERRE, EST REFELLERE A

maxim meaning 'to refer errors to their principles, is to refute them.

ESTOPPEL 'to stand still, to halt' a bar or waiv.er. a restraint or impediment imposed by the law; the prev.ention of further action or claim by a party. in real estate law, an *estoppel certificate* is a sworn statement by a party to the transaction as to some important fact; e.g., the principal amount of a mortage. The statement is binding upon him for all purposes thereafter. *Promissory estoppel* prev.ents a party who has made a promise upon which another party has relied, from repudiating that promise. an impediment or bar arising from a man's own conduct; whereby he is prohibited from averring or proving anything in contradiction to what he has either expressly avowed, or has by his conduct led others to believe to be the case. *Successors Of Moine & Co. Ltd v. East Asiatic Co. Ltd & Singapore Harbour Board [1954] 20 MLJ at Pg. 114; (Estoppel); T. Chelliah v. Laxman Singh & Anor [1954] 20 MLJ at Pg. 211; (Contract Estoppel); Koh Kok Eng v. Regina [1955] 21 MLJ at Pg. 17; (Road Traffic Ordinance 1941)*

ET AL 'and others'. It is the abbreviation of et alii, meaning "and others".

ET CETERA 'the other, the rest', And so forth; and more of the same'. And others of the same kind. *Abdul Kadir AND Another v. T. Kaderbhoy [1949] 15 MLJ 43 Pg. 49*

ET DE HOC PONIT SC SUPER and of this he puts himself upon the country.

These words were the proper conclusion in a plaintiffs pleading where he concluded his traverse.

ET HOC PARATUS EST VERIFICARE and this he is prepared to verify. These words were the formal conclusion of a pleading in confession and avoidance.

ET SEQ (ET SEQUITUR) 'to follow'. And the following; and as follows. Used to indicate that notes or pages of a text follow sequentially after a specified number or that one element of a list follows another. *Nicholas & ors. v. Gan Realty Sdn Bhd. & ors. [1970] 2 MLJ 89, at 91 (Temporary injunction), The Sultan of Johore v. Tungku Abubakar & ors. [1950] 16 MLJ at Pg. 22 ;(Land, Trust, Constitutional - Sovereign Ruler); Yong Kuan Teik v. Dev.An Nair [1965] 2 MLJ 162 Pg. 164;*

ET UXOR 'and wife'. usually used instead of naming a man's wife as a party in a case.

ET VIR 'and husband'. It is usually used instead of naming a woman's husband as a party in a case.

ETCETERA so forth or the like that refers to a limitation, it is submit-ted, and not an enlargement of the powers of the officers and inspectors as already expressed in the section.

EVENTUS EST QUI EX CAUSA SEQUITUR; ET DICITUR EVENTUS QUIA EX CAUSIS EVENIT an event is that which follows from the cause, and is called an event because it eventuates from causes.

EVENTUS VARIOS RES NOVA SEMPER HABET a new matter always produces various events. It also means a new matter always induces various events.

EX ABUNDANTE CAUTELA; 'from excessive caution'. *In Re Tan Lian Boh, Deed. Wee Sin Choe & Anor v. The Official Assignee & The Attorney-General [1951] 17 MLJ at Pg. 189; (Will), E. v. Comptroller-General of Inland Revenue [1970] 2 MLJ 117, at 119 (Income Tax Law), Eng Song Hai v. Public Prosecuter [1954] 20 MLJ at Pg. 38; (Criminal Procedure Code); Yap Yoon Lin v. Regina [1954] 20 MLJ at Pg. 61; Chong Fong Yeen & Anor v. Tan Kriam Wah [1951] 17 MLJ at Pg. 217; (Debtor and Creditor (Occupation Period) Ordinance); Re Arbitration Between Tan Chu Ing & ors [1939] 8 MLJ 182 at Pg. 182; (Rules of The Supreme Court); Wong Poh Oi v. Gertrude Guok & Anor [1966] 2 MLJ 134 at Pg. 135; Rex v. Li Kim Poat & Another [1933] 2 MLJ 164 Pg.166; Tai Lee Oil Mill Co. & ors. v. Ng Ok Ling [1967] 1 MLJ 285 –Pg.290; Leonard J.K.B. v. Official Asssignee, Singapore [1941] MLJ 26; Tan Geok Kwang v. Public Prosecutor [1949] 15 MLJ 87 Pg.88*

EX AEQUO ET BONO 'In equity and good conscience'. From what is fair and good. A man is bound to pay money which ex oequo et bono he holds for the use of another. *Ng Siew San v. Melaka [1973] 2 MLJ 154 Pg.158*

EX ANTE 'of before'; essentially, meaning "before the event", usually used when forecasting future events.

EX ANTECIDENTIBUS ET CONSEQUENTIBUS FIT OPTIMA INTERPRETATIO a passage will be best interpreted by reference to that which precedes and follows it. From that which goes before, and from that which follows, is derived the best interpretation. It is a true rule of construction that the sense and meaning of the parties in any particular part of an instrument may be collected from what goes before and what follows; every part of it may be brought into action in order to collect from the whole one uniform and consistent sense.

EX CAPITE DOLL (OR) FRAUDIS on the ground of fraud.

EX CATHEDRA 'from the chair'. where chair refers to authority or position. authority derived from one's position.

EX CAUTELA *Nyalchand Motichand & Co. v. A.S.Mohamed Mydin and v.V.Arusay Rowther, Third Party [1951] 17 MLJ at Pg. 201; (Common Law)*

EX CONCESSIS 'from what has been conceded already'. often used in a "guilt by association" context.

EX CONTRACTU «from a contract,» is a legal term that indicates a consequence of a contract. Ex contractu is often to denote the source of a legal action (often as opposed to ex delicto). Source of a legal action can be ex contractu or ex delicto. Where a cause of action for a suit arises from a breach of promise laid down in a contract, the action is ex contractu. Where cause of action arise from a breach of duty it is ex delicto. *Goh Yew & Anor v. Soh Kian Tee [1970] 1 MLJ 138, 141 (Inability to Perform Contract), Low Ai Bee v. Ralph Eu Peng Lee [1974] 1 MLJ 74 Pg.75*

EX CONTRACTU, QUASI EX CONTRACTU

EX DEBITIO JUSTITIAE arising as a matter of right; a debt of justice. Contrasted with ex gratia. matter of right; a debt of justice. Contrasted with ex gratia. It also means from or as a debt of justice; in accordance with the requirement of justice, of right; as a matter of right. Or from a debt of justice; from that which is owing; from one's right ; as of right. As a debt of justice; as a legal obligation; from a lawful or just debt. A remedy which the applicant obtains as of right, such as habeas corpus. From what is due of right; from or as a debt of justice; in accordance with the requirement of justice; a right the refusal of which wil cause injustice; as a matter of right; for example a writ of habeus corpus.'... at the hearing mutual mistake was not mentioned until final address and it was too late for the defendant to reply ... (he) may claim ex dubito justitiae to have the plaintiff's case presented in an intelligent form...' per *Pretheroe CJ in M Pakiam v YP Devathanjam [1952] 18 MLJ 58.* Whether power of court to stay an action under a arbitration clause is a matter of discretion and not

ex debito justitiae. *Heyman & Anor v Darwin Ltd [1942] All ER 337 at 335, Alagappa Chettiar v Palanivelpillai & Others [1967] 1 MLJ 208 (s 6 Arbitration Act 1952). United Asian Bank Bhd v Balakrishnan (t/a Balakrishnan Restaurant) & Ors [1992] 1 MLJ 587 at 591 Per VC George J*

EX DEBITO JUSTITIAE 'As a matter of right'. The phrase is applied to remedies that the court is bound to give when they are claimed, as distinct from those that it has discretion to grant. *King Hock Ching v. Ung Siew Ping [1974] 2 MLJ 16 Pg.17, Palka Utama Shipping Co. Ltd v. "Sri Melati" (Owners) & Parties Interested[1976] 1 MLJ 283 Pg. 286, Tan Chwee Geok & Anor v. Khaw Yen-Yen & Anor [1975] 2 MLJ 188 Pg. 190*

EX DELICTO 'from a transgression'. It is the consequence of a crime or tort.

EX DEMISSIONE upon the demise. In England, before the passing of the Common Law Procedure Act of 1852, an action on ejectment was a complicated one and a testimony to the ingenuity of the common law practitioners. Originally, an action in ejectment was available only to enforce possessory rights under a lease or other such chattel interest. An action for recovery of land by one entitled to the freehold was a real action and was extremely complex in procedure. In order to make an action in ejectment applicable to such actions for recovery of land, the courts permitted the plaintiff to introduce the fiction that he had leased the land to John Doe who was dispossessed by the casual ejector, Richard Roe, during the currency of the lease. The action was commenced by the party claiming title delivering a declaration to the defendant in possession, stating the arrangement of the lease to John Doe and the dispossession of John Doe by Richard Roe. Attached to this declaration was a notice to the defendant that Richard Roe had no title to the land and that if the defendant did not appear in the action, Richard Roe would suffer judgment and accordingly the defendant would be then turned out of possession. The action was entitled: Doe on the demise or lease Jones v Browm or Doe d. Jones v Brown.

EX DILUTURNITATE TEMPORIS, OMNIA PRAESUMUNTUR SOLEMNITER ESSE ACTA from length of time (after lapse of time) all things are presumed to have been done in due form. It also means from lapse of time, all things are presumed to have been done rightly and regularly. This maxim applies as well where matters are in contest between private persons as to matters public in their nature. Deeds, wills, and other attested documents which are more than thirty years old, and are produced from the proper custody, prove themselves, and the testimony of the subscribing witness may be dispensed with. The law will presume strongly in favour of the validity of a marriage, especially where a great length of time has elapsed since its celebration. It will also presume in favour of honesty and against fraud, and this presumption acquires weight from the length of time during which

a transaction has subsisted. But there is only a presumption and Coke (Co Lott 232b) adds 'Donec probetur in contrarium' - until the contrary is proved.

EX DOLO MALO NON ORITUR ACTIO No action can arise from or be based on a bad deed or on deceit. The principle, which directs a court not to consider an action based on an illegal or immoral act. *P.M. Hendry v. George John De Cruz [1949] 15 MLJ 79 Pg.80*

EX FACIE 'shape, form, figure' that are clear on the first glance. They are seen clearly, without doubt or question or those elements, which are clear from the face of a document. *Ahmad Bin Udoh & Anor v. Ng Aik Chong [1969] 2 MLJ 117 (Contract); Re Ding Do Ca, DECD [1966] 2 MLJ 220 at Pg. 222; Low Pin v. Likok Finance Co. Ltd. [1966] 1 MLJ 167 at Pg. 168; Lam Soon Cannery Co. v. Hooper & Co. [1966] 1 MLJ 198 at Pg. 202; Lam Soon Cannery Co. v. H.W. Hooper & Co. [1965] 1MLJ 135 Pg. 137; Gov. Inda Mudaliar Sons v. Gov.Indasamy [1967] 2 MLJ 5 Pg.6, Comptroller – General of Inland Revenue, Malaysia v. T [1970] 2 MLJ 35, at 38 (Income Tax Law)*

EX FACIE 'on the face'. if a contract is blatantly and obv.iously incorrect or illegal, it can be considered void ex facie without any further analysis or arguments.

EX FIDA BONA 'good business norms'.

EX GRATIA 'As a matter of fav.or'. Pleasantness, kindness, thankfulness. Willingly'. Out of a sense of fairness. An action done as a fav.or, not because it was required, due or owed. A decision made not in recognition of right but out of a sense of fairness and justice. *Acme Canning Corporation Ltd v. Lee Kim Seng [1977] 1 MLJ 252 Pg. 254*

EX HYPOTHESI 1 'according to assumptions'. by the hypothesis; upon the supposition; upon the theory or facts assumed. *Murugappa Chettiar v. S. Seeniv. Asagam [1940] 9 MLJ 217 at Pg. 219, 221; (Mortgage); In Re Tan Soh Sim (f) Deceased: The Official Administrator, Federation Of Malaya v. Tan Saw Keow & 17 Others [1950] 16 MLJ at Pg. 129; (Probation); Ng Siew Eng & Anor v. Loh Tuan Woon [1955] 21 MLJ at Pg. 90; (Negligence); Meenachi Sundram & Anor v. Kunjan Pillai [1955] 21 MLJ at Pg. 130; (Landlord And Tenant); Chua Sai Ngoh (f) v. Beh Ai Meng [1955] 21 MLJ at Pg. 169; (Land Law); Chong Fook Kam & Anor v. Shaaban Bin Hussien [1967] 2 MLJ 54 Pg.58*

EX IMPROV.ISO '(Done) without forethought or preparation'. Suddenly, spontaneously. *Muller & Phipps (M) Sdn Bhd Penang Port Commision [1974] 2 MLJ 39 Pg.41*

EX IMPROVISO without preparation. Indeed, the judge had no hesitation in saying that, without it, it was impossible to ask the jury to act as handwriting experts and to pass a verdict which might be a conviction. It cannot be said, in the circum-stances, that this

evidence was evidence upon any matter which arose ex improviso, if those Latin words are given the meaning which was originally attributed to them. Nor can it be said that it was evidence the necessity of which no human ingenuity could foresee. It was evidence the necessity of which was obvious.

EX In law Latin the word 'ex' or 'e' as it occurs before consonants is a preposition, used at the beginning of many phrases and maxims, meaning 'from' 'out of', 'of', 'by', 'By virtue of', 'on', 'on account of', 'according to', 'with', 'at or in', and it is sometimes used in conjunction with other words as an adverb. As a prefix, it may denote removal or cessation, or it may be equivalent to 'without', 'reserving' or 'excepting'. It is also sometimes used as an abbreviation of Exhibit.

EX INJURIA JUS NON ORITUR law does not arise from injustice a principle in international law that unjust acts cannot create laws.

EX IPSA CORPORA *Wah Tat Bank Ltd & ors v. Chan Cheng Kum & ors [1967] 2 MLJ 263 Pg.264*

EX JURE NATURE *Yong Joo Lin & ors v. Fung Pol Fong [1941] MLJ 56; Sochalingam Chettiar v. Samasundaram Chetiiar [1941] MLJ 88*

EX JURE *Re Chan See, Deed; Kui Ti Eng (w) ors. v. Singapore Fishery Ltd. [1955] 21 MLJ at Pg. 141; (Workmen's Compensation Ordinance)*

EX LEGE, LEGIBUS according to law. The fiduciary duty may arise, not only from trust, but also ex lege and ex conventione. The duty was recognised by the civil law, and it is, I think, acknowledged in the jurisprudence of all civilised communi-ties. The duty is, to use the Latin phrase, that the person subject to it must not become auctor in rem suam. It applied to tutors and curators in the civil law, and it applies to tutors and curators in the Scots law. It applies also to judicial factors appointed by the courts in Scotland, and to partners and to agents under a contract of agency, and, of course, to trustees under a settlement or under a will. That by no means exhausts the area of its operation, but for illustrative purposes the examples I have given will suffice. Some who are subject to the duty are never entitled to remuneration; some are ex lege entitled to payment for their services; some are entitled to payment ex conventione; and some are entitled to payment if the settlor or testator so directs. The rule is the same for all: it is not that reward for services is repugnant to the fiduciary duty, but that he who has the duty shall not take any secret remuneration or any financial benefit not authorized by the law, or by his contract, or by the trust deed under which he acts, as the case may be. In England, moreover, the court has power to order payments to be made to trustees for whom the truster has made no such provision, a power which it is difficult to reconcile with a general principle that remuneration is repugnant to trusteeship.

EX MERO MOTU 'From a mere motion'. Of one's own freewill. complete motion Of his own doing; voluntarily; without being asked. On motion of the court without application by either party. *Public Prosecutor v. Datuk Haji Harun Bin Haji Idris & ors [1977] 1 MLJ 180 Pg. 200, Public Prosecutor v. Syed Abdul Bahari Shahabuddin [1976] 1 MLJ 87 Pg. 88*

EX MULTITUDINE SIGNORUM, COLLOGITUR IDENTITAS VERA true identity is gathered from a great number of signs or marks. It also means a thing described by a great number of marks is easily identified though, as to some, the description may not be strictly correct.

EX NECESSITATE (EX NECESSITATE REI) 'from the urgency of the case'. from the necessity of the thing. many acts may be done ex necessitate ret, which would not be justifiable without it; and sometimes property is protected, ex necessitate rei, which, under, other circumstances, would not be so. For example, property put upon the land of another from necessity, cannot be distrained for rent. see distress; necessity. *Hendrik christiaan v.An Hoogstraten v. Low Lum Seng [1940] 9 MLJ 138 at Pg. 144; International Law*

EX NECESSITATE LEGIS from the necessity of the law. By implication of the law.

EX NON SCRIPTO JUS VENT QUOD USUS COMPROBAVIT law arises from custom which use the sanctioned.

EX NUNC 'from now on'. term used in contract law to specify terms that are v.oided or confirmed in effect only in the future and not prior to the contract, or its adjudication. c.f. ex tunc.

EX OFFICIO 'By virtue of his office'. Any prerogative or jurisdiction which a person in office has, by virtue of that office, he is said to exercise ex officio. From the office, by virtue of the office; powers necessarily held or implied by virtue of an office or title. Powers which need not be specified but which may be exercised nevertheless because they are necessary to the administration of the office by the officeholder. *Lee Chick Yet v. Chen Siew Hee & ors [1977] 2 MLJ 218 Pg. 219*

EX PARTE 'On one part'. Evidence given on one side only is called ex parte. referring to motions, hearings or orders granted on the request of and for the benefit of one party only. This is an exception to the basic rule of court procedure that both parties must be present at any argument before a judge, and to the otherwise strict rule that an attorney may not notify a judge without prev.iously notifying the opposition. Ex parte matters are usually temporary orders (like a restraining order or temporary custody) pending a formal hearing or an emergency request for a continuance. Most jurisdictions require at least a diligent attempt to contact the other party's lawyer of the time and place of any ex parte hearing. *Salt V. Mohammedan and Hindu Endowment Board [1941] MLJ 183,* H.M.T v.

Director –General Of Inland Revenue [1975] 2 MLJ 22 Pg. 24; Public Prosecutor v. H. Chamras Tasaso [1975] 2 MLJ 44 Pg. 45; Mak Sik Kwong v. Minister of Home Affairs,Malaysia [1975] 2 MLJ168 Pg. 170; Mak Sik Kwong v. Minister of Home Affairs,Malaysia (No 2)[1975] 2 MLJ175 Pg. 177,182; Tan Chwee Geok & Anor v. Khaw Yen-Yen & Anor [1975] 2 MLJ 188 Pg. 190; Damodaran v. V.Esudev.An [1975] 2 MLJ 231 Pg. 234; Ipoh Garden Sdn Bhd v. Ismail Mahyuddin Enterprise Sdn Bhd [1975] 2 MLJ 241 Pg. 241; Re Datuk James Wong Kim Min [1975] 2 MLJ 244 Pg. 244; Madhav.An Nair & Anor v. Public Prosecutor [1975] 2 MLJ 264 Pg. 267;

EX POST FACTO 'Done after another thing'. A law enacted purposely to take cognizance of an offence already committed, is, so far as that indiv. idual offence is concerned, an ex postfacto law. The phrase applies to any law that criminalizes an act that was innocent when committed; any law that makes a crime greater or more serious than when it was committed; or any rule of evidence which adv.ersely affects a criminal defendant's rights as they existed prior to the rule. Article I, Section 9 of the U.S. Constitution precludes the passage of such a law or rule by any state or by the federal Government. The prov.ision has been construed to apply only to crimes, not to civ.il rights. DATUK HAJI HARUN BIN HAJI IDRIS & ORS V. PUBLIC PROSECUTOR[1978] 1 MLJ 240 =PG 245. LING BENG SUNG V. KHONG THAI SAWMILL (MIRI) SDN BHD [1976] 1 MLJ 59=PG 69

EX POST FACTO 'from a thing done afterward'. commonly said as "after the fact." *Ex post facto* law a retroactive retroactive law. e.g. a law that makes a past act illegal that was not illegal when it was done.

EX POST 'from after'. based on knowledge of the past.

EX PROCEDENTIBUS ET CONSEQUENTIBUS EST OPTIMA INTERPRETATIO the best interpretation is made from that which precedes and follows.

EX PROPRIO MOTU 'one's own motion, movement', of his own decision; of his own accord. *Re Mohamed Yusoff Meera Hussain & Anor. [1954] 20 MLJ at Pg. 46,47,48; (Bankruptcy); Re Chops Loh Ban Chuan AND Chuan Bee; Ex Parte Lim Eng Hoe [1933] 2 MLJ 286 Pg. 287*

ex rel [arising] out of the narration [of the relator] abbrev.iation of ex relatione. used when the government brings a case that arises from the information conveyed to it by a third party ("relator").

EX TUNC 'from then'. term used in contract law to specify terms that are v.oided or confirmed in effect from the execution of the contract. c.f. ex nunc.

EX TURPI CAUSA NON ORITUR ACTIO No disgraceful, foul, immoral, or obscene matter can be the basis of an action. This principle is often cited by courts which refuse to consider claims based upon fraud or illegality. *Webster Automatic Packeting Factory Ltd. v.S. Chop Kim Leong Thye [1933] 2 MLJ 61 Pg. 62*

EX TURPI CAUSA NON ORITUR from an immoral cause, no action arises'. An action does not arise from a base cause. *Chang Min Tat J in Win Hin Tin Mining Co Ltd v Lee Chow Beng [1968] 2 MLJ 251.* Meeting of Minds Without Pleadings [1993] 1 MLJ cxv at cxviii Choong Yeow Choy- I take the rule to be that any person who contributes to the performance of an illegal act, knowing that the subject-matter is to be applied, cannot recover the price of such subject-matter, and that the old notion, if any such ever existed, which I do not wish to affirm, that the price must be intended to be paid out of the profits of the illegality, has ceased to be part of the law, if ever it was so. I do not think that for this purpose we should make any distinction between an illegal an immoral act. The rule now is, ex turpi causa non oritur actio, and whether such turpitude be an immorality or an illegality, the effect is the same; ...,Reverting to the circumstances of our instant appeal, we consider that the fact that the first re-spondent had no valid work permit, per se, cannot affect his claim for loss of earnings in Singapore. This is so as unlike Chua's case Administratrix of the estate of *Teoh Tek Lee, deceased) & Anor v Government of Malaysia & Anor [1994] 1 MLJ 394],* the first respondent was working legally in Singapore initially. He had a valid work permit issued by the Singapore authorities but unfortunately that expired four months before the accident. We have been told that the obligation to renew the work permit lies squarely with the first respondent's employer and since there is no evidence that they had done so, we consider that the first respondent had not been culpably responsible for the predicament that he had found himself to be in. Under these circumstances, we consider that the maxim ex turpi causa non oritur actio lacked moral justification and to that end is not applicable to the instant appeal before us. As to the maxim's application in actions based on tort, we echo what was said by the Supreme Court in Chua's case 'that the maxim has a limited application in tort. The maxim's principal role lies mainly and most exclusively in actions on contract'. *Tan Lye Seng & Anor v Nazori bin Teh & Anor [1998] 3 MLJ 873 at 879 Per Siti Norma Yaakob JCA,* We have decided after most anxious consideration that any claim for loss of earnings from any illegal source should not be allowed on the ground that it is against public policy. We think that we would also follow, on this point, the decisions of *Ooi Han Sun & Anor v Bee Hua Meng [1991] 3 MLJ 219 (folld); Burns v Edman [1970] 2 QB 541, [1970] 1 All ER 886, [1970] 2 WLR 1005 (folld); Lebagge v Buses Ltd [1958] NZLR 630 (folld) and Dhalmin v Protea Assurance [1974](4) SA 906 (A) (folld), and approve the dictum in question in Yaakob Foong v Lai Mun Keong & Ors [1986] 2 MLJ 317 (folld).* We therefore uphold the decision of the learned judge in the court below and that of the learned registrar at the first instance that the claim for that part of damages as related to earnings from the illegal operations of the taxi should be disallowed; because ex turpi causa non oritur actio or, in other words, such claim would be against public policy. We would like to emphasize the timely caution of the learned Chief Justice of Singapore in Ooi, that the maxim has a limited application in tort. The maxim's principal role lies mainly and almost exclusively in actions on contract. *Chua Kim Suan (Administratrix of the estate of Teoh Tek Lee, decd) v Government of Malaysia & Anor [1994] 1 MLJ 394 at 401 Per Peh Swee Chin SCJ. In his judgment in Scott v Brown, Doering, McNab & Co, Slaughter and May v Brown, Doering, McNab & Co Lindley LJ ([1891-94] All ER Rep at 657, [1892] 2 QB at 728) thus expressed a well-established principle of law. Tay Kian Hock (t/a Hock Yen Co) v Kewangan Bersatu Bhd [2002] 4 MLJ 411 at 421 Per Kang Hwee Gee J*

EX V.I TERMINI By force of the term; as a bond Ex v.i termini Imports a Sealed Instrument. *Public Prosecutor v. Yeong Yin Chong [1976] 2 MLJ 268 Pg.269*

EXCEPTIO EJUS REI CUJUS PETITUR DISSOLUTIO NULIA EST a plea of that matter, the dissolution of which is the object of the action, is of no effect. It also means there is no exception of that thing of which the dissolution is sought.

EXCEPTIO NULLA EST VERSUS ACTIONEM QUAE EXCEPTIONEM PERIMIT there is (can be) no plea against an action which destroys (the subject or matter of) the plea. It also means there is no exception against an action which entirely destroys an exception.

EXCEPTIO PROBAT REGULAM DE REBUS NON EXCEPTIS an exception proves the rule concerning things not excepted.

EXCEPTIO SEMPER ULTIMA PONENDA EST an exception is always to be last.

EXCESSIVUM IN JURE REPREBATUR. EXCESSUS IN BE QUALIBET JURE, REP-ROBATUR COMMUNI excess in law is reprehended. Excess in anything is reprehended in common law. It also means prolixity in law is reprehended. Prolixity in any fact is reprehended at common law.

EXCESSUS IN RE QUALLBET JURE REPROBATUR COMMUNL excess in anything is condemned by the common law.

EXCOMMUNICATIO RECIDIENDO an obsolete writ whereby persons excommunicated and committed to prison for their obstinacy were unlawfully delivered from prison, before they had given caution to obey the authority of the Church, were to be sought out and imprisoned again.

EXCURSUS a digression in which some point or detail is discussed at length; an appendix devoted to the discussion of some marginal question. Finally, and as an excursus, it must be considered what the possible consequences would be of those judgments entered which include post judgment interest at more than the statutory rate of 8%. Due to the uncertainty of the law and the existence of conflicting views in this subject, there must be countless number of such judgments existing which have yet to be satisfied. If the views put forward in this article are held to be correct, how would the validity of those judgments be affected? A Matter of Interest [1986] 2 MLJ clxxiii at clxxxix Per Yong Pung How CJ

EXCUSAT AUT EXTENUAT DELICTUM IN CAPITALIBUS QUOD NON OPERATUR IDEM IN CIVILIBUS that may excuse or palliate a wrongful act in capital cases which would not have the same effect in civil injuries. It also means that excuses or extenuates an offense of wrong in capital cases which do not operate similarly in civil cases

EXECUTED ESTATE an estate in possession, by which a present interest passes, as distinguished from an executor estate, one depending on some future contingency. It also means an execution is the end and the fruit of law.

EXECUTIO JURIS NON HABET INJURIAM the law will not in its executive capacity work a wrong'. (Broom) The execution of the process of the law does no injury. If an action be brought in a Court which has jurisdiction upon insufficient grounds or against the wrong party, no injury is thereby done for which an action can be maintained; he is not to be esteemed a wrong-doer who merely avails himself of his legal rights. On the other hand, if an individual, under colour of the law, does an illegal act, or if he abuses the process of the Court to make it an instrument of oppression or extortion, this is a fraud upon the law, by the commission of which liability will be incurred.

EXECUTIONE FACIENDA a general name for writs of execution, the various forms of which were prescribed in the table of Regis-team Judicale.

EXEMPLA ILLUSTRANT NON RESTRIGUNT LEGEM examples make the law clearer, do not restrict it.

EXEMPLI GRATIA 'for the sake of example'. usually abbreviated "e.g.".

EXEQUATUR a written official recognition and authorization of a consular officer, issued by government to which he is accredited. Boyle v Fleming, D.C. Canal Zone, 219 Supp 277 283. In French practice, this term is subscribed by judicial authority upon a transcript of a judgment from a foreign country, or from another part of France, and authorizes the execution of the judgment within the jurisdiction where it is so indorsed.

EXILIUM EST PATRIAE PRIVATIO, NATALIS SOLI MUTATIO, LEGUM NATIVARUM AMISSIO Exile is a deprivation of our natal soil and country, and aeloss of our native laws.

EXIT it goes forth. This word is used in docket entries as a brief mention of the issue of process. Thus, 'exit fi. fa', denotes that a writ of fieri facias has been issued in the particular case. The 'exit' of a writ is the facet of its issuance. Way out ; opposite of entrance.

EXLEX 'without legal authority'. *Hendrik Christiaan v. An Hoogstraten v. Low Lum Seng [1940] 9 MLJ 138 at Pg. 145; International Law*

EXPEDIT REPUBLICAE NE SUS RE QUIS MALE UTATUR it is for the public good that no one should use his property badly. It also means it is for the public good that no one should use his property badly.

EXPRESSA NOCENT, NON EXPRESSA NON NOCENT things expressed are (maybe) prejudicial ; things not expressed are not. It also means things expressed harm, things not expressed do not.

EXPRESSA NON PROSUNT QUAE NON EXPRESSA PRODERUNT things expressed do no good, which, not expressed do no harm.

EXPRESSIO UNIUS EST EXCLUSIO ALTERIUS The statement of one thing or fact suggests the exclusion of all others. The expression of one thing in a statute or document will be interpreted to mean that another thing which is not specifically mentioned will be excluded; e.g., a statute which is applicable to "doctors, nurses, nurses aids, and other hospital employees" will be construed as excluding the employees of nursing homes. *Chow Yew Hon & ors v. Oon Kim Meng [1975] 2 MLJ 19 Pg. 22, Ackson's Malaya Berhad v. Penang Port Commission [1973] 2 MLJ 27 Pg.28; Ng Siew San v. Menaka [1973] 2 MLJ 154 Pg. 161*

EXPRESSIO, EORUM QUAE TACITE INSUNT NIHIL OPERATUR the expression of what is tacitly implied is inoperative'. (Broom Leg Max) Express mention of those things which are tacitly implied has no effect. It also means the expressing of those things which are tacitly implied, is inoperative.

EXPRESSUM FACIT CESSARE TACITUM A thing expressed takes priority ov.er a thing implied. A law which is plainly and clearly written must be followed as written. *Mohd Sultan Maicar v. Prudential Assurance Co. Ltd [1941] MLJ 20*

EXTANT 'existing'. refers to things that are currently existing at a given point, rather than things that are no longer so.

EXTORTIO EST CRIMEN QUANDO QUIS COLORE OFFICII EXTOR QUET QUOD NON EST DEBITUM, VEL SUPRA DEBITUM, VEL ANTE TEMPUS QUOD EST DEBITUM extortion is a crime, when, by color of office, any person extorts that which is not due, or above due, or before the time when it is due.

EXTRA LEGEM '*extra*, contract, rule, law'. Outside the law. Beyond the protection of the law. *K.S Roberts v. Public Prosecutor [1970] 2 MLJ 137, at 138 (Obscene Publication)*

EXTRA LEGEM POSITUR EST CIVILITER MORTUUS one who is put out of the law (ie, outlawed) is civilly dead. It also means he who is placed out of the law is civilly dead.

EXTRA TERRITORIUM JUS DICENTI IMPUNE NON PARETUR One who exercises jurisdiction out of his territory is not obeyed with impunity. *Re Datuk James Wong Kim Min [1976] 2 MLJ 245 Pg. 252*

F

FACIE CURIAE (IN FACIE CURIAE) 'Facing the court'. Before the court. *Narayanasamy v. The King [1941] MLJ 101*

FACIO UT DES; FACIO UT FACIAS i do so that you may give; I do so that you may do. These are forms of consideration for a contract where the consideration is mutual

FACTA TENENT MULTA QUAE FIERI PROHIBENTUR deeds contain many things which are prohibited to be done.

FACTO In fact; as where anything is actually done, etc.

FACTUM PROBANS A fact, which acts as proof. A fact which has probativ.e value or which tends to prov.e the existence of another fact. *Lim Ah Oh and Anor. v. Rex [1950] 16 MLJ at Pg. 269, 270; (Criminal Procedure Code)*

FACTUM That which is done. A deed, act, exploit or accomplishment. An integral fact which is essential to the resolution of a problem or question. An act which is integral to a legal issue or definition. *Fraud in the factum* is a deception which induces a party to perform an act or to execute a document. *Attan Bin Abdul Gani v. Public Prosecutor [1970] 2 MLJ 143, at 145 (Bribery and Corruption)*

FACULTAS PROBATIONUM NON EST ANGUSTANDA the facility of proofs is not to be narrowed.

FAEDER-FEOH property brought by a wife to her husband which reverted to her on his death in case his heir refused to consent to her second marriage or to her family if she returned to them.

FAIT ACCOMPLI An accomplished, presumably irrev.ersible deed or fact. *Liew Yu Fatt v. Teck Guan & Co. Ltd. [1966] 1 MLJ 87 at Pg. 89; Notes [1932] 1 MLJ 83 Pg. 84; Low Pui Heng v. Tham Kok Cheong & ors. [1965] 1 MLJ 212 Pg. 214; Merchantile Bank Ltd v. Yoon Siew Kang [1967] 2 MLJ 226 Pg.233, Liew Yu Fatt v. Teck Guan & Co. Ltd. [1966] 1 MLJ 87 at Pg. 89*

FALSA DEMONSTRATIO 'to lead astray, deceive, to indicate, point out'. A false or deceptiv.e statement or description. *Syed Omar Alsagoff & Anor v. State Of Johore [1975] 1 MLJ 241 Pg. 242*

FALSA DEMONSTRATIONE LEGATUM NON-PEREMITUR a legacy is not destroyed by an incorrect description. It also means a legacy will not fail from a false description.

FALSA GRAMMATICA NON VITIAT CHARTAM false grammar does not vitiate a charter.

FALSA GRAMMATICA NON VITIAT CONCESSIONEM erroneous or incorrect spelling or ungrammatical expression does not vitiate a grant or false spelling or false grammar does not vitiate a grant.

FALSA ORTHOGRAPHIA, SIVE FALSA GRAMMATICA, NON VITIAT CONCESSIONEM erroneous or incorrect spelling or ungrammatical expression does not vitiate a grant'; 'False spelling or false grammar does not vitiate a grant. It also means bad spelling, or bad grammar does not vitiate a grant.

FALSUS IN UNO FALSUS IN OMNIBUS;false in one thing, false in ev.erything. A Roman legal principle indicating that a witness who willfully falsifies one matter is not credible on any matter. The underlying motiv.e for attorneys to impeach opposing witnesses in court: the principle discredits the rest of their testimony if it is without corroboration. *Public Prosecutor v. Datuk Haji Harun Bin Haji Idris (No. 2)[1977] 1 MLJ 15 Pg. 21*

FALSUS IN UNO, FALSUS IN OMNIBUS A maxim false in one thing, false in all. It also means false in one, false in all.

FAMA fame; character; reputation; a slanderer.

FATETUR FACINUS QUI JUDICIUM he who flees from judgment confesses his guilt. It also means he who flees judgment confesses his guilt.

FATUM fate; a superhuman power; an event or cause of loss, beyond human foresight or means of prevention.

FAUTE DE MIEUX 'For lack of something better'. *Lau Yau Weng and Lau Yau Chi v. The Bank of Malaya Ltd. [1933] 2 MLJ 250 Pg. 255*

FAVOR CONTRACTUS 'Favor of the contract'. A concept in treaty law that prefers the maintaining of a contract ov.er letting it expire for purely procedural reasons.

FAVORABILIORES REI POTIUS QUAM ACTORES HABENTUR defenders are held to be in a more favourable position than pursuers. The condition of the defendant is to be favored rather than that of the plaintiff.

FAVORABILIORES SUNT EXECUTIONES ALIIS PROCESSIBUS QUIBUSCUNQUE executions are preferred to all other processes whatever. Executions are more preferred than all other processes whatever.

FELIX QUI POTUIT RERUM COGNOSCERE CAUSAS happy is he who can apprehend the causes of things.

FELO DE SE 'Felon of himself'. A suicide. This archaic term stems from English common law, where suicide was legally a felony, thus a person who committed suicide was treated as a felon for purposes of estate disposal.

FELONIA IMPLICATUR IN QUALIBET PRODITIONE felony is implied in every.

FELONIA, EX VI TERMINI, SIGNIFICANT QUODLIBET CAPITALE CRIMEN FELLEO ANIMO PERPETRATUM felony, by force of the term, signifies any capital crime perpetrated with a malignant mind. (

FEME SOLE 'an unmarried woman, never married, widowed, or div.orced'. A married woman who is independent of her husband with respect to property is also called a femme sole. *Koh v. Koh [1965] 1 MLJ 99 Pg. 100*

FEMINE NON SUNT CAPACES DE PUBLICIS OFFICIIS women are not able to hold public offices.

FEODUM NOVUM a new fee. Acquired by the tenant himself directly and for the first time.

FEODUM SIMPLEX QUIA FEODUM IDEM EST QUOD HEREDITAS, ET SIMPLEX IDEM EST QUOD LEGITIMUM VEL PURUM, ET SIC FEODUM SIMPLEX IDEM EST QUOD HEREDITAS LEGITIMA, VEL HEREDITAS PURA a fee-simple, so called because fee is the same as inheritance and simple is the same as legit-imate or pure; and thus fee-simple is the same as a legitimate or pure inheritance.

FEODUM TALLATUM, IE HAEREDITAS IN QUANDUM CERTITUDINEM LIMITATA fee tail is an inheritance limited to certain bounds.

FERA wild animal.

FERAE NATURAE Wild animals of nature Wild animals residing on unowned property do not belong to any party in a dispute on the land.

FERE SECUNDUM PROMISSOREM INTERPRETAMUR we generally infer in favour of the promissor.

FERIA a week day, as distinguished from Sunday; a holiday; a day exempt from judicial process.

FESTINATIO JUSTITIAE EST NOVERCA INFORTUNII swift justice is the stepmother of misfortune. It also means 'hasty justice is the step-mother of misfortune.'

FESTINUM REMEDIUM the speedy remedy.

FIAT JUSTITIA ET PEREAT MUNDUS 'Let there be justice, though the world perish'. Often used as a motto, notably by Ferdinand I, Holy Roman Emperor.

FIAT JUSTITIA RUAT CAELUM 'Let justice be done though the heavens fall'. Also sometimes a motto, a legal maxim that justice must be done regardless of the result otherwise.

FIAT 'Let it be done'. A warrant issued by a judge for some legal proceedings.

FIAT let it be done. An authoritative sanction or authorisation; a command that something should be done. An order or decree by a judge or the Attorney General on behalf of the Crown for certain proceed-ings to begin. Where a statute provides that the consent of the Attorney General is necessary, a fiat must be obtained before further steps can be taken. In a matter in which a member of the public does not have standing to commence an action the person may request the Attorney General to grant a fiat to a relator action. The Attorney General's decision whether to grant a fiat is not justiciable.

FIAT UT PETITUR let it be done as asked. The phrase was the form for granting the relief asked for in a petition.

FICTIO LEGIS INIQUAE OPERATUR ALICUI DAMNUM VEL INJURIAM a legal fiction does not properly work loss or injury.

FICTIO LEGIS NEMINEM LAEDIT 'a fiction of law injures no one or a legal fiction must injure no one or fiction are only to be made for necessity and to avoid mischief.

FICTIO a fiction; a legal fiction.

FIDES 'Trust, confidence, reliance (related to FIDELIS, *supra*) used in *bona fide*, in

FIDUCIA in civil law, one form of mortgage or pledge whereby property was transferred from the debtor to the creditor with an implied understanding that upon the repayment of the debt, it

will be re-transferred back to the debtor. (Latin for Lawyers)

FIERI FACIAS 'May you cause to be done'. A writ ordering the local law enforcement to ensure that damages awarded by the court are properly recovered. A writ of execution.

FIERI to be made; to be done.

FILIATIO NON POTEST PROBARI affiliation cannot be proved.

FILIUS POPULI the son of the people. A bastard.

FILLIUS a son; a child, As distinguished from heir, filius is a term of nature, haeres a term of law. In the civil law the term was used to denote a child generally. A distinction was sometimes made, in the civil law, be-tween 'filii' and 'liberi', the latter word including grandchildren (nepotes), the former not.

FILUM AQUAE the middle line of a stream or body of water.

FILUM an imaginary thread or line passing through the middle of a stream or road.

FINALIS CONCORDIA final agreement. In order to constitute a final order it is necessary that the order should be one by which the suit or the proceeding is finally disposed of whichever way the decision went. The decision of an important or vital issue which may ultimately affect the fate of the proceeding is by itself not enough. Final order is one which leaves nothing more to be done in the proceedings and by its own force, affects the rights of the parties to those proceedings. An order is final if it accounts to a final decision relating to the rights of the parties in dispute in a civil proceeding. If after the order, the civil proceeding still remains to be tried and the rights in dispute between the parties have to be determined, the order is not a final order. Order of High Court rejecting application for condonation of delay in filing appeal is not final order since there was no adjudication of the rights of the parties.

FINIS FINEM LITIBUS IMPONIT a fine puts an end to litigation.

FINIS REI ATTENDEDUS EST the end of a thing is to be attended to.

FINIS UNIUS DIEI EST PRINCIPIUM ALTERIUS the end of one day is the beginning of another.

FINITIO an ending; death, as the end of life.

FIRMA a contract of lease; also the rents reserved; a messuage with the house or lands connected therewith.

FIRMARIUS the lessee under a firma.

FIRMIOR ET POTENTIOR EST OPERATIO LEGIS QUAM DISPOSITIO HOMINIS the operation of law is firmer and more powerful than the will of man. Thus

an agreement entered into between two persons cannot, in general, affect the rights of a third par-ty; so, if it be agreed between A and B that B shall discharge a debt due from A to C, such an agreement cannot prevent C from suing A for its recovery.

FLAGRANTE DELICTO in the very act of committing the crime, the crime being manifest; as, where a thief is taken with the mainour, that is, with the things stolen upon him in manu in his hand.

FLUMINA ET PORTUS PUBLICA SUNT, IDEOQUE JUS PISCANDI OMNIBUS COM-MUNE EST rivers and ports are public; therefore the right of fishing there is common to all. It also means navigable rivers and ports are public; therefore the right of fishing there is common to all.

FLUMINIBUS navigable rivers.

FLUVIUS a river, public rivers for public passage; flood, or flood-tide.

FOEMINAE NON SUNT CAPACES DE PUBLICIS OFFICIIS women are not to be admitted to public offices.

FOENERATION lending money at interest; the act of putting out money to usury.

FOENUS interest on money lent.

FONS ET ORIGO 'source and origin'. *Re Yap E. Boon [1933] 2 MLJ 217 Pg. 220*

FORISFACERE, IE, EXTRA LEGEM SEU CONSUETUDINEM FACERE to do something outside law or custom.

FORISFACTUM forfeiture or forfeited goods.

FORISFACTUS a criminal who has forfeited his life by committing a capital offence.

FORISJUDICATIO depriving of a person of anything by a judgment of court.

FORMA LEGALIS FORMA ESSENTIALIS legal form is essential form.

FORMA PAUPERIS 'In the form of a poor Man'. Where any person has just cause of suit, but is so poor that he is not worth five pounds when all his debts are paid, the court, on oath made to that effect, and a certificate from counsel that he has good ground of action, will admit him to sue in forma pauperis, without paying any fees to counsel, attorney, or the court. *Deraman & ors v. Mek Yam [1977] 1 MLJ 52 Pg. 56, Teo Tong v. Tan Sai Hoon [1940] 9 MLJ 86 at Pg. 86; (Civil Procedure Code); E Peterson v. S. "Ban Ho Liong" Tan Lark Sye & Ong Wai Soey [1940] 9 MLJ 259 at Pg. 263; (Succession); Yeo Hock Cheng v. Rex [1939] 8 MLJ 73 at Pg. 73; (Evidence) ; Angullia v. Rahimaboo [1939] 8 MLJ 80 at Pg. 86; (Testamentary Capacity); Anthony Lucas v. S. The Malayan Cultures Co. Ltd. [1933] 2 MLJ 21 Pg. 21*

FORTIOR ET AEQUIOR EST DISPOSITIO LEGIS QUAM HOMINIS the will of the law is stronger and more equal than that of man.

FORTIORI 'From stronger reasoning'. With much greater probabihty. If a pound of gunpowder can blow up a house, a fortiori a hundredweight must be able to do it. *Datin Siti Hajar v. Murugasu [1970] 2 MLJ 153, at 154 (Right of Way); Dev.I v. Francis – A Critique [1970] 1 MLJ x, at xii, Hup Aik Tin Mining Co. v. Kam Hoy Trading [1969] 1 MLJ 93 (Partnership); Disclose Defence At Police Court [1932] 1 MLJ 29 Pg. 30; Lau Yau Weng and Lau Yau Chi v. The Bank of Malaya Ltd. [1933] 2 MLJ 250 Pg. 253; E. Mohamedi v. H. Mulchand & Anor. [1934] 3 MLJ 47 at Pg. 48; Tan Joo Hern and Anor. v.S. The Sze Hai Tong Banking Insurance Co. Ltd. and ors. [1934] 3 MLJ 127 at Pg. 128; (Trust – Trustees's Power); Abdul Rahman Talib v. Seeniv.Asagam & Anor [1965] 1 MLJ 142 Pg. 147; Mohamed Sidin v. Public Prosecutor [1967] 1 MLJ 106 Pg.108*

FORTIS ATTACHIAMENTUM, VALIDIOR PRAESUMPTIONEM 'strong attachment, the stronger presumption'. When determining whether a chattel is a fixture: "size doesn't matter, how much or degree chattel is attached to 'land' and to 'what'"

FORTIUS CONTRA PREFERENTES *V.Iruthasalam & ORS. v. Phang Quee [1965] 1 MLJ 133*

FORUM ACTORIS OR REI the forum of the plaintiff's or the defendant's domicile. It also means the jurisdiction where the subject matter of a dispute is located. Court of the matter. The court of a country in which the subject matter of the dispute is situated.

FORUM NON CONVENIENS 'Disagreeable forum'. A concept wherein a court refuses to hear a particular matter, citing a more appropriate forum for the issue to be decided.

FRACTIO a breaking; a division; fraction; a portion of a thing less than the whole.

FRANGENTI FIDEM, FIDES FRANGATUR EIDEM ket faith be broken to him who breaks it.

FRATER FRATRI UTERINO NON SUCCEDET IN HAEREDITATE PATERNA full brothers succeed in preference to half- brother. It also means a brother shall not succeed a uterine brother in the paternal inheritance. Or a brother shall not succeed a brother by the mother's side in the paternal inheritance.

FRATERNIA a fraternity, brotherhood, or society of religious persons.

FRAUDEM LEGIS 'to cheat law or rule'. To commit a fraud upon the law. *Stephen Kalong Ningkan v. Tun Abang Haji Openg & Tawi Sli (NO 2) [1967] 1 MLJ 46 Pg.47, Yeap Hock Seng V. Minister for Home Affairs, Malaysia [1975] 2 MLJ 279 Pg. 282*

FRAUS fraud.

FRIBUSCULUM a temporary separation between husband and wife, caused by a quarrel or estrangement, but not amounting to a divorce, because not accompanied with an intention to dissolve the marriage.

FRUCTUS INDUSTRIALS 'vegetation,like crops, that grows by human efforts'. In property law, a co-owner profting from her or his fructus industriales is solely responsible for any losses that may occur.

FRUSTRA FIT PER PLURA QUOD FIERI POTEST PER that is done vainly by many things, which might be accomplished by fewer. It also means that is uselessly done by more (words) which may be done by fewer.

Frustration 'to disappoint, deceive'. to thwart or make impossible or difficult. to prevent or impede. to make ineffectual, as to frustrate the purposes of a law. the term *frustration of purpose* is used in contract law to define a supervening event which completely defeats the purpose for which one of the parties entered into the contract and which entitles that party to avoid the contract. the event must have been unforeseeable at the making of the contract and must deprive the party of all benefit under the contract. *Tye Ong Kiat & Anor v. Tan Guan Hoo [1951] 17 MLJ at Pg. 73; (Debtor and Creditor-Contract of Sale)*

FUGAM FECIT he has flied. Where a man indicted for treason or felony fled, at common law he forfeited his goods and lands.

FUMUS BONI IURIS 'Smoke of a good right'. Refers to having a sufficient legal basis to bring legal action.

FUNCTUS OFFICIO 'having discharged his duties'. said of one who no longer holds his former office. *Mary Ng v. Singapore Improvement Trust [1954] 20 MLJ at Pg. 32; (Land Law); Public Prosecutor v. Tan Yook Kee & Anor [1939] 8 MLJ 126 at Pg. 126; (Criminal Procedure Code); Public Prosecutor v. Utam Singh [1939] 8 MLJ 194 at Pg. 194; (Road Traffic Enactment); Abdul Mormin v. Public Prosecutor [1939] 8 MLJ 248 at Pg. 248, 249; (Civil Procedure Code); Public Prossecutor v. Huntsman [1996] 1 MLJ 93 at Pg. 96; Ho Chick Kwan v. S. The Hon'ble, The British Resident, Selangor [1932] 1 MLJ 99 Pg. 99; Megat Ibrahim v. S. The British Resident of Perak & Anor. [1933] 2 MLJ 154 Pg.158, Public Prosecutor v. Musa [1970] 1 MLJ 101, at 101, 102, 103, 104 (Internal Security); Manggai v. Government Of Sarawak & Anor. [1970] 2 MLJ 41, at 41, 43; 1) Kuluwante v. Government of Malaysia & Anor [1978] 1 MLJ 92 Pg. 96; Ramli Bin Salleh v. Inspector Yahya Bin Hashim [1973] 1MLJ 54 Pg. 54; Musa Bin Salleh v. Public Prosecutor [1973] 1MLJ 167 Pg. 168; Public Prosecutor v. Huntsman [1996] 1 MLJ 93 at Pg. 96 (Practice and Procedure)*

FUNDATIO EST QUASI FUNDI DATIO; ET APPELLATIONE FUNDI, AEDIFICIUM ET AGER CONTINENTUR fundation is, as it were, the giving of the revenues or fund; and by the term 'fundus', lands and buildings are contained.

FUNDI PATRIMONIALES lands or inheritance.

FUNDUS land; the foundation of a thing.

FUNDUS MARIS *B. Hoon & ors. v. The Government of The State Of Penang & ors. [1970] 1 MLJ 244, at 245, 248 (Land Law)*

FURIOSI NULLA VOLUNTAS EST a madman has no will or a madman has no free will. There must be as an essential ingredient in a criminal offence some blameworthy condition of mind, and such condition of mind cannot justly be imputed to madmen who are under a natural disability of distinguishing between good and evil.

FURIOSUS ABSENTIS LOCO EST a madman is considered as absent.

FURIOSUS NULLUM NEGOTIUM CONTRAHERE POTEST a lunatic cannot make a contract.

FURIOSUS SOLO FURORE PUNITUR a madman is punished by his madness alone. It also means a madman is only punished by his madness.

FURIOSUS STIPULARE NON POTEST, NEC ALIQUID NEGOTIUM AGREE, QUI NON INTELLIGIT QUID AGIT a mad man who knows not what he does, cannot make a bargain, not transact any business.

G

GENERALIA SPECIALIBUS NON DEROGANT 'universal things do not detract from specific things'. This well-known proposition of law says that when a matter falls under any specific provision, then it must be governed by that provision and not by the general provision. The general provisions must admit to the specific provisions of law. It is a basic principle of statutory interpretation. *Thanimalai & Government of Malaysia V. Lee Ngo Yew[1975] 1 MLJ 125 Pg. 127; Rangasamy Pillai v. Comptroller Of Income Tax [1970] 1 MLJ 233, at 233, 234, 235 (Bankruptcy); Pengurus Wilayah Utara, Bahagian Kederaan Mara, Kedah v. Hasnah [1970] 2 MLJ 130, at 131 (Employee); Public Prosecutor v. Kirubakaran [1974] 2 MLJ 23 Pg.24, Public Prosecutor V. Toh Ah Keat [1977] 2 MLJ 87 Pg. 88; Public Prosecutor V. Sandra Margaret Birch [1977] 1 MLJ 129 Pg. 130;*

GENERALIA PRAECEDUNT, SPECIALIA SEQUUNTUR things general precede, things special follow.

GENERALIA SPECIALIBUS NON DEROGANT general things do not derogate from special. It also means special Acts are not repealed by general Acts unless there be some express reference to the previous legislation, or a necessary inconsistency in the two Acts standing together, which prevents the maxim from being applied. *Public Prosecutor v Toh Ah Keat [1977] 2 MLJ 87 at 88 Per Hashim Yeop A Sani J.* The relevant maxim in the present appeal is generalia specialibus non derogant - general statement of provisions do not derogate from special statements or provision or conversely, generalia specialibus derogant - special provisions derogate from general. The Government Proceedings Act 1956 was en-acted generally the rights of the Government to sue, its liability, jurisdiction and procedure. Section 10(1) provides in non-specific and general terms that all debts due and claims owing to the government shall enjoy preferential payment over other competing debts or claims which arise subsequent to the date of accrual of such government claim. The phrase 'all debts due'; 'claims of every kind'; 'from such persons to any person whomsoever' are plainly general words and general words and general words are to be understood generally - generalia verba sunt generalita intelligenda. *Director of Customs, Federal Territory v Ler Cheng Chye (Liquidator of Castwell Sdn Bhd, in liquidation) [1995] 2 MLJ 600 at 610 Per Wan Yahya FCJ.* On the need to accord precedence to a specific provision, I had occasion to say in Folin & Brothers Sdn Bhd v Wong Foh Ling & Wong Swee Lin & Ors [2001] 2 MLJ 23, especially at 41-42 of the report, the following: In my judgment, the specific provision must necessarily take precedent over the general provision. I am fortified in my view by certain passages that appeared in the judgments of other learned judges in the following cases: (1) In Barker v Edger & Ors [1898] AC 748, PC, at 754, Lord Hobhouse had this to say: 'The general maxim is, generalia specialibus non derogant. When the Legislature has given its attention to a separate subject, and made provision for it, the presumption is that a subsequent general enactment is not intended to interfere with the special provision unless it manifests that intention very clearly. Each enactment must be construed in that respect according to its own subject-matter and on its own terms. This case is a peculiarly strong one for the application of the general maxim. (2) In Luggage Distributors (M) Sdn Bhd v Tan Hor Teng & Anor [1995] 1 MLJ 719 (CA), Gopal Sri Ram JCA delivering the judgment of the Court of Appeal at pp 758-759 remarked that: 'There is another compelling reason for holding that the respondents have no caveatable interest in the land. It lies in the rule of construction expressed in the maxim generalibus specialia derogant. Where there are two provisions of written law, one general and the other specific, then, whether or not these two provisions are to be found in the same or different statutes, the special or specific provision excludes the operation of the general provision. Thus, in Commissioner of Income Tax v Shahzada Nand & Sons AIR 1966 SC 1342, where (at p 1347) Subba Rao J said: 'Another rule of construction which is relevant to the present enquiry is expressed in the maxim generalia specialibus non derogant, which means that when there is a conflict between a general and a special provision, the latter shall prevail.

The said principle has been stated in Craies on Statute Law (5ᵗʰ Ed), at 205, thus: The rule is, that whenever there is a particular enactment and a general enactment in the same statute and the latter, taken in its most comprehensive sense, would overrule the former, the particular enactment must be operative, and the general enactment must be taken to affect only the other parts of the statute to which it may properly apply. PP v Chew Siew Luan [1982] 2 MLJ 119. This very case was also reported in two other popular local law journals, namely, Current Law Jour-nal vide [2001] 1 CLJ 604 and All Malaysia Reports vide [2000] 1 AMR 429. The maxim generalibus specialia derogant is of universal application and it is very efficacious. In Re Wong Chong Siong ex p Arab Malaysian Finance Bhd [1998] 7 MLJ 208, I reiterated that (see 212 of the report): The maxim generalibus specialia derogant is a popular terminology for interpretation and it has been used by judges in Commonwealth countries. Reference to some of these judgments would be fruitful. Thus, Griffiths CJ in Goodwin v Phillips (1908) 7 CLR 1 said at 7 of the report: ... where the provisions of a particular Act of Parliament dealing with a particular subject matter are wholly inconsistent with the provisions of an earlier Act dealing with the same subject matter, then the earlier Act is repealed by implication. It is immaterial whether both Acts are penal Acts or both refer to civil rights. The former must be taken to be repealed by implication. Another branch of the same proposition is this, that if the provisions are not wholly inconsistent, but may become inconsistent in their application to particular cases, then to that extent the provisions of the former Act are excepted or their operation is excluded with respect to cases falling within the provisions of the later Act. In PP v Chew Siew Luan [1982] 2 MLJ 119, Raja Azlan Shah CJ (Malaya) (as His Majesty then was) said: Generalibus specialia derogant is a cardinal principle on interpretation. It means that where a special provision is made in a special statute, that special provision excludes the operation of a general provision in the general law. Earlier on in the same vein, his Lordship Raja Azlan Shah Ag LP (as His Majesty then was) said in PP v Chu Beow Hin [1982] 1 MLJ 135 at 137 : Where a special provision is made in a special statute, that special provision excludes the operation of a general provision in the general law -- generalibus specialia derogant.'Finally, Reilly J in Corporation of Madras v Electric Tramways Ltd AIR 1931 Mad 152 said: There is the old maxim generalia specialibus non derogant; that is general provisions do not derogate from special provisions. If the legislature makes a special Act dealing with a particular case and later makes a general Act, which by its terms would include the subject of the special Act and is in conflict with the special Act, nevertheless unless it is clear that in making the general Act the legislature has had the special Act in its mind and has intended to abrogate it, the provisions of the general Act do not override the special Act.If the special Act is made after the general Act, the position is even simpler. Having made the general Act if the legislature afterwards makes a special Act in conflict with it, we must assume that the legislature had in mind its own general Act when it made the special Act and made the special Act, which is in conflict with the general Act, as an exception to the general Act. These propositions appear to me to be beyond discussion at the present day.'Without a doubt applying that maxim, the Bankruptcy Rules 1969 takes precedence over the RHC.Likewise here, the sale and purchase agreements made in accordance with Schedule 'H' to the Housing Regulations which were in turn made under the Housing Act must take precedence over the Contracts Act 1950. Being a specific piece of social legislation enacted solely to protect house buyers from un-scrupulous developers, the standard sale and purchase agreements signed by the plaintiffs must take precedence over the Contracts Act 1950 and must be given effect accordingly. Hariram a/l Jayaram & Ors v Sentul Raya Sdn Bhd [2003] 1 MLJ 22 at 39 Per Abdul Malik Ishak J. So one sees that as a general principle, special Acts are not repealed by general Acts unless there is some express reference to the previous legislation or unless there is a necessary inconsistency in the two Acts standing together. There is one final extract worth referring to rom 36 Halsbury's Laws of Eng-land (3rd Edn) at 467-468, para 711, under the heading 'Repeal of particular enactment by general. If it is difficult to imply a repeal where both enactment are in the affirmative, the difficulty increases where the earlier enactment is particular, and the later general, in nature. In such a case the maxim generalia specialibus non derogant applies. If Parliament has considered all the circumstances of, and made special provision for, a particular case, the presumption is that a subsequent enactment of a purely general character would not have been intended to interfere with that provision and if, therefore, such an enactment, though inconsistent in substance, is capable of reasonable and sensible application without extending to the case in question, it is prima facie to be construed as not so extending. The special provision stands as n exceptional proviso upon the general. If, however, it appears from a consideration of the general enactment in the light of admissible circumstances that Parliament's true intention was to establish thereby a rule of universal application, then the special provision must give way thereto. So one has to see what were the purposes of the Land Drainage Act 1930 and the Land Drainage Act 1961. Was the earlier Act dealing with an individual case and the later with general principles? Was the intention of Parliament to establish a rule of universal application in the 1961 Act? It is not without inter-est to look at the long titles of the two Acts.

GENERALIBUS SPECIALIA DEROGANT special things derogate from general. The same principle was referred to at 119-120 in the case of PP v Chew Siew Luan [1982] 2 MLJ 119, wherein Raja Azlan Shah CJ stated: Generalibus specialia derogant is a cardinal principle on interpretation. It means that where a special provision is made in a special statute, that special provision excludes the operation of a general provision in the general law. (See also PP v Chua Boew Hin). The provisions of s 3 of the Criminal Procedure Code which counsel for the respondent seeks to rely on has no relevance whatsoever to the matter before us. Perwaja Steel Sdn Bhd v Majlis Daerah Kemaman, Terengganu [1994] 3 MLJ 15 at 22 Per Mokhtar Sidin J. There is another reason for holding that the respondents have no caveatable interest in the land. It lies in the rule of construction expresses in the maxim generalibus specialia derogant. Where there are two provisions of written law, one general and the other specific, then, whether or not thease two provisions are to be found in the same or different statutes, the special or specific provision excludes the opration of the general provision. Luggage Distributors (M) Sdn Bhd v Tan Hor Teng [1995] 1 MLJ 719 at 758 Per Gopal Sri Ram JCA

GENERALIS CLAUSULA NON PORRIGITUR AD EA QUAE ANTEA SPECIALITER SUNT COMPREHENSA a general clause does not extend to those things which are before specially provided for.

GENEROSUS gentleman; a gentleman.

GERENS bearing, (as) gerens datum (bearing date).

GERULUS messenger.

GESTUM a deed or act; a thing done. Some writers affected to make a distinction between 'gestum' and 'factum'. But the best authorities pronounced this subtitle and indefensible.

good faith; *mala fides,* in bad faith. *Des Raj V. Fidar Nath [1977] 1 MLJ 159 Pg. 160*

GRATIS DICTUM 'said to no purpose'. Irrelevant to the present question. *Murugappa Chettiar v. S. Seeniv.Asagam [1940] 9 MLJ 217 at Pg. 233; (Mortgage);*

GRATIS free; without reward. It also means free of charge. The defendant being an illegal occupier is in no better or worse position than a squatter. A squatter has no rights. He enters into illegal occupation of another's land with an intention of staying as long as he can, gratis, without a care in the world. He might attempt to justify or excuse his conduct by various pleas and ploys. But once the court finds that his occupation is illegal or that he is a squatter, the plea of homelessness must not sway the court from its duty to the owner of the land.

grav.amen Things weighing down The basic element or complaint of a lawsuit.

Guardian-ad-litem 'a guardian appointed by a court to protect the interests of a minor or incompetent in a particular matter'. state law and local court rules govern the appointment of guardian ad litems. typically, the court may appoint either a lawyer or a court appointed special advocate volunteer to serve as guardian ad litem in juvenile matters, family court matters, probate matters, and domestic relations matters. the guardian ad litem is not expected to make diagnostic or therapeutic recommendations but is expected to provide an information base from which to draw resources. as authorized by law the guardian ad litem may present evidence and ensure that, where appropriate, witnesses are called and examined, including, but not limited to, foster parents and psychiatric, psychological, medical, or other expert witnesses. when a person involved in a suit cannot adequately represent his or her own interests, the court may appoint a guardian ad litem to protect the person's interests. unlike typical guardians or conservators, guardians ad litem only protect their wards' interests in a single suit. generally, courts appoint guardians ad litem to represent legal infants and adults who are actually or allegedly incapacitated. courts most frequently appoint guardians ad litem in parents› disputes ov.er custody of their children. for example, the federal child abuse prevention and treatment act requires states to appoint guardians ad litem for children in abuse or neglect proceedings. *Dan Sin Wah v. Chan hai swee [1951] 17 MLJ at Pg. 191, 192; (Land Code)*

H

HABEAS CORPORA JURATORURN

that you have the body of the jurors. Formerly, in England, this was a writ directed to the sheriff com-manding him to produce the jurors named in the panel before the court, to ensure their attendance.

HABEAS CORPUS

'You are to bring up the body'. The English subject's writ of right. Where a person has been imprisoned, having offered sufficient bail, which has been refused though the case is a bailable one' the judges of the court of Chancery or the Queen's Bench may award this writ, for the discharge of the prisoner, on receiving bail. *E. Gopal & Anor v. Awang Bin Mona [1978] 2 MLJ 251 Pg. 253, Ooi Ah Phua v. Officer-In-Charge Criminal Investigation, Kedah/Perlis [1975] 2 MLJ 198 Pg. 198; Zainab Binti Othman v. Superintendent of Prison, Pulau Jerajak, Penang[1975] 2 MLJ 221 Pg. 221; Re Datuk James Wong Kim Min [1975] 2 MLJ 244 Pg. 244; Yeap Hock Seng v. Minister For Home Affairs,Malaysia [1975] 2 MLJ 279 Pg. 279; Ooi Ah Phua v. Officer-In-Charge,Criminal Investigation, Kedah,Perlis [1975]1 MLJ 93 Pg. 93, Re Tan Boon Liat Allen & Anor [1977] 2 MLJ 108 Pg. 108; Lui Ah Yong v. Superintenden Of Prisons,Penang [1977] 2 MLJ 226 Pg. 226; Re Tan Boon Liat @ Allen & Anor [1977] 1 MLJ 39 Pg.39; Subramaniam v. Menteri Hal Ehwal Dalam Negeri & ORS [1977] 1 MLJ 82 Pg. 82*

HABEAS CORPUS AD FACIENDUM AT RECIPIENDUM, OR, HABEAS CORPUS CUM CAUSA

a writ which lies in civil cases, to remove a suit from an inferior to a superior jurisdiction.

HABEAS CORPUS AD PROSEQUENDUM, TESTIFICANDUM, DELIBERANDUM

these issue when it is necessary to remove a prisoner, in order to prosecute, or bear testimony, in any court.

HABEAS CORPUS AD RESPONDENDUM

when a man hath cause of action against one, who is confined by the process of some inferior court; in order to remove the prisoner, and charge him with the action in the court above

HABEAS CORPUS AD SATISFACIENDUM

This is was formerly a judicial writ issued 'when a prisoner hath had judgment against him in an action, and the plaintiff is desirous to bring him up to some superior court to charge him with execution. Habeas corpus ad testifiendum: Formerly, in England, this was a writ issued for the purpose of bringing a prisoner before court in order that he may testify. We have the best witness in an accused who confesses the charge.

HABEAS CORPUS AD SUBJICIENDUM

by way of eminence called the writ of habeas corpus, (q. v.) is a writ directed to the person detaining another, and commanding him to produce the body of the prisoner, with the day and cause of his caption and detention, ad faciendum, subjiciendum, et recipiendum, to do, submit to, and receiv.e, whatsoev.er the judge or court awarding such writ shall consider in that behalf. *Loh Kooi Choon v. Government of Malaysia [1977] 2 MLJ 187 Pg. 191, Re Onkar Shrian [1970] 1 MLJ 28, at 32 (Criminal Procedures)*

HABEAS CORPUS CUM CUASA 'you should hav.e the body with the cause'. a writ issued from a superior court to an inferior court requiring that a defendant be produced along with the cause for which the defendant has been taken and held. *Re Onkar Shrian [1970] 1 MLJ 28, at 33 (Criminal Procedures)*

HABENDUM the clause usually following the granting part of the premises of a deed which defines the extent of the ownership in the thing granted to be held by the grantee. The office of the Habendum is to limit the es-tate so that the general implication of the estate which by construction of law passeth in the Premises is by the Habendum controlled and qualified. Re Mehah Binti Muhamed & Ors Presumed decd [1972] 1 MLJ 212 at 213 Per Chang Min Tat J

HABERE FACIAS POSSESSIONEM that you cause to have possession. This was a writ of execution commanding the sheriff to put in pos-session the successful plaintiff in action for ejectment.

HABERE FACIAS SEISINAM a judicial writ that lay where one had recovered judgment for possession of lands, and this writ was then directed to the sheriff commanding him to give the plaintiff seisin of that land, and it was not returnable.

HABERE FACIAS VISUM that you cause to have a view. This was a writ directing the sheriff to view the lands and premises in question in an action.

HAEMA – TOMA An accumulation of blood under the tissues to produce a solid swelling. *Hoe Gan Tai v. Fong Chee Yan [1970] 1 MLJ 75, at 76*

HAEREDEM APPELLATIONE VENIUNT HAEREDES HAEREDUM IN INFINITUM under the term 'heirs' are included the heirs of heirs to infinity.

HAEREDES PROXIMI next of kin, nearest heirs. Nearest or next heirs. The children or descendants of the deceased; heirs begotten.

HAEREDES REMOTIORES remote heirs.

HAEREDES SUCCESSORES QUE SUI CUIQUE LIBERI every man's Children are his heirs and successors.

HAEREDITAS DAMNOSA an inheritance which is more of a burden than a benefit.

HAEREDITAS an inheritance; an estate by descent or succession.

Haeres v.iv.entis (nemo est haeres v.iv. etis) Literally means 'no one is the heir of a liv.ing person'. a person becomes an actual, complete heir of another only when the ancestor dies. before a person can be an heir, his/her ancestor or person from who s/he inherits must be dead. In Re Westerling [1951] 17 MLJ at Pg. 43; (Extradition), *Hoon Wee Thim v. Pacific Tin Consolidated Corporation [1966] 2 MLJ 240 at Pg. 244*

HERMAPHRODITUS, TAM MASCULO QUAM FOEMINAE COMPARATUR, SECUN-DUM PRAE V ALENTIAM SEXUS INCALESCENTIS an hermaphrodite is to be considered male or female, according to the predominancy of the prevailing sex

HONESTUS good character or standing.

HONORABILIS respectful.

HOSPITIUM hospitability; the relationship between a host and his or her guest. An inn or guest-house. An inn building and those parts of the inn building that are so intimately related to the inn as to be regarded as part of the inn building: Williams v Linnitt [1951] 1 KB 565. An innkeeper in the hospitium of the inn.

HOSTES SUNT YUI NOBIS VEL QUIBUS NOS BELLUM DECERNIMUS CAETERI PRODITORES VEL PRAEDONES enemies are those with whom we are at war; all others are traitors or robbers

HOSTIS HUMANI GENERIS 'Enemy of the human race'. A party considered to be the enemy of all nations, such as maritime pirates.

HUMANUM EST ERRARE It is the lot of humanity to err.

I

IBI SEMPER DEBET FIERI TRIATIO, UBI JURATORES MELIOREM POSSUNT HEBERE NOTITIAM a trial should always be had where the jury can get the best information.

IBID (IBIDEM,ID) 'in the same place or Case'. *PI. AR. Arunasalan Chettiar & ors. v. PI. Palaniappa [1969] 1 MLJ 58 (Hindu Law)*

ICONA an image. Iconoclasm means breaking of images or idols. Iconoclast means breaker of images or idols ; one who assails cherished beliefs.

ICTUS ORBIS a bruise or contusion that does not involve a break or laceration on the skin surface.

ID PERFECTUM EST QUOD EX OMNIBUS SUIS PARTIBUS CONSTAT; ET NIHIL PERFECTUM EST DUM ALIQUID RESTAT AGENDUM that is perfect which is complete in all its parts ; and nothing is perfect whilst anything remains to be done.

ID QUOD COMMUNE EST, NOSTRUM ESSE DICITUR that which is common is said to be ours. Id quod est magis remotum non trahit ad se quod est magis junctum sed e contrario in omni casu. That which is more remote does not draw to itself that which is nearer, but on the contrary in every case.

IDEM (abbreviation Id) (in reference) means the same author on authority. Or the same; used to indicate a references previously made.

IDEM AGENS ET PATIENS ESSE NON POTEST to be at once the person acting and the person acted upon is impossible. The same person cannot be both the agent and the patient.

IDEM EST NON ESSE AT NON APPARERE *B. H Oon & ors. v. The Government of The State of Penang & ors. [1970] 1 MLJ 244, at 248,249 (Land Law); Dev.I v. Francis – A Critique [1970] 1 MLJ x, at xii*

IDEM EST SCIRE AUT SCIRE DEBERE AUT POTUISSE to be bound to know or to be able to know is same as to know. Idem per idem. The same for the same. An illustration or an example that really adds nothing to the matter under consideration.

IDES the calendar of the Romans had a peculiar arrangement. They gave particular names to three days of the month. The first was called the 'calends'. In the four months of March, May, July, and October the seventh day was called 'nones' and in the four former the fifteenth days were called 'ides', and in the last the thirteenth were thus called (as) 'Ides of March' (Shakespeare).

IDIOTA INQUIRENDO VEL EXAMINANDO formerly this was a

writ directed to the sheriff of the county 'to call before him the parties suspected of idiocy, and examine them by the oath of twelve men, whether he had sufficient wit to dispose of his own lands, and to certify this into the Chancery ; for the king had power by his prerogative to dispose of his subject's estate who or were defective in their understandings.

IGNORAMUS '*ignorare*, to be unaware of, not to know'. Literally we do not know. Formerly used by lawyers in the sense of, "we choose not to know." In this sense, the word was subscribed by a grand jury on a bill of indictment if the jury chose not to indict after hearing the evidence. Nowadays, the jury writes "no bill" or "not found" instead. Also, an ignorant person, a fool. A word formerly written by the grand jury on the back of a bill preferred to them, when they collllidered the evidence too defectiv.e or too weak to support an indictment. Now, in such cases, they indorse in English "no bill," "no true bill," or "not found," and the bill is thus said to be "thrown out." *Loh Teck Chong v. Public Prosecutor [1966] 1 MLJ 7 at Pg. 8; Public Prosecutor v. Lee Yoke Kai [1967] 1 MLJ 213 -p215*

IGNORANTIA JURIS NEMINEM EXCUSAT Ignorance of the law excuses no one. *Re Estate of Choong Lye Hin Decd[1977] 1 MLJ 96 Pg. 99, Wong Ah Suan v. Chii Poh Get & Anor [1966] 1 MLJ 142 at Pg. 143, 144*

IGNORANTIA EXCUSATUR, NON JURIS SED FACTI ignorance of fact may excuse, but not ignorance of law.

It also means Ignorance of fact excuses; ignorance of law does not excuse. The word us in this Maxim means the settled general law of the Country. A person is not bound to know the true solution of a doubtful point of law, nor the true position regarding private rights, even his own.

IGNORANTIA JUDICIS EST CALAMITAS INNOCENTIS the ignorance of the judge is the misfortune of the innocent

IGNORANTIA LEGIS NEMINEM EXCUSAT ignorance of law excuses no one.it also means ignorance of the law does not afford excuse.

IMPENSAE expenses ; outlays, Divided into necessary (necessariae), useful (utiles), and tasteful or ornamental.

IMPERITIA CULPAE ADNUMERATUR want of skill is reckoned as a fault; negligence for which one professes skill makes him responsible. Inexperience is accounted a fault.

IMPERIUM power; authority.

IMPLACITARE to implead; to sue.

IMPONERE to force upon; levy; as, to impose a tax. imponere,'to put or place upon'.

IMPRIMATUR 'Let it be printed'. An authorization for a document to be printed. Used in the context of

IMPRIMIS In the first place; as, imprimis, I direct my just debts to be paid.. *Lau Tai Thye, Etc. v. Leong Yin Khean & ors. [1934] 3 MLJ 110 at Pg. 110; (Family Law – Claim For Declaration of Status)*

IMPROBI REMORES DISSIPATI SUNT REBELLIONIS PRODROMI wicked rumors spread abroad are the forerunners of rebellion.

IMPROMPTU readily. A witticism or composition produced at the moment.

IN ABSENTEM (ABSENTIA) 'in the absence'. Its meaning varies by jurisdiction and legal system. In common law legal systems, the phrase is more than a spatial description. It suggests recognition of violation to a defendant's right to be present in court proceedings in a criminal trial. *Lau Yau Weng & Lau Yau Chi v. The Bank of Malaya Ltd. [1933] 2 MLJ 250 Pg. 253, Re Chai Kai Wooi[1970] 1 MLJ 34, at 35 (Advocates and Solicitors)*

IN ALTA PRODITIONE NULLUS POTEST ESSE ACCESSORIUS SED PRINCIPALIS SOLUMMODO in high treason, no one can be an accessory; all are principals. It also means in high treason there is no accessory, but principal alone.

IN AMBIGUA VOCE LEGIS EA POTIUS ACCIPIENDA ESK SIGNIFICATIO, QUAE VITIO CARET ; PRAESERTIM CUM

approv.al by a religious body or other censoring authority.

ETIAM VOLUNTAS LEGIS EX HOC COLLIGI POSSIT in an ambiguous law that interpretation shall be preferred which is most consonant to equity, especially where it is in conformity with the general design of the legislature.

IN ARTICULO MORTIS 'at the moment of death'. Often used in probate law, as well as for testimony in the sense of a dying declaration.

IN CAMERA 'In the chamber'. Conducted in private, or in secret. The opposite of in open court.

IN CIVILE EST, NISI TOTA SENTENTIA INSPECTA, DE ALIQUA PARTE JUDICARE it is improper to pass an opinion on any part of a passage without examining the whole. It also means it is unjust to judge of any part unless the whole sentence is examined.

IN CURIA 'In court'. Conducted in open court. The opposite of in camera.

IN ESSE 'In actual being'. That which exists. In being; in existence. Contrasted with *in posse*, which means in the future, not yet in existence. A child is *in posse* before birth, *in esse* after birth. *Melah Binti Indot v. Tambysah Bin Hj Kassim & ors [1941] MLJ 72*

IN EXTENSO 'in full', or 'at large'. without abridgment. used in reference to written documents. A text, such as a judicial opinion, which is recited or reproduced *in extenso* is reproduced in its entirety or verbatim. *Arthanarisami Chettiar & 2 Others v. Public Prosecutor [1940] 9 MLJ 67 at 67; (Criminal); he Sultan Of Johore v. Tungku Abubakar & ors. [1950] 16 MLJ at pg 9; (Land, Trust, Constitutional- Sovereign Ruler); Assa Singh v. Mentri Besar, Johore [1969] 2 MLJ 31 (Unlawful Detention), Assa Singh v. Mentri Besar, Johore [1969] 2 MLJ 31 (Unlawful Detention), Goh Yoke v. Public Prosecutor [1970] MLJ 1 63, at 66 (Defence of Insanity); Tee Than Song v. Caltex Oil Malaysia Ltd. [1970] 1 MLJ 68, at 69 (Interlocutory Injunction)*

IN EXTREMIS *'exterior,* at the outer limits, at the edge'. in extremity; in extreme circumstances; at or close to the end. imminent death; especially, in anticipation of death. a dying declaration is a disposition or statement *in extremis.* the dying declaration of the victim is admissible as evidence in a trial for homicide. the term is also used to describe any extreme or urgent circumstance. *Naranjan singh v. Public Prosecutor [1949] 15 MLJ 71 Pg.123*

IN FIERI 'to make, do'. In progress or process, in the process of being made or done; incomplete, inchoate. A trial is *in fieri* until the verdict is in and judgment is entered. In the course of execution; a thing commenced but not completed. A record is said to be in fieri during the term of the court, and, during that time, it may be amended or altered at the sound discretion of the court. *Kersah La'usin v. Sikin Menan [1966] 2 MLJ 20 at Pg. 22*

IN FLAGRANTE DELICTO 'In blazing offense'. Caught in the actual act of committing a crime. Often used as a euphemism for a couple caught in the act of sexual intercourse, though it technically refers to being "caught in the act" of any misdeed.

IN FORMA PAUPERIS 'in the form of a poor man'. where any person has just cause of suit, but is so poor that he is not worth five pounds when all his debts are paid, the court, on oath made to that effect, and a certificate from counsel that he has good ground of action, will admit him to sue in forma pauperis, without paying any fees to counsel, attorney, or the court. *Teo Tong v. Tan Sai Hoon [1940] 9 MLJ 86 at Pg. 87; (Enlarge Appeal); Sunny Tay, Etc. v. Seow See Neo & Anor. [1934] 3 MLJ 83 at Pg. 87; (Family Law – Chinese Marriage); Jambalingam Saminathan v. A. Saminathan [1941] MLJ 68*

IN FUTURO 'later, in the future'. contrasted with *in praesenti*, at present, at this moment. *Regina v. Lim Heng Soon & ors [1954] 20 MLJ at Pg. 151; (Municipal Ordinance); Tok Jwee Kee v. Tay Ah Hock & Son Ltd. & Town Council, Johore Bahru [1969] 1 MLJ 197;(Planning Law); District Council Central, Province Wellesley v. Yegappan [1966] 2 MLJ 177 at Pg. 177; Re Man Bin Mihat [1965] 2 MLJ 1 Pg. 1*

IN GREMIO 'In the bosom of the law'. This is a figurative expression, by which is meant, that the subject is under the protection of the law; as, where land is in abeyance. *Chai Sau Yin v. Kok Seng*

Fatt [1966] 2 MLJ 54 at Pg. 58, Credit Corporation (M) Sdn Bhd v. National Insurance Co. Ltd [1975] 2 MLJ 104 Pg. 105

IN HAEC VERBA 'In these words'. Used when including text in a complaint verbatim, where its appearance in that form is germane to the case, or is required to be included

IN INFINITUM 'Without end'; to the end; indefinitely. A continuous succession of things or events. That which is infinite or endless is reprehensible in law. *Malay Rights in Malay Reservation Lands Pg. xv.ii*

IN INVITOS (INVITO) 'being unwilling' or against or without the assent or consent *The Eastern Shipping Co. Ltd. of Penang v. His Majesty's Attorney General For The S.S. [1934] 3 MLJ 99 at Pg. 109*

IN INVITUM against an unwilling party, against one who is not assenting, against an adverse party (Latin for Law-yers). Against unwilling party; against one assenting. A term applied to proceedings against an adverse party, to which he does not consent.

IN LIEU *Government Of Malaysia v. Rosalind Oh Lee Pek Inn [1973] 1 MLJ222 Pg.225, Government of Malaysia v. Iznan Bin Osman [1975] 2 MLJ 61 Pg. 63, Itam Binti Saad v. Chik Binti Abdullah [1974] 2 MLJ 53 Pg.54, Public Prosecutor v. Looi Yew Chun & Two Others [1951] 17 MLJ at Pg. 31*

IN LIMINE 'threshold, home, dwelling'. At the very beginning or threshold. A *motion in limine* is a pretrial motion, which seeks to prevent opposing counsel from referring to evidence which may be irrelevant or prejudicial until the court has had an opportunity to rule on the evidence at the proper juncture in the trial. *Cheong Kong Enterprise Co. Sdn. Bhd. v. Foong Seong Mines Ltd. & ors. [1969] 2 MLJ 247 (Specific Performance), Cheong Kong Enterprise Co. Sdn. Bhd. v. Foong Seong Mines Ltd. & ors. [1969] 2 MLJ 247 (Specific Performance); Shaik Sahied Bin Abdullah Bajerai v.S. S.S.T. Sockalingam Chettiar [1933] 2 MLJ 81 Pg. 82 ; Kuppusamy v. Golden Hope Rubber Estate Ltd. [1965] 1 MLJ 178 Pg. 180; Government of Malaysia & Anor v. Chin Keow [1965] 2 MLJ 91 Pg. 94; Tan Kheng Ann & ors. v. The Public Prosecutor [1965] 2 MLJ 108 Pg. 120*

IN LOCO PARENTIS 'in the place of a parent'. It is used to refer to a person or entity assuming the normal parental responsibilities for a minor. This can be used in transfers of legal guardianship, or in the case of schools or other institutions that act in the place of the parents on a day-to-day basis.

IN MITIUS 'In the milder'. It is a type of retroactive law that decriminalizes offenses committed in the past. Also known as an amnesty law.

IN OMNIBUS 'In all'. It is used to mean "in every respect." It is something applying to every aspect of a situation.

IN PAIS This phrase, as applied to a legal transaction, primarily means that it hastaken place without legal proceedings. Thus a widow was said to make a request in paisfor her dower when she simply applied to the heir without issuing a writ (Co. Litt. 326.)So conv.eyances are div.ided into those by matter of record and those by matter in pais. In some cases, howev. er, "matters in pais" are opposed not only to "matters of record," but also to "matters in writing," i. e., deeds, as where estoppel by deed is distinguished from estoppel by matter in pais. Lian Seng Construction Co. v. Yuzin [1970] 1 MLJ 108, at 111; B. H Oon & ors. v. The Government of The State of Penang & ors. [1970] 1 MLJ 244, at 247

IN PARI DELICTO 'equal fault, crime; in equal fault' or to be equally culpable or guilty. The general rule is that illegal transactions or contracts are not legally enforceable by anyone. But when parties to an illegal agreement are not *in pari delicto*, i.e., are not equally at fault, the agreement may be enforceable in equity by the less guilty party. A party may, for example, hav.e participated in the illegal agreement only because he was compelled to do so under fraud or duress. In tort law, the party most responsible for the wrong may be liable for all the damages without contribution by others who may be less responsible. *Ahmad Bin Udon & Anor v. Ng Aik Chong [1970] 1MLJ 82, at 82,83, 84 (Contract Void)*

IN PARI DELICTO MELIOR EST CONDITIO POSSIDENTIS 'in equal fault (better is the condition of the possessor)'. Is a legal term used to indicate that two persons or entities are equally at fault, whether the malfeasance in question is a crime or tort. *Ahmad Bin Udon & Anor v. Ng Aik Chong [1970] 1MLJ 82, at 83 (Contract Void)*

IN PARI MATERIA 'on the same topic' or 'pertaining to the same subject matter'.' On a similar or intertwined subject matter'. A rule of statutory construction which provides that all relevant legislation, whether sections of one statute or parts of several statutes, dealing with a particular subject or directed to a common purpose, should be read and interpreted together to determine the legislative intent. The rule may be applied also in the interpretation of instruments and contracts. *Tan Chye Choo & ors v. Chong Kew Moi [1966] 2 MLJ 4 at Pg 7; Wearne Brothers (M) Ltd v. Jackson [1966] 2 MLJ 155 at Pg. 155; Tan Hua Lam v. Public Prosecutor [1966] 1 MLJ 147 at Pg. 150; Shaik Sahib Bin Omar, Etc v. The Municipal Commissioners [1932] 1 MLJ 53 Pg. 54, 55; Ena Mohamed Tamby [1932] 1 MLJ 128 Pg.133; Gulwant Singh v. Abdul Kahlik [1965] 2 MLJ 55 Pg. 58*

IN PERSONAM 'into or against the person'. Relief or recovery against a person, not against his property. pleadings or actions *in personam* require jurisdiction ov.er the person of the defendant, usually acquired either by personal service or by substituted service. the decisions of equity courts are generally *in personam* in that they order the defendant himself either to do or to refrain from doing some act.

A remedy in personam, is one where the proceedings are against the person, in contradistinction to those which are against specific things, or in rem. *Director-General Of Inland Revenue v. T.M. Sdn Bhd 1 MLJ 71 Pg.73, In Re Maria Huberdina Hertogh; Adrianus Petrus Hertogh And Anor v. Amina Binte Mohamed and Ors. (1951) 17 MLJ at Pg. 172; (Guardianship of Infants, Marriage Law); Kersah La'usin v. Sikin Menan [1966] 2 MLJ 20 at Pg. 22; Re Tan Teng Trading Etc V. Re Chop Hoe Seng [1932] 1 MLJ 159 Pg.163; Muttiah V.S. Chang Kiam Ho[1933] 2 MLJ 239 Pg. 239; Malay Rights in Malay Reservation Lands Pg. xv.ii*

IN PLENO 'In full'.

IN PROPE PERSONA 'On one's own person'. One who represents themselv. es in court without the [official] assistance of an attorney.

IN PROPRIA PERSONA 'In one's own proper person'. Alternate form of in prope persona. One who represents themselv.es in court without the [official] assistance of an attorney.

IN RE 'in the matter of'. In the matter of, concerning, in the affair of. Used in the title of a legal proceeding or action which is not inherently adv.erserial but which requires the determination of some right or matter or an interest in property; e.g., *In re Estate of Murphy*. Also used more generally, as in the heading of a letter or memorandum, to indicate the subject matter dealt with by the writer. *Re Tan Teng Trading Etc*

v. Re Chop Hoe Seng [1932] 1 MLJ 159 Pg.163; Re Ang Teck Say [1934] 3 MLJ 25 at Pg. 25; (Bankruptcy); Re Chop Kwong Fook Seng [1934] 3 MLJ 34 at Pg. 36

In rem 'a thing, fact or object'. Concerning a thing or item of property, rather than a person. an action in which the plaintiff seeks recovery against or affecting property or things. the judgment in an action *in rem* determines the rights of all parties claiming an interest in the property involved. (examples of actions *in rem*: action to partition real estate; action to foreclose a mortgage; attachment.). *In Re Maria Huberdina Hertogh; Adrianus Petrus Hertogh and Anor v. Amina Binte Mohamed and ors. (1951) 17 MLJ at Pg. 172; (Guardianship of Infants, Marriage Law); The Saint Chirstopher [1969] 1 MLJ 214; (Procedural Law); Re Tan Teng Trading Etc v. Re Chop Hoe Seng [1932] 1 MLJ 159 Pg. 163; Tan Yow Kee v. Chop Teck Hwai & Anor. [1933] 2 MLJ 53 Pg. 54; Drouth v. The Ship "G.G. Paul Doumer" [1934] 3 MLJ 72 at Pg. 73; (Arbitration); Karupanan v. Empire Theatre [1941] MLJ 81, Temenggong Securities Ltd& Anor v. Registrar of Titles & ors [1974] 2 MLJ 45=Pg.47; Sea Breeze Navigation Co. S.A. v. Owners Of Ship "Hsing An" [1974] 1 MLJ 45 Pg.45*

IN SITU 'In its site', or 'position'. In its place or location. In its original place; in its proper position. Used to describe the location of a parcel of property. *Hoon Wee Thim v. Pacific Tin Consolidated Corporation [1966] 2 MLJ 240 at Pg. 244; Pacific Tin Consolidated*

Corporation v. Hoon Wee Thim [1967] 2 MLJ 35 Pg. 39; Rex v. Lim Kang Chui [1949] 15 MLJ 211 Pg.212, Yahaya Bin Mohamad v. Chin Tuan Nam [1975] 2 MLJ 117 Pg. 122

IN SOLIDUM 'For the whole'. Where a group of persons share liability for a debt, such as co-signers to a loan, the debtor can sue a single party in solidum, that is, to recover the entire amount owed.

in terrorem clause clause "in order to frighten" a clause in a will that threatens any party who contests the will with being disinherited. also called a no-contest clause.

IN TERROREM 'in terror'. by way of warning. any power of enforcing the execution of a bond, or of inflicting punishment, or of revealing a secret, may be held in terrorem against another. The rod and fool's cap are exhibited in terrorem. In apprehension, fright or fear. a clause or prov.ision, usually in a lease, deed or will which is intended by the maker of the instrument to induce or coerce someone into not taking some action, as not to contest a will provision. for example, a testator may provide that a gift will be forfeit if the recipient contests the will. in most jurisdictions, provisions of this kind are unenforceable as against public policy. they are always unenforceable if the action they try to force or induce is illegal or impossible. Leong & Anor v. Lim Beng Chye [1955] 21 MLJ at Pg. 155, 156; (Will); In Re Settlement Of Shaik Salleh Bin Obeid Bin Abdat & Anor [1954] 20 MLJ at

Pg. 10; (Trust); Dorothy Kwong Chan v. Ampang Motors Ltd. @ Anor [1969] 2 MLJ 70 (Hire Purchace Agreement)

IN TOTO 'In the whole'. Entirely. *Chop Seng Heng v. Thev. Annasan & ors [1975] 2 MLJ 3 Pg. 4, Corespondence – Lee Wah Bank Ltd v. Singapore Bank Employees' Union [1970] 1 MLJ xxv., at xxv., xxv.i, xxv.ii; Yew You & Anor. v. Mah Poay Koh & Anor. [1970] 1 MLJ 57, at 58 (Negligence); Yeow Tiong Kok v. Collector of Land Revenue, Port Dickson [1970] 1 MLJ 116, at 120 (Land Acquisition); Kong Cheng Whum v. Tengku Besar Zabaidah [1970] 1 MLJ 179, at 182 (Rent in Excess Payment); Gan Poh v. Union Omnibus Co. Ltd [1970] 1 MLJ 188, at 190 (Claim for Damages Sustained during Employment);Mahesan v. Public Prosecutor [1970] 1 MLJ 255, at 260 (Bribery and Corruption); Ng Eng Kooi & Anor. v. Public Prosecutor [1970] 1 MLJ 267, at 268, 273 (Quantum of Proof)*

IN V.ACUO 'In a vacuum'. *New zealand insurance co. Ltd v. Sinnadorai [1969] 1 MLJ 184; (Insurance); Majumder v. Attorney-General of Sarawak [1967] 1 MLJ 101 –Pg.103, Re Will of P. M. Framroz, DECD.; Chartered Bank (M) Trustee Ltd. v. S.F. Framroz & ors. [1970] 1 MLJ 171, at 171 (Construction of Will)*

INCLUSIO UNIUS EST EXCLUSIO ALTERIUS 'the inclusion of the one implies the exclusion of the other'. In other words, to include one thing is to exclude another. *Menaka v. Lum Kum Chum [1977] 1 MLJ 91 Pg. 94*

INCLUSIO UNIUS EXCLUSIO ALTERIUS the inclusion of one is the exclusion of another; the mention of one is the exclusion for another. It also means The mention of one is the exclusion for another. The general rule considered in illegality in money lending transaction) *Menaka v Lum Kum Chum [1977] 1 MLJ 91*. If the words are equally susceptible other parts of the statute are to be referred to: Fateh Chand Agarwalla [1916] 44 Cal 477 (expressions in the parts of the Penal Code).

INCOGNITO a sovereign traveling incognito though he enjoys as sovereign the right of exterritoriality is entitled to be treated as private person, if he so wishes. But when he chooses to put an end to such incognito, he is entitled to all the prerogatives of a sovereign. Thus the king of Holland in 1873 was condemned by a police Court in Switzerland to a fine, which was at once annulled on his making known his royal position (Rivier, Droit des Gens, Paris, 1896, i, 418. In diplomacy a distinction is made between simple and strict [incognito, the former being a diplomatic fiction used to dispense with ceremonial functions.

INCOMMUNICADO unable to communicate.

INDEBITATUS indebted.

INDEBITUS not owed, not due.

INDICIA 'Indications'. Often used in copyright notices. Refers to distinctive markings that identify a piece of intellectual property.

INDICIA (INDICIUM) 'Indications; signs or circumstances which tend to suggest that a fact or relationship may exist, but which are not in and of themselv.es sufficient to establish the existence of that fact or relationship'. *Indicia of partnerhip* are circumstances which would suggest that someone is a partner in a firm. *Indicia of title* are documents which suggest ownership but do not confirm it; e.g., the carbon copy of a bill of sale. An owner of property who allows another to display or use the *indicia of ownership* may enable that person to convey good title to a third party without notice. Circumstantial evidence may be described as *indicia* from which a fact or happening may be inferred or from which a reasonable conclusion may be drawn. This term is very nearly synonymous with the common law phrase, "circumstantial evidence." It was used to designate the facts giving rise to the indirect inference, rather than the inference itself; as, for example, the possession of goods recently stolen, vicinity to the scene of the crime, sudden change in circumstances or conduct, &c. Indicia may be defined to be conjectures, which result from circumstances not absolutely necessary and certain, but merely probable, and which may turn out not to be true, though they have the appearance of truth. Denisart, mot Indices. Howev.er numerous indicia may be, they only show that a thing may be, not that it has been. An indicium, can have effect only when a connexion is essentially necessary with the principal. Effects are known by their causes, but only when the effects can arise only from the causes to which they. Are attributed. When several causes may have produced one and the same effect, it is, therefore, unreasonable to attribute it to any one of such causes. A combination of circumstances sometimes conspire against an innocent person, and, like mute witnesses, depose against him. There is danger in such cases, that a jury may be misled; their minds prejudiced, their indignation unduly excited, or their zeal seduced. Under impressions thus produced, they may forget their true relation to the accused, and condemn a man whom they would have acquitted had they required that proof and certainty which the law demands. *Bata Shoe Company (Malaya) Ltd v. Employees [1967] 1 MLJ 120 –Pg.121; Ong Lock Cho v. Quek Shin & Sons Ltd [1941] MLJ 78*

INDICIA a symbol: token: sign or mark. plural of Indicium. In Malaysia in Yeop Cheng Hock v Kajima - Taisei Joint Venture [1973] 1 MLJ 230 (refd), Syed Agil Barakbah J (as he then was) specified the indicia that attach to a licensee in the following terms at 232 of the report. Toh Kheng Heng & Anor v Ahmad Fauzi bin Mohd Taufek [1994] 1 MLJ 356 at 367 Per Sel-venthiranathan JC

INFRA 'Underneath, below, following'. Used in a text, *infra* refers to items, facts, terms or citations, which come after the point or place of reference. Contrasted with *supra*, which refers to items, facts, terms or citations which come before or precede the point or place of reference. The opposite of supra, above. Thus we say primo gradu est supra, pater, mater; infra, filius, filia. In the first degree of kindred in the ascending line; above, is the father and the mother; below, in the descending line, the son and daughter. In another, sense, this word signifies within; as, infra corpus comitatus, within the body of the county; infra proesidia, within the guards. It also signifies during; as infra furorem during the madness. *Building Society of Malaya Ltd v. Joseph Michael [1973] 1 MLJ 119 Pg.120, Zainab Binte Ismail v. Marimuthu & Anor [1955] 21 MLJ at Pg. 23; (Courts Ordinance 1948)*

INFRA 'Below or Under'.

INIQUITAS injustice, iniquity, unfairness.

INITIO 'at the very beginning'. the opening phases of a lawsuit are said to be *in initio litis. Chung Peng Chee v. Cho Yew Fai & ors [1954] 20 MLJ at Pg. 101; (Trust)*

INJURIA an unauthorised interference on the plaintiff, a legal wrongdoing.

INNUENDO 'By nodding'. An intimation about someone or something, made indirectly or vaguely suggesting the thing being implied. Often used when the implied thing is negative or derogatory.

INOPS poor, helpless, in need, needy, without resources.

INSIMUL jointly, together.

INTER ALIA 'Among other things'. Used when quoting only a portion of a statute or regulation, or a part of a judge's opinion, or a document or writing; e.g., "the statute provides *inter alia...*". It is used to indicate that something is one out of a number of possibilities. For example, "he filed suit against respondents in state court, alleging, inter alia, a breach of contract." *Bank of Canton Ltd v. Dart Sum Timber (PTE) Ltd [1978] 2 MLJ 5 Pg. 6; Re An Advocate & Solicitor [1978] 2 MLJ 7 Pg. 12; Union Workshop (Construction) Co. v. Ng Chew Ho Construction Co. Sdn Bhd [1978] 2 MLJ 22 Pg. 23; Loh Koon Moy & Anor v. Zaibun Sa Binti Syed Ahmad[1978] 2 MLJ 29 Pg. 30; H.A Gomez V. Government of Malaysia[1978] 2 MLJ 69 Pg. 69, Chop Seng Heng v. Thev.Annasan & ors [1975] 2 MLJ 3 Pg. 4; Joseph v. Government of Sarawak & Anor[1975] 2 MLJ 38 Pg.38; Yaw Kee v. Tan Chee Yim & Anor [1975] 2 MLJ 51 Pg.52; Chew Chee Sun v. Public Prosecutor[1975] 2 MLJ 58 Pg. 60; Employees Provident Fund Board v. M.S Ally & Co. Ltd [1975] 2 MLJ 89 Pg. 93*

INTER ALIA 'Among others'. Used to indicate an item cited has been pulled from a larger or more complete list.

INTER ALIOS 'Among or between others (other persons)'. Between other parties, who are strangers to the proceeding in question. *Lam Kee Ying Sdn Bhd v. Lam Shes Tong & Anor [1974] 2 MLJ 83 Pg.86; Government of Malaysia v. Lionel [1974] 1 MLJ 3 Pg. 4*

INTER ARMA ENIM SILENT LEGES 'For among arms, the laws fall silent'. A concept that during war, many illegal activities occur. Also taken to mean that in times of war, laws are suppressed, ostensibly for the good of the country.

INTER between, among.

INTER MARITOS *Hujah Lijah Binti Jamal v. Fatimah Binti Mat Diah [1950] 16 MLJ at Pg. 65; (Harta Sepencarian)*

INTER PARTES 'side, party'. An instrument or document in which two parties join for a common purpose, such as a deed or contract. This, in a technical sense, signifies an agreement professing in the outset, and before any stipulations are introduced, to be made between such and such persons as, for example, "This Indenture, made the _____ day of _____ 1848, between A B of the one part, and C D of the other." It is true that every contract is in one sense inter partes, because to be valid there must be two parties at least; but the technical sense of this expression is as abov.e mentioned. This being a solemn declaration, the effect of such introduction. is to make all the covenants, comprised in a deed to be cov.enants between the parties and none others; so that should a stipulation be found in the body of a deed by which "the said A B covenants with E F to pay him one hundred dollars," the words "with E F" are inoperativ.e, unless they have been used to denote for whose benefit the stipulation may have been made, being in direct contradiction with what was previously declared, and

108

C D alone can sue for the non-payment; it being a maxim that where two opposite intentions are expressed in a contract, the first in order shall prevail. When there are more than two sides to a contract inter partes, for example, a deed; as when it is made between A B, of the first part; C D, of the second; and E F, of the third, there is no objection to one covenanting with another in exclusion of the third. *Jit Kaur v. Pari Singh [1974] 2 MLJ 199 Pg.200, Khong Kim Ching v. Hassan Bin Din & ors [1973] 2 MLJ173 Pg. 173*

INTER RUSTICOS 'Among rustics'. Refers to contract, debts, or other agreements made between parties who are not legal professionals.

INTER SE (INTER SESE) 'among or between themselv.es'. A matter which concerns only the parties inv.olv.ed and no one else; e.g., the relationship between the trustee under a trust instrument and the designated beneficiaries. *Gerald Fernandez v. Attorney – General, Malaysia [1970] 1 MLJ 262, at 262, 263 (Extradition); Gold Clause and Containerisation [1970] 2 MLJ xliii, at xlv., In Re Jasper Bertram Young, Deceased. [1954] 20 MLJ at Pg. 81; (Company Law); Kundan Singh & ors v. Public Prosecutor [1939] 8 MLJ 22 at Pg. 22; (Criminal); Puran Singh v. Kehar Singh & Anor [1939] 8 MLJ 57 at Pg. 61; (Land); Official Assignee v. Leong Cheong Wai [1939] 8 MLJ 148 at Pg. 154; (Bankruptcy); Murugappa Chettiar v. Letchumanan Chettiar [1939] 8 MLJ 183 at Pg. 183; (Land); Sim Lim Investments Ltd. v. Attorney General [1969] 1 MLJ 6 (Company Law)*

INTER VIVOS iterally means 'Between' or 'among the living'. Between or among the living. A transaction between one living person and another, hence a transaction intended to be consummated during life, as opposed to a transaction *causa mortis*, or one in comptemplation of, or intended to take effect upon, death. The term is used to describe a v.ariety of transactions, all during the life of the initiating party; e.g., an *inter v.iv.os* gift, an *inter v.iv. os* transfer, or an *inter v.iv.os* trust. Between living persons; as, a gift inter v.iv.os, which is a gift made by one living person to another; see Gifts inter v.iv. os. It is a rule that a fee cannot pass by grant or transfer, inter v.iv.os, without appropriate words of inheritance. *Ali Mat Bin Khamis v. Jamaliah Binti Kassim [1974] 1 MLJ 18 Pg.19*

INTERESSE the notion of loss or damage suffered by the claimant as opposed to the usurious conception of reward for money lent.

INTEREST REIPUBLICAE UT SIT FINIS LITIUM 'In concerns the commonwealth that there be an end of law suits'. In the interest of society as a whole, litigation must come to an end. *T.N. Nathan v. Public Prosecutor [1978] 1 MLJ 137 Pg. 138*

INTERIM 'in the meantime, for the time being' an act or condition which is short-term or temporary and which comes before a more permanent act, e.g., *interim financing; interim order; interim appointment; interim statement* etc. for example, one appointed between the time that a person is made bankrupt, to act in the place of the assignee until the assignee shall be appointed, is an assignee ad interim. *Liew Ngun Yin v. Lee Pak Yin & ors [1939] 8 MLJ 248 at Pg. 248; (Partnership); Suppiah Chettiar v. Ong Pee Koi & Another [1951] 17 MLJ at Pg. 52; (Japanese Judgments and Civil Proceedings Ordinance 1946)*

INTRA FAUCES TERRA 'Within the jaws of the land'. This term refers to a nation's territorial waters.

INTRA LEGEM 'Within the law'. Used in various contexts to refer to the legal foundation for a thing.

INTRA 'within, inside, near'. Within. Used as part of another word to convey the notion of occurring within, as in *intragalactic* (within a single galaxy); *intracranial* (within the skull); or *intramural* (within the student body). *"Malayan legislation". a Review [1932] 1 MLJ 62 Pg. 63*

INTRA V.IRES 'force, power, strength'. within one's strength or power. an act or deed which is within the power or authority of the person committing it; e.g., the act of presiding at a meeting is *intra v.ires* for the president or chairman of a corporation; the sale of its goods is *intra v.ires* for a corporation engaged in manufacturing. Husin Bin Mandot v. Public Prosecutor [1940] 9 MLJ 22 at Pg. 23; (Criminal); *In Re K. Mohamed Ibrahim & Company Ex Parte Ramchand*

[1940] 9 MLJ 90 at Pg. 92; (Bankruptcy); Lee See Chian v. The Public Prosecutor [1940] 9 MLJ 148 at Pg. 148, 150; (Criminal); Public Prosecutor v. Utam Singh [1939] 8 MLJ 194 at Pg. 194; (Road Traffic Enactment); The Singapore Harbour Board v. The Firestone Tire & Rubber Co. (S.S) Ltd [1950] 16 MLJ at Pg. 132,133; (Bailment, Negligence, Tort)

INTRA VEL ULTRA VIRES *B. v. Comptroller-General Inland Revenue [1973] 1 MLJ 123 Pg.127; Comptroller –General of Inland Revenue v. N.P. [1973] 1 MLJ 165 Pg.166*

INTROMISSIO introduce; insert.

INTUITUS a view; regard; contemplation; with a different view.

IPSE DIXIT 'He himself said it." He said it on his ipse dixit. A mere saying or assertion without proof. authority or precedent except the statement itself. A bald, unproved statement. Sometimes used in place of *dictum*. Asserted but unproven. *Hashim & Anor v. Public Prosecutor [1966] 1 MLJ 229 at Pg. 231; Loh Teck Chong v. Public Prosecutor [1966] 1 MLJ 7 at Pg. 8, Hashim & Anor v. Public Prosecutor [1966] 1 MLJ 229 at Pg. 231; Loh Teck Chong v. Public Prosecutor [1966] 1 MLJ 7 at Pg. 8; Public Prosecutor v. Lee Yoke Kai [1967] 1 MLJ 213 Pg. 215; Pacific Tin Consolidated Corporation v. Hoon Wee Thim [1967] 2 MLJ 35 Pg.38*

IPSISSIMA V.ERBA 'the very words'. is a legal term referring to material, usually established authority, that a writer or speaker is quoting or referring to. It refers to an established authority, that a writer or speaker is quoting or referring to. When an attorney or judge refers to the exact words used by some authority it can be termed ipsissima verba. in most of the judgments, judges quote valid sentences that refer to similar issue and use them as precedents. the use of the very words of an authority is ipsissima v.erba. *Public Prosecutor v. Thum Soo Chye [1954] 20 MLJ at Pg.98; (Evidence Ordinance 1950- Criminal Procedure Code); Public Prosecutor v. Raman I, Raman II & Ayappan [1940] 9 MLJ 163 at Pg. 165; Criminal Procedure Code*

IPSO FACTO 'in fact itself'. 'absolutely', or 'actually'. By that very fact itself; in and of itself; the inevitable result. The end of a marriage results *ipso facto* from a decree of divorce. By the very act. These words are often applied to forfeitures, indicating that when any forfeiture is incurred, it shall not be necessary to declare such forfeiture in a court of law, but that the penalty shall be incurred by the doing of the act prohibited. And so, when it is enacted

that any proceeding shall be *ipso facto* void, it means that such a proceeding is to have not even *prima. facie* validity, but may be treated as void for all purposes *ab initio. Ban Hong Joo Mines Ltd v. Chen & Yap Ltd. [1969] 2 MLJ 85 (Contract); Subramaniam Chettiar & Ors. v. J.C. Chang Ltd. [1969] 2 MLJ 179 (Contract); Tengku Besar Zabaidah v. Kong Cheng Whum [1969] 2 MLJ 228 (Tenancy), Haw Par Bros. (PTE) Ltd v. Dato Ah Kow[1973] 2 MLJ169 Pg.169; Song Toh Chu v. Chan Kiat Neo[1973] 2 MLJ206 Pg. 206; Lee Mooi v. Nam Sing Mining, Kepong [1973] 1 MLJ 113 Pg.114*

IRROTULATIO a record.

IUDEX NON CALCULAT 'The judge does not calculate'. A principle that calculation errors made by the court do not invalidate the judgement on a technicality. Also taken to mean that the judge does not tally up the arguments of both sides and decide in favor of the more numerous, but rather weighs all of the evidence without regard to the number of arguments made.

J

JACTUS thrown; cast; defeated. In the civil law. The throwing of goods overboard to lighten a vessel; jettison; the thing thrown in overboard. The word 'jactus' is used in the maritime law to designate a portion of a cargo or vessel which is drawn overboard at time of peril for the purpose of preventing the loss of the vessel and cargo.

JRAULEM *Legis* Stephen Kalong Ningkan v. Tun Abang Haji Openg & Tawi Sli (NO 2) [1967] 1 MLJ 46 Pg.50

JUDEX ADULTERII ANTE OCULOS HABERE DEBET ET INQUIRERE, AN MARITUS PUDICE VIVENS, MULLERI QUOQUE BONOS MORES COLENDI AUTOR FUERIT. PERINIQUUM ENIM VIDETUR ESSE, UT PUDICITIAM VIR AB UXORE OXIGAT, QUAM IPSE NON EXHIBEAT a judge, in a case of adultery, should carefully examine, whether the husband by living chastely himself had also been an example of good conduct to his wife. For it seems perfectly unjust that the husband should require that chastity in his wife which appears not in himself. earnest money towards a contract. The practice of giving something to signify the conclusion of the contract - sometimes a sum of money, sometimes a ring or other object - to be re-paid or re-delivered on the completion of the contract, ap-pears to be one of great antiquity, and very general prevalence. It may not be unimportant to observe, as evidence of his antiquity, that our own word 'earnest' has been supposed to flow from a Phoenician source, the arra or arrha of the Latins and the arrhes of the French ... Taking these early authorities into consideration, I think we may conclude that the deposit in the present case is the earnest or arrha of our earlier writers; that the expression used in the present contract, that the money is paid as a deposit and in part payment of the purchase money, relates to the alternatives, and declares that, in the event of the purchaser making default, the money is to be forfeited, and that, in the event of the purchase being completed, the sum is to be taken in part payment.'

JUDEX AEQUITATEM SEMPER SPECTARE DEBET a judge ought always to regard equity.

JUDEX BONUS NIHIL EX ARBITRIO SUO FACIAT, NEC PROPOSITIONE DOMESTI-CAE VOLUNTATIS, SED JUXTA LEGES ET JURA PRONUN CIET a good judge should do nothing of his own arbitrary will nor on the dictate of his personal inclination but should decide according to law and justice it also means a good judge does nothing from his own judgment, or from a dictate of private will; but he will pronounce according to law and justice. *Teng Boon How v Pendakwa Rakyat [1993] 3 MLJ 553 at 562 Per Edgar Joseph Jr SCJ*

JUDEX EST LEX LOQUENS the judge is the speaking law.

JUDEX HABERE DEBET DUOS SALES, SALEM SAPICUTIAE, NE SIT INSIPIDUS, ET SALEM CONSCIENTIEA, NE SIT DIABOLUS a judge should have two salts, the salt of wisdom, lest he be insipid; and the salt of conscience, lest he be devilish.

JUDEX the judicial power which examines the truth of the fact, the law arising upon it and if an injury has been done, applies the remedy (In old English Law). A judge, one who declares the law, or administers justice between contending parties. In Roman law, a judge, being a private individual appointed as such for a specific trial.

JUDEX NON POTEST ESSE TESTIS IN PROPRIA CAUSA a Judge cannot be a witness to his own cause. It also means a Judge cannot be a witness in his own cause.

JUDEX NON POTEST INJURIAM SIBI DATAM PUNIRE a judge cannot punish an injury (a wrong) done to himself.

JUDEX NON REDDIT PLUS QUAM QUOD PETENS IPSE REQUIRIT a judge cannot give more than the petitioner (or suitor) himself asks. It also means a judge does not give more than that which the plaintiff requires. Or a Judge does not give more than what he that seeks does himself require.

JUDGMENTS, EX TEMPORE by lapse of time; without preparation. The reason why the cases did not find their way into the local law reports is because in most cases the decisions were given ex tempore — off the cuff, so to speak. Ex tempore judgments, even when reduced into writing, are not always useful.

JUDICARE to judge; to decide or determine judicially; to give judgment or sentence.

JUDICATIO judging; the pronouncing of sentence after hearing a cause.

JUDICES NON TENENTUR EXPRIMERE CAUSAM SENTENTIAE SUAE judges are not bound to explain the reason of their sentence.

JUDICIA SUNT TANQUAM JURIS DICTA, ET PROVERITATE ACCIPIUNTUR judgments are, as it were, the sayings of the law, and are received as truth'.

JUDICIA; JUDICIA PUBLICA Judicial proceedings, trials. Also criminal trials.

JUDICIIS POSTERIORIBUS FIDES EST ADHIBENDA credit is to be given the latest.

JUDICIS (NOSTRUM) EST JUDICARE SECUNDUM ALLEGATA ET PROBATA It is the duty of a judge to determine according to what is alleged and proved. It also means it is the duty of a judge to decide according to facts alleged and proved.

JUDICIS EST JUS DICERE, NON DARE it is the province of a judge to declare the law, not to give it. It also means it is for the judge to administer, not to make law.

JUDICIS OFFICIUM EST OPUS DIEI IN DIE SUO PERFICERE it is the duty of a judge to finish the work of each day within that day.

JUDICIS OFFICIUM EST UT RES ITA TEMPORE RERUM QUAERERE it is the duty of a judge to inquire into the times of things, as well as into things themselves. It also means it is the duty of a judge to inquire as well into the time of things as into things themselves; by inquiring into the time you will be safe.

JUDICIUM A NON SUO JUDICE DATUM NULLIUS EST MOMENTI judgment given by one who is not the proper judge is of no force. It also means a judgment given by a judge without jurisdiction is of no importance.

JUDICIUM judgement. A decision before a judex or judge; a court or judicial tribunal.

JUDICIUM NON DEBET ESSE ILLUSORIUM; SUUM EFFECTUM HABERE DEBET a judgment ought not be illusory; it ought to have its consequence.

JUDICIUM REDDITUR IN INVITUM, IN PRAESUMPTIONE LEGIS judgment in presumption of law is given contrary to inclination.

JUDICIUM SEMPER PRO VERITATE ACCIPITUR a judgment is always accepted as true.

JURA ECCLESIASTICA LIMITATA SUNT INFRA LIMITES SEPARATORS ecclesiastical laws are limited within separate bounds.

JURA EODEM MODO DESTRUUNTUR QUO CONSTRUUNTUR laws are abrogated by the same means as those by which they are made.

JURA NATURE SUNT IMMUTABILIA the laws of nature are unchangeable.

JURA NOVIT CURIA 'The court knows the law'. Concept that parties to a case do not need to define how the law applies to their case. The court is solely responsible for determining what laws apply.

JURA PUBLICA EX PRIVATO PROMISCUE DECIDI NON DEBENT public rights ought not to be promiscuously determined in analogy to a private right or public rights ought not to be promiscuously decided out of a private transaction.

JURA SANGUINIS NULLO JURE CIVILI DIRIMI POSSUNT rights of blood cannot be destroyed by any civil right.

JURAMENTUM EST INDIVISIBLE, ET NON EST ADMITTENDUM IN PARTE VERUM ET IN PARTE FALSUM an oath is indivisible; it is not to be held partly true and partly false. It also means an oath is indivisible, and is not to be received as partly true and partly false.

JURARE EST DEUM IN TESTEM VOCARE, ET EST ACTUS DIVINI CULTUS to swear is to call God to witness, and is an act of religion. (Inst 165) To swear is to call God to witness, and is an act of Divine worship.

JURAT '(He) swears'. Appears at the end of an affidav.it, where the party making the affirmation signs the oath, and the information on whom the oath was sworn before is placed.

JURAT that the affiant swore before the officer taking the affidavit; a certificate of the officer who administered the oath that the affiant had subscribed and sworn before him; that part of an affidavit where the officer certifies that it was sworn before him. the jurat of an officer authorised to receive and file oaths is the certificate of the officer who administered the oath that the affiant had subscribed and sworn to the same before such officer. The 'Jurat' is not a certificate to a deposition in the ordinary sense of the term, but a certificate of the fact that the witness appeared before the commissioner and sworn to the truth of what he had stated. The primary meaning of the word 'jurat' is 'sworn' but the derivative signification is 'proved'.

JURATO CREDITUR IN JUDICIO he who makes oath is to be believed in judgment. It also means in judgment credit is given to the swearer.

JURATORES DEBENT ESSE VICINI, SUFFICIENTES, ET MINUS SUSPECTI Jurors ought to be neighbours, of sufficient estate, and free from suspicion

JURE GENTIUM 'a clan, a people, all people'. By the law of nations. According to International Law. *Public Prosecutor v. Lee Chin Chai [1974] 2 MLJ 174 Pg. 175*

JURE HUMANO by human law; founded on the rights of man, and deriving its obligation from the assent of the people.

JURI NON EST CONSONUM QUOD ALIQUIS ACCESSORIUS IN CURIA REGIS CON-VINCATUR ANTEQUAM ALIQUIS DE FACTO FUERIT ATTINCTUS it is not consonant to justice that any accessory should be convicted in the King's court before any one has been attainted to the fact. It also means it is not consonant to justice that any accessory should be convicted in the king's court before someone has been attainted of the fact.

JURIDICUS relating to the courts or to the administration of justice; juridical; lawful.

JURIS EFFECTUS IN EXECUTIONE CONSISTIT the effect of law depends upon execution.

JURIS ET DE JURE 'Of law, and from law'. Incontrovertible and fundamental presumptions of law. One cannot argue against, or try to otherwise refute these.

JURIS of law; of right.

JURISDICTIO jurisdiction; authority to judge, or administer justice.

JURISPRUDENTIA jurisprudence. It is the science of law which treats the principles of positive and substantive law and le-gal relations. Its function is to ascertain the principles on which legal rules are based, to classify them in their proper order and show the relation in which they stand to one another. It is not merely a history of law; its function is to separate the essential elements of legal principles from its historical accidents on a comparative study of the legal institutions of various countries. It has no direct concern with questions of moral or political policy, but when a new and doubtful case arises to which two different rules seem, when taken literally, to be equally applicable, it may be, and often is, the function of jurisprudence to consider the ultimate effect which would be produced if each rule were applied to an indefinite number of similar cases, and to choose that rule, when so applied, as will produce the greatest advantage to the community.

JUS ACCRESCENDI PRAEFERTUR ONERIBUS the right of survivorship is preferred to incumbrances.

JUS ACCRESCENDI PRAEFERTUR ULTIMAE VOLUNTATI the right of survivorship is preferred to the last will.

JUS ACCRESCENDRI 'Right of survivorship'. In property law, on the death of one tenant, that tenant's interest passes automatically to the surviving tenant(s) to hold jointly until the estate is held by a sole tenant. The only way to defeat the right of survivorship is to sev.er the joint tenancy during the lifetime of the parties, jus accrescendi takes priority ov.er a will or interstate accession rules.

JUS AD BELLUM 'Laws to war'. Refers to legalities considered before entering into a war, to ensure it is legal to go to war initially. Not to be confused with ius in bello (q.v.), the "laws of war" concerning how war is carried out.

JUS ALBINATUR alien law.

JUS CIVILE 'Civil law'. A codified set of laws concerning citizenry, and how the laws apply to them.

JUS COGENS 'Compelling law'. Internationally agreed laws that bear no dev.iation, and do not require treaties to be in effect. An example is law prohibiting genocide.

JUS COMMUNE 'Common law'. Not actually referring to common law, this term refers to common facets of civ.il law that underlie all aspects of the law.

JUS CONSTITUI OPORTET IN HIS QUAE UT PLURIMUM ACCIDUNT NON QUAE EX laws ought to be made with a view to those cases which happen most frequently, and not to those which are of rare or accidental occurrence.

JUS DESCENDIT ET NON TERRA a right descends, not the land.

JUS EST NORMA RECTI: ET QUICQUID EST CONTRA NORMAM RECTI EST INJURIA law is a rule of right; and whatever is contrary to the rule of right is an injury.

JUS EX INJURIA NON ORITUR a right does not arise out of an injury.

JUS EX NON SCRIPTO the unwritten law. This would refer to custom or usage.

JUS GENTIUM 'Laws of nations'. Customary law followed by all nations. Nations being at peace with one another, without having to have an actual peace treaty in force, would be an example of this concept.

JUS HABENDI ET RETINENDI the right to have possession of property and to retain the profits thereof.

JUS HABENDI the right to be put in actual possession of a thing.

JUS HAEREDITATIS the right of inheritance.

JUS IN BELLO 'Law in war'. Laws governing the conduct of parties in war.

JUS IN PERSONAM 'A right against a person'; a right which gives its possessor a power to oblige another person to give or procure, to do or not to do, something. It means the right to enforce a particular person's obligation by instituting an action against such person. In other words it means that the person entitled has a right, availing against a determinate person, to the acquisition of a right availing against the world at large, and, by consequence, his/her right is a right to an act of conveyance or transfer on the part of the person obliged. A right of legal action against or to enforce a legal duty of a particular person or group of persons. *Malayan Credit Ltd. v. Mohamed Kassim [1965] 2 MLJ 134 Pg. 135*

JUS IN RE 'A right in a thing. A right existing in a person with respect to an article or subject of property, inherent in his relation to it, implying complete ownership with possession, and available against all the world. Property, title. The right which a man has in a thing by which it belongs to him. It is a complete and full right. Is the absolute domain which a man has in a thing by which it belongs to him/her. It is the real and complete right ov.er a property. Jus in re is the right on a property and jus in rem is the right against a property. Jus in rem is inherent in a person's relation to the property.

JUS IN RE ALIENA 'A right in the property of another'. (see encumbrance). It is contrasted with jus in re propria – a right in one's own property. Is the right of enjoyment which is incident not to full ownership or property but to certain limited ownerships in or rights ov.er or in respect of the thing. *The Halcyon Isle [1978] 1 MLJ 189 Pg. 190*

JUS IN RE ALIENA a right in another person's property such as an easement.

JUS IN REM "a right to a thing." It is a personal right to possession of property that usually arises from a contractual obligation (as a lease). Jus ad rem is a mere imperfect or inchoate right. It is a right exercisable by one person ov.er a particular article of property in virtue of a contract or obligation incurred by another person in respect to it and which is enforceable only against or through such other person. The right a man has in relation to a thing; it is not the right in the thing itself, but only against the person who has contracted to deliv.er it. Jus ad rem is descriptive of a right without possession. On the other hand jus in re is descriptive of a right accompanied by possession. It is thus distinguished from jus in re which is a complete and absolute dominion ov.er a thing available against all persons. a right exercisable by one person ov.er a particular article of property in virtue of a contract or obligation incurred by another person in respect to it and which is enforceable only against or through such other person. It is thus distinguished from *jus in re* which is a complete and absolute dominion ov.er

a thing av.ailable against all persons. *Malayan Credit Ltd. v. Mohamed Kassim [1965] 2 MLJ 134 Pg. 135*

JUS INTER GENTES 'Law between the peoples'. Laws governing treaties and international agreements.

JUS JURANDI FORMA VERBIS DIFFERT RE CONVENIT HUNC ENIM SENSUM HABERE DEBET UT DEUS INVOCETUR the form of taking an oath though it differs in words, agrees in meaning; for it ought to have this sense, that the deity be invoked.

JUS JURANDUM INTER ALIOS FACTUM NEC NOCERE NEC PRODESSE DEBET an oath made by others ought neither to hurt nor profit.

JUS JURANDUM an oath.

JUS LATII the right of the latins, which seems to have been mainly a right to the use of their own laws, a right to exemption from the edicts of the practor.

JUS 'Law, right'. Essentially: Law.

JUS right, justice; law; power or authority. Jus is a term with two meanings in the first instance it means law considered in the abstract, or law taken as a system, an aggregate, a whole, or someone particular system or body of particular laws; and in the second instance it means a right in general or in the abstract. It is said that the word 'Just' is derived from the Latin 'Justus' which is from the latin 'Jus', which means a right, and, more technically, a legal right, a law. In the maxim 'Ignorantia juris haud excusat' the word 'Jus' is used in the sense of denoting General Law, the ordinary law of the country. But when 'jus' is used in the sense of denoting a private right, that maxim has no application.

JUS NATURAL 'Natural law'. Laws common to all people, that the av.erage person would find reasonable, regardless of their nationality.

JUS NON HABENTI TUTE NON PARETUR one who has no right cannot be safely obeyed. It also means it is not safe to obey him who has no right.

JUS PRIMAE NOCTIS 'Right of the first night'. Supposed right of the lord of an estate to take the virginity of women in his estate on their wedding night.

JUS PUBLICUM ET PRIVATUM EST QUOD EX NATURALIBUS PRAECEPTIS, AUT GENTIUM AUT CIVILIBUS EST COLLECTUM ET QUOD IN JURE SCRIPTO JUS AP-PELLATUR, ID IN LEGE ANGLIAE RECTUM ESSE public and private law is that which is collected from natural principles, either of nations or in states; and that which in the civil law is called jus in the law of England is said to be right. Public and private law is that which is collected from natural principles, either of nations or in States; and what in written law is called 'jus' by the law of England is said to be right.

JUS QUAESITUM TERTIO 'rights on account of third parties'. Generally, a contract cannot confer rights on a third party. howev.er, rights can be conferred on third parties by means of a trust. jus quaesitum tertio means rights on account of third parties. contracts may be formed for the benefit of third parties. in order to confer a jus quaesitum tertio on a third party it must appear from the terms of the instrument that the object of the maker was to benefit the third party's interests. it must be clear from the wording of the contract that both contracting parties intended to confer a benefit on the third party. third party must be intimated of the benefit contract. third party is entitled to enforce performance of the contract according to its terms. moreov.er, the third party can recov.er damages for non- performance. to be enforceable, the contract conferring third party benefit must be irrevocable. *G. Ramchand v. Lam Soon Cannery Co. Ltd [1954] 20 MLJ At Pg. 241; (Contract)*

JUS RESPICIT AEQUITATEM the law regards equity'.

JUS SANGUINIS 'law of the soil'. in some countries, jus soli system or birthright citizenship is followed. according to this principle, citizenship of a person is determined by the place where a person was born. jus soli is the most common means to acquire citizenship of a nation. the system through which a person acquires citizenship through their parents or ancestors is called jus sanguinis. in the U.S., jus soli system is followed to determine citizenship.

this means whoever is born in the U.S. and is subject to its jurisdiction is automatically granted u.s. citizenship. the principle that a person's nationality at birth is the same as that of his natural parents. *Lui Ah Yong V. Superintenden of Prisons,Penang [1977] 2 MLJ 226 Pg. 228*

JUS SOIL the law of the place of one's birth. A right acquired by virtue of the soil or place of birth. Under this right, the nationality of a person is determined by the place of birth rather than parentage. Nationality is conferred by the state in which the birth takes place. Every person born in Singapore after 16 September 1963 is a Singapore citizen provided one his parents was a Singapore citizen or a permanent resident of Malaysia ... This modified operation of the jus soil principle has two other usual disqualifications - his father, not being a Malaysian citizen pos-sessed diplomatic immunity; or was an enemy alien and the place of birth occurred in a place under enemy occupation. (see Citizenship in Malaysia [1964] MLJ xlviii by S Jayakumar dan FA Trindade at xlix)

JUS SOLI 'Right of soil'. Social law concept wherein citizenship of a nation is determined by place of birth.

JUS SUPERVENIENS AUCTORI ACCRESCIT SUCCESSORI a right growing to the possessor accrues to the successor.

JUS TERTII 'Law of the third'. Arguments made by a third party in disputes ov.er possession, the intent of which is to question one of the principal parties' claims of ownership or rights to ownership. In cases involving two parties with conflicting claims to possession of a parcel of real property, both parties may be precluded from relying on *jus tertii*, i.e., the rights of a third party. The right of a third party. If A., who *facie* is liable to restore property to B., alleges that C. has a paramount title, A. is said to set up the *jus tertii*. This may not be done by an agent as against his principal. *The Official Assignee of The Property Of Loh Chuk Poh v. The Over Sea Chinese Bank [1934] 3 MLJ 76 at Pg. 82 Maruthappan v. Claude Da Silva [1965] 1 MLJ 94 Pg. 97*

JUS TRIPLEX EST; PROPRIETATIS, POSSESSIONIS, ET POSSIBILITATIS right is threefold; of property, of possession, of possibility.

JUSTAE NUPTIAE JUSTUM MATRIMONIUM *Chua Mui Nee v. Palaiappan [1967] 1 MLJ 270 Pg. 272*

JUSTICIA justice.

JUSTITIA DEBET ESSE LIBERA, QUIA NIHIL INIQUIUS VENALI JUSTITIA ; PLENA, QUIA JUSTITIA NON DEBET CLAUDICARE ; ET CELERIES, QUIA DILATIO EST QUAEDAM NEGATIO justice ought to be free, because nothing is more iniquitous than venal justice; full, because justice ought not to halt; and speedy, because delay is a kind of denial. It also means justice ought to be un-bought, because nothing is more hateful than venal justice; full, for justice ought not to be defective; and quick, for delay is a certain denial.

JUSTITIA EST DUPLEX: VIZ SEVERE PUNIENS, ET VERE PRAEVENIENS Justice is two fold, viz: severely punishing, and really or efficiently preventing. Justice is double; punishing with severity, preventing with lenity.

JUSTITIA FIRMATUR SOLIUM by justice the throne is established or that justice strengthens the throne.

JUSTITIA statute law; ordinance.

JUSTITIA NEMINI NEGANDA EST justice is to be denied to none.

JUSTITIA NON EST NEGANDA, NON DIFFERENDA justice is neither to be denied nor postponed.

JUSTITIA NON NOVIT PATREM NEC MATREM; SOLAM VERITATEM SPECTAT JUSTITIA justice knows not father nor mother; justice looks at truth alone. Justice knows neither father nor mother, but regards truth alone.

JUSTUM NON EST ALIQUEM POST MORTEM FACERE BASTARDUM QUI TOTO TEMPORE VITS SUE PRO LEGITIMO HABEBATUR it is not just to make anyone a bastard after his death when for his whole life he was taken to be legitimate.

Juxta 'near; following; according to'. *Tan Boon Teek v. Public Prosecutor [1950] 16 MLJ at Pg. 44, 45;*

L

LACUNA (LACUNAE) 'An empty space or a missing part; a gap'. *Lacuna (law), the lack of a law or legal source addressing a situation. Assa Singh v. Mentri Besar, Johore [1969] 2 MLJ 31 (Unlawful Detention), Leong Hoi Kow v. Chan Ho Yat [1951] 17 MLJ at Pg. 67; (Landlord and Tenant); Assa Singh v. Mentri Besar, Johore [1969] 2 MLJ 31 (Unlawful Detention); Haji Ariffin v. Government of Pahang [1969] 1 MLJ 9 (Administrative Law); Hati Talib v. Public Prosecutor [1969] 1 MLJ 94 (Murder); Rawther v. Abdul Kareem [1966] 2 MLJ 201 at Pg. 202*

LAESA MAJESTAS high treason; injury to Her Majesty.

LAICUS a member of the laity; a layman, one not ordained. Which means that an ordinary layman; a person who has left the ministry for want of a family life. Such a person is said to have become 'laicised, as it is called. Anyone can change his career if he likes.

LAPIS MARMORIUS a marble stone at the Westminster Hall on which was placed a marble chair for the use of the sovereign at the coronation dinner and at other times of the Lord Chancellor.

LATITATIO hidden, concealment of the person.

LATOR a messenger; also the maker of laws.

LATRO a robber.

LAUDARE to cite, to show one's title or authority.

LAUDUM a judgment, arbitration, an award.

LEGARE legation - diplomatic mission headed by a minister; also, the minister's official residence and office.

LEGATUM a legacy; a gift from a deceased person.

LEGATUS REGIS VICE FUNGITUR A QUO DESTINATUR ET HONORANDUS EST SICUT ILLE CUJUS VICEM GERIT an ambassador tills the place of the King by whom he is sent and is to be honored as he is whose place he fills.

LEGEM accusative of lex, law.

LEGES ANGLIAE SUNT TRIPARTITAE - JUS COMMUNE, CONSUETUDINES AC DE-CRETA COMITIORUM the laws of England are threefold - common law, customs, and decrees of parliament.

LEGES ET CONSTITUTIONES FUTURIS CERTUM EST DARE FORMAM NEGOTIIS NON AD FACTA PRETERITA REVOCARI; NISI NOMINATIM ET DE PRETERITO TEMPORE

ET ADHUC PENDENTIBUS NEGOTIIS CAULUM SIT law and statutes are regarded as regulating future negotiations not as revoking past transactions; unless they are expressly make to apply to past time and existing obligations.

LEGES HUMANAE NASCUNTUR, VIVUNT, MORIUNTUR 'The laws of man are born, live, and die'. Illustrates that laws are made, are in force for a period, and then become obsolete.

LEGIBUS SUMPTIS DESINENTIBUS, LEGE NATURE UTENDUM EST when laws imposed by the state fail, we must act by the law of nature. It also means laws imposed by the State failing, we must act by the law of nature.

LEGIS HABET V.IGOREM; *Legality and The Rule Of Law [1970] 1 MLJ xiv., at xlv.*

LEGISLATORUM EST VIVA VOX, REBUS ET NON VERBIS LEGEM the voice of legislators is a living voice, to impose laws on things, and not on words.

LEGITIMATIO PER SUBSEQUENS MATRIMONIUM the process of making a bastard legitimate by the subsequent marriage of his parents.

LEGITIME IMPERANTI PARERE NECESSE EST one lawfully commanding must be obeyed. It also means it is necessary to obey one legitimately commanding.

LETTRES DE CACHET literally mean s 'letters of the sign/signet'. Were letters signed by the king of France, countersigned by one of his ministers, and closed with the royal seal, or *cachet*. They contained orders directly from the king, often to enforce arbitrary actions and judgments that could not be appealed. A letter under the sov.ereign's seal, often authorizing imprisonment without trial. *Assa Singh v. Mentri Besar, Johore [1969] 2 MLJ 31*

Lex LOCI domicilii 'the law of the place of domicile'. it is the law of the place of a party's dwelling house. lex loci domicilii is applied in case related to will, marriage, div.orce, separation and contract. in re harwood, 104 misc. 653 (n.y. misc. 1918), the court held that the v.alidity of a last will is gov.erned entirely and solely by the lex loci domicilii of the testator. when it is sufficient at his/her domicile at the time of death, such will is v.alid in ev.ery other country in which the testator's mov.able property is situated. the law of the domicile by which the rights of persons are sometimes gov.erned (as where a person dies leav.ing personal property). *In Re Maria Huberdina Hertogh; Adrianus Petrus Hertogh and Anor v. Amina Binte Mohamed and Ors. [1951] 17 MLJ at Pg.167,171, 173; Indarjit Singh v. Jinder Pal [1975] 2 MLJ 128 Pg. 129*

LEX ANGLIAE EST LEX MISERICORDIAE the law of England is a law of mercy.

LEX ANGLIAE LEX TERRA EST the law of England is the law of the land.

LEX ANGLIAE NUNQUAM MATRIS SED SEMPER PATRIS CONDITIONEM IMITARI PARTUM JUDICAT the law of England rules that the offspring shall always follow the condition of the father never that of the mother.

LEX BENEFICIALIS REI CONSIMILI REMEDIUM PRAESTAT a beneficial law affords a remedy for a similar case.

LEX COMMUNIS'Common law'. Alternate form of jus commune. Refers to common facets of civ.il law that underlie all aspects of the law.

LEX EST EXERCITUS JUDICIUM TUTISSIMUS DUCTOR t the law is the safest leader of the army of judges.

LEX EST SUMMA RATIO INSITA A NATURA QUAE JUBET EA, QUAE FACIENDA SUNT, PROHIBETQUE law is the perfection of reason implanted in its by nature, which enjoins what should be done, and forbids what we should not do.

LEX ET CONSUETUDO PARLIAMENTI the law and customs and customs of Parliament. It also means the rules by which Parliament governs itself; the law and custom (or usage) of parliament.

LEX FORI'market-place, public square, courthouse, court'. the law of the court or forum; the law of the jurisdiction in which an action is commenced or is pending. the *lex fori* will control all procedural and substantiv.e matters required for decision except in those instances in which some principle of conflicts resolution requires the court to look at the law of another jurisdiction. The law of the court or forum. Law of the jurisdiction where an action is pending. The law of the *forum*, that is, the law of the place in which any given case is tried. *Pi. Ararunasalan Chettiar & Ors. v. Pi. Palaniappa [1969] 1 MLJ 58; The "Halcyon Isle "[1977] 1 MLJ 145 Pg.146*

LEX HOSTILIA DE FURTIS a Roman law which did away with the necessity of the owner's intervention in commencing a prosecution for theft.

LEX LATA 'The law borne'.The law as it has been enacted

LEX a body or collection of various laws peculiar to a given nation or people.

LEX LOCI 'place, location'. The law of the place. Generally followed by a word or phrase which specifies the place which is intended; e.g., *lex loci contractus*. If no word is added, the assumption is that *lex loci* means *lex loci contractus. Koninklijke Bunge N. V. v. Sinitrada Co. Ltd [1973] 1MLJ 194 Pg.197*

LEX LOCI CELEBRATIONIS the law of the place where a contract is entered into. The law of the place where a contract is made. The law of the place where a judicial act occurs such as where a marriage was celebrated or a contract was made.

LEX LOCI CONTRACTUS 'the place in which a contract is made. In cases inv.olv.ing conflicts of laws, the *lex loci contractus* generally controls issues of substance and the *lex fori* controls issues of procedure. The law of the place where an agreement is made. Generally, the v.alidity of a contract is to be decided by the law of the place where, the contract is made; if v.alid, there it is, in general, v.alid ev.erywhere. Story, Confl. of Laws, §242, and the cases there cited. And v.ice v.ersa if v.oid or illegal there, it is generally v.oid ev.erywhere. There is an exception to the rule as to the univ.ersal v.alidity of contracts. The comity of nations, by v.irtue of which such contracts deriv.e their force in foreign countries, cannot prev.ail in cases where it v.iolates the law of our own country, the law of nature, or the law of God. When the contract is entered into in one place, to be executed in another, there are two loci contractus; the locus celebrate contractus, and the locus solutionis; the former gov.erns in ev.erything which relates to the mode of construing the contract, the meaning to be attached to the expressions, and the nature and v.alidity of the engagement; but the latter gov.erns the performance of the agreement. *Koninklijke Bunge N. V. v. Sinitrada Co. Ltd [1973] 1MLJ 194 Pg.197*

LEX LOCI REI SITAE (LEX SITUS) The law of the place in which the thing is situated. The law of the site of the subject matter, usually with reference to real property. *The Commissioner of Stamps v. Oei Tjong Swan [1933] 2 MLJ 107 Pg. 108*

LEX NEMINEM COGIT AD VANA SEU INUTILIA PERAGENDA the law will not force anyone to do a thing vain and fruitless or the law does not require anyone to do vain or useless things. When the condition of an obligation is possible at the time of its making, but before it can be performed becomes impossible by an act of God, the law, or the obligee, the obligation is saved.

LEX NIL FRUSTRA FACIT the law does nothing in vain. It also means the law will not attempt to do, or compel one to do, an act which would be vain.

LEX NON COGIT AD IMPOSSIBILIA The law never compels the impossible. *Shaik Sahied Bin Abdullah Bajerai v. S. S.S.T. Sockalingam Chettiar [1933] 2 MLJ 81 Pg.83; King Lee Tee v. Norwich Fire Insurance Society, Ltd. [1933] 2 MLJ 187 Pg.190; Re Ang Teck Say [1934] 3 MLJ 25 at Pg. 25, 26, 27*

LEX NON CURAT DE MINIMIS the law does not regard small matters. It also means the law cares not about trifles.

LEX NON DEBET DEFICERE CONQUERENTIBUS IN JUSTITIA EXHIBENDA the law wills that, in every case where a man is wronged and endamaged, he shall have remedy. It also means the law ought not to fail in dispensing justice to those with a serious grievance.

LEX NON FAVET DELICATORUM VOTIS law pays little attention to more fastidiousness. It also means the law favours not the wishes of the dainty.

LEX NON INTENDIT AD IMPOSSIBILIA the law does not intend anything impossible.

LEX NON NOVIT PATREM, NEC MATREM; SOLAM VERITATEM the law knows neither father nor mother; only the truth.

LEX NON ORITUR EX INJURIA the law does not arise from an unlawful act.

LEX POSTERIOR DEROGAT PRIORI 'later law removes the earlier'. More recent law overrules older ones on the same matter.

LEX RETRO NON AGIT 'the law does not operate retroactively'. A law cannot make something illegal that was legal at the time it was performed.

LEX SCRIPTA 'written law' or the law that specifically codifies something, as opposed to common law or customary law.

LEX SCRIPTA SI CESSET ID CUSTODIRI OPORTET QUOD MORIBUS ET CONSUE-TUDINE INDUCTUM EST, ET SI QUA IN RE HOC DEFECERIT TUNE ID QUOD PROX-IMUM ET CONSEQUENS EI EST if the written law be silent, that which is drawn from usage and custom ought to be ob-served, and if in that anything is defective, then that which is next and analogous to it.

LEX SEMPER INTENDIT QUOD CONVENIT RATIONI the law always intends what is agreeable to reason.

LEX SPECIALIS DEROGAT LEGI GENERALI 'specific law takes away from the general law'. where sev.eral laws apply to the same situation, the more specific one(s) take precedence ov.er more general ones.

LEX SPECTAT NATURE ORDINEM the law regards the order and course of nature. It also means the law regards the order of nature. Thus, the law will not permit a man to demand that which he cannot, recover, and where the thing sued for by tenants in common is in its nature entire, as in detinue for a horse, they must of necessity join in the action, contrary to the rule which in other cases obtains, and according to which they must sue separately.

Libel 'a little book'. the original declaration of an action in the civil law. They are articles drawn out in a formal allegation in the ecclesiastical court, setting forth the complainant's ground of complaint or the charge on which, in Scotland, a civil or criminal prosecution takesplace. an obscene, blasphemous, or seditious publication, whether by printing. writing, signs, or pictures. a defamatory publication upon a person by writings, pictures, or the like. all contumacious matter that tends to degrade a man in the opinion of his neighbours, or to make him ridiculous, will, if fublished, amount to libel. Thus libel differs from slander, in that slander consists in oral defamation only, whereas a libel must consist of matter published, also the scope of the offence of libel is more extensiv.e than that of slander. libel may be punished criminally, whereas a person guilty slander can only be proceeded against civ.illy. A little book, a short declaration or memorandum] a defamatory statement expressed in writing, printing, pictures, art, or signs. any statement that injures the reputation of another. any accusation or attribution in writing or art which holds a person up to ridicule or exposes him to public contempt, shame or ridicule. *H.G.Hammett v. Northern Malaya Newspaper Ltd [1951] 17 MLJ at Pg. 219*

LIBELLUS a little book. Feudal law. An instrument of alienation or conveyance, as of a fief, or a part of it. Libellus supplex. A petition, especially to the emperor, all petitions to whom must be in writing. Li-bellum rescribere, to mark on such petition the answer to it. Libellum agere, to assist or counsel the em-peror in regard to such petitions. Libellus accusatorius, an information and accusation of a crime. Libellus divortii, a writing of divorcement. Libellus rerum, an inventory. Libellus or oratio consultoria, a message by which emperors laid matters before the senate. Libellus appellatorius, an appeal.

LIBERAM LEGEM AMITTERE to lose one's free law. A form of punishment anciently pronounced against conspirators. It involved be-coming discredited or disabled as juror and witness, forfeiting goods and chattels and lands for life; having those lands wasted, houses razed. trees uprooted and one's body committed to prison.

LIBERTAS EST RES INESTIMABILIS liberty is an inestimable thing.

LIBERTAS INESTIMABILLS RES EST freedom is a priceless thing.

LIBERTINUM INGRATUM LEGES CIVILES IN PRISTINAM REDIGUNT SERVITUTEM; SED LEGES ANGLIE SEMEL MANUMISSUM SEMPER LIBERUM JUDICANT the civil laws reduce an ungrateful freeman to his original slavery, but the laws of England regard a man once freed as ever after free.

LIBERUM VETO 'free veto'. an aspect of a unanimous v.oting system, whereby any member can end discussion on a proposed law.

LICEST SAEPIUS REQUISITUS although frequently requested. A phrase used in pleading whereby the plaintiff alleged that the defend-ant failed to pay the debt due although frequently requested to do so.

LICET DISPOSITIO DE INTERESSE FUTURO SIT INUTILIS, TAMEN POTEST FIERI DECLARATIO PRAECEDENS QUAE SORTIATUR EFFECTUM, INTERVENIENTE NOVO ACTU although the grant of a future interest is inoperative, yet it may become a declaration precedent, taking effect upon the intervention of some new act. It also means although the grant of an interest yet to come into existence is inoperative, yet it may become a declaration precedent, which will take effect on the intervention of some new act. This principle does not apply to an existing reversionary interest. But it does apply, for instance, to the wife's after-acquired property clause in a marriage settlement. A covenant by a wife to bring in her af-ter-acquired property does not operate on that property; even when it is acquired, but it must be conveyed by the wife to the trustees or the tenant for life under the settlement.

LICITA BENE MISCENTUR, FORMULA NISI JURIS OBSTET lawful acts (done by several authorities) are well mingled (ie become united or consolidated into one good act), unless some form of law forbid. Things permitted are properly united unless the form of law oppose.

LICITARE to offer a price at a sale; to bid; to bid often; to make several bids, one above another.

LIEN As applied to personalty, a lien is understood to be the right of a bailee to retain the possession of a chattel entrusted to him until his claim upon it been satisfied. As applied to realty, a *lien* for unpaid purchase-money is his right to enforce his claim upon the land sold; a right which is recognised in a court of equity, subject to the doctrines of that court for the protection of *bmui .fole* purchasers for valuable consideration without notice. *Liew Siew Yin & Another v. Lee Pak Yin & Another [1940]*

9 MLJ 135 at Pg.136; Puran Singh v. Kehar Singh & Anor [1939] 8 MLJ 57 at Pg.58; Liew Yu Fatt v. Teck Guan & Co. Ltd [1966] 1 MLJ 87 at Pg. 90, Lim Su Sang v. Teck Guan Construction & Development Co. Ltd [1966] 2 MLJ 29 at Pg. 32; Yong Mok Hin v. United Malay States Sugar [1966] 2 MLJ 286 at Pg. 289; Liew Yu Fatt v. Teck Guan & Co. Ltd [1966] 1 MLJ 87 at Pg. 90

LIEW (IN LIEU) 'Instead of'. For example, a "deed in **lieu** of foreclosure» is a deed to a house offered to the lender by the homeowner so that the lender will not foreclose. *Kamunting (Perak) Rubber & Tin Co. Ltd. v. Abraham [1965] 1 MLJ 20 Pg. 21*

LIGEANTIA EST VINCULUM FIDEI; LIGEANTIA EST LEGIS ESSENTIA allegiance is the bond of fealty, and the essence of law.

LIGEANTIA NATURALIS NULLIS CLAUSTRIS COERCETUR, NULLIS METIS RE-FRAENATUR, NULLIS FINIBUS natural allegiance is restrained by no barriers, reined by no bounds, compressed by no limits. Thus both at common law and under the Treason Act, 1351 (which is declaratory of it) it is treason to aid the Queen's enemies by acts performed outside the realm.

LINGUA FRANCA 'the frankish language'. It is a language common to an area that is spoken by all, even if not their mother tongue. It is a term that is gotten from the name given to a common language used by traders in the mediterranean basin dating from the Middle Ages.

LINGUA language, tongue or speech.

LIS ALIBI PENDENS 'lawsuit elsewhere pending'. It refers to requesting a legal dispute be heard that is also being heard by another court. to av.oid possibly contradictory judgements, this request will not be granted.

LIS INTER PARTES legal suit between parties. *Mak Sik Kwong v. Minister Of Home Affairs, Malaysia [1975] 2 MLJ168 Pg. 173*

LIS a controversy or dispute, suit or action. In Roman law, a proceeding or an issue the subject of a proceeding. The word 'lis' is a stage in the process of arriving at an administrative decision. It commences with the show cause notice and then takes a quasi-judicial character. State of Madras v Tiruneveli Municipal Council [1967] 1 MLJ 47]. In Re Application By Ong Eng Guan For An Order Of Prohibition In Re Appointment Of S H D Elias [1959] MLJ 92 at 93 Per Rose CJ

LIS MOTA The cause of the suit or action. By this term is understood the commencement of the controv.ersy, and the beginning of the suit. The cause or motiv.ation of a legal action or lawsuit. The literal translation is "litigation mov.ed". *Lim Ah Toh v. Ang Yau Chee & Anor. [1969] 2 MLJ, Lim Ah Toh v. Ang Yau Chee & Anor. [1969] 2 MLJ 195*

LIS PENDENS 'suit pending'. often used in the context of public announcements of legal proceedings to come.

LIS PENDENS 'to be in progress'. Notice that an action is pending. A statement to all that a court has before it a suit or action affecting the named parties, or a parcel of land, in which the court is being asked to determine or resolv.e a dispute set forth and described in the pleadings. The purpose of the statement is to give notice of the action to all and to bind purchasers or encumbrancers of any property inv.olv.ed in the action to the court's decision. A notice of *lis pendens* or notice of pendency is a document filed in a public record office which has the effect of. A pending suit; an expression used especially of pending suits relating to land as affecting the title to the land in question. *Damodaran v. Vesudevan [1975] 2 MLJ 231 Pg. 231; Re Choe Kuan Him [1975] 2 MLJ 274 Pg.275, Singapore Pak Hock Pai Athletic Association v. Yiu Pek Heng [1973] 2 MLJ 6 Pg.6*

LITERA a letter; the letter; as distinguished from the meaning of a writing; a term applied in the plural to various instruments in writing; public and private.

LITERATIM letter by letter.

LITIGARE to litigate; to carry on a suit (litem agere), either as plaintiff or defendant; to claim or dispute by action; to test or try the validity of a claim by action.

LITIGIUM litigation: the contest between the parties to a suit.

LITURA an obliteration or blot in a will or other instrument.

LOANNIS DASKALELIS *The Halcyon Isle [1978] 1 MLJ 189 Pg.191*

LOCALE 'a place or locality'. Especially when v.iewed in relation to a particular ev.ent or characteristic. *Lee Pak Yin & Another v. Liew Siew Yin & Another [1940] 9 MLJ 80 at Pg. 81*

LOCATIO letting for hire.

LOCO PARENTIS (IN LOCO PARENTIS) 'In the place of a parent'. One who has assumed parental status and discharged parental duties, usually temporary in character, ov.er a ward, without the formality of a decree of adoption or other permanent placement. Sometimes a group of companies; local unions are consolidated into national unions, which are in turn joined into international unions. It is frequently important in cases of dev.ises and bequests, to ascertain whether the testator did or did not stand towards the dev.isee or legatee, in loco parentis. In general, those who assume the parental character may be considered as standing in that relation but this character must clearly appear. The fact of his so standing may be shown by positiv.e proof, or the express declarations of the testator in his will, or by circumstances; as, when a grandfather or an uncle; takes an orphan child under his care, or supports him, he assumes the office of a parent. The law places a master in loco parentis in relation to his apprentice. *Re Joseph De Cruz James & Anor [1973] 2 MLJ117 Pg.119*

LOCUM a substitute.

LOCUM TENENS holding the place of another. A deputy or substitute. It also holding someone's place; a deputy. One who holds office in place of another or temporarily performs the professional duties of another. Legal practitioners carrying on private practice on their own account or in partnership have a professional obligation to either perform professional work personally or to adequately supervise the performance of that work by staff. Where a sole practitioner is absent on leave or because of illness, he or she may utilise the services of a locum to carry on the work of the firm. The locum will generally be an experienced legal practitioner holding a practicing certificate entitling him or her to practice on his or her own account. The local law society usually maintains a list of practitioners who are prepared to act as locum tenants. A person who acts as a lawful substitute in an office; one who holds the place of another, one who law-fully executes the office of another. The contentions of the parties and the decision of the commissioners in the other four cases were sub-stantially the same, except that the fourth and fifth taxpayers in their final contentions submitted that any profits or gains arising to them in respect of locum tenses work, as well as domiciliary visits, were proper to be regarded as profits or gains of their

130

profession assessable under Sch E. The Crown contended that these payments, made in the course of the part-time appointments, were properly to be regarded as emoluments of an office or employment assessable under Sch E and not as profits or gains assessable under Sch D the commissioners found that the remuneration received by the two taxpayers in respect of their temporary appointments act as locum tenens was in each case the profit of an office within the meaning of Sch E to the Income Tax Act 1918 (as amended by s. 18 of the Finance Act 1922), and s 158 of the Income Tax Act 1952; and that the two taxpayers' temporary appointments to act as locum tenens were a necessary part of the exercise of their profession and merely incidental thereto, notwithstanding that a great deal of their time taken up by them and the part-time appointments.

LOCUS CLASSICU A passage from a classic or standard work that is cited as an illustration or instance. *Seet Soon Guan v. Public Prosecutor [1955] 21 MLJ at Pg. 227*

LOCUS DELICTI 'place of the crime'. shorthand v.ersion of lex locus delcti commissi. the "scene of the crime".

LOCUS IN QUO 'the place in which'. meaning, the place or position which was prev.iously occupied. The place in which anything is alleged to be done. In pleadings, designates the place where an action occurred or an offense was committed. The place in which. In pleadings it is the place where any- thing

is alleged to hav.e been done. *Goh Khiok Phiong v. Regina [1954] 20 MLJ at Pg. 224,225; Thambiah v. The Queen [1966] 1 MLJ 70 at Pg. 71; Mohamed Bin Salleh v. Public Prosecutor [1967] 1 MLJ 185, Goh Leng Kang V. Teng Swee Lin & Ors [1977] 1 MLJ 85 Pg. 85*

LOCUS place.

LOCUS POENITENTIAE contracts, crim. law. Literally this signifies a place of repentance; in law, it is the opportunity of withdrawing from a projected contract, before the parties are finally bound; or of abandoning the intention of committing a crime, before it has been completed. Associated with contractual law which means opportunity to withdraw from a contract or obligation before it is completed or to decide not to commit an intended crime. This signifies repentance in the context of criminal law and prov.ides an opportunity of withdrawing from a projected contract, before the parties are finally bound or of abandoning the intention of committing a crime. *Ahmad Bin Udoh & Anor v. Ng Aik Chong [1969] 2 MLJ 117*

LOCUS PRO SOLUTIONE REDITUS AUT PECUNIAE SECUNDUM CONDITIONEM DIMISSIONIS AUT OBLIGATINIS EST STRICTE OBSERVANDUS the place for the payment of rent or money according to the condition of a lease or bond, is to be strictly observed. It also means the place, according to the condition of a lease or bond, for the payment of rent or money, is to be strictly observed.

LOCUS REGIT ACTUM the place governs the act; the act is governed by the law of the place where it is done. The principle that a legal act or transaction validly undertaken in a country in compliance with its legally prescribed formalities, should also be valid in another country where it is to be performed or executed. Locus regit actum applies even if the act or transaction is deficient in terms of the other formalities required by the law of the latter country.

LOCUS STANDI IN JUDICIO *Hendrik Christiaan v.An Hoogstraten v. Low Lum Seng [1940] 9 MLJ 138 at Pg.146*

LOCUS STANDI 'A place for standing." A position assumed in argument. Signifies a right of appearance in a court of justice or before parliament on any given question. In other words In other words, it signifies a right *to be heard,* as opposed to a right to succeed on the merits. A litigant's standing in court. The right to appear and be heard before a body such as a court, a legislature, a committee, etc. *District Council Central, Province Wellesley v. Yegappan [1966] 2 MLJ 177 at Pg. 177, Kesatuan Pejerja2 Kenderaan Sri Jaya v. The Indutrial Court & Ors. [1970] 1 MLJ 78, at 80; Kuala Lumpur, Klang & Port Swettenham Omnibus Co. Berhad v. Transport Workers' Union [1970] 2 MLJ 148, at 148 Devi v. Francis – A Critique [1970] 1 MLJ x, at xi; DEVI v. Francis – A Reply [1970] 1 MLJ xlv.i*

LONGUM TEMPUS ET LONGUS USUS QUI EXCEDIT MEMORIA HOMINUM SUFFICIT PRO JURE long time and long use, exceeding the memory of men, suffices for right. It also means long time and long use, which exceeds the memory of man, suffices in law.

LUGET BRITANNIA NON GREMIO DARI FOVERE *Lawyers and Literary Men [1932] 1 MLJ 155 Pg.157*

M

MAGNITUDO DELICTI *Rex v. S. Teo Woo Tin [1932] 1 MLJ 124 Pg. 126*

MALA FIDE 'bad faith'. Bad faith, in bad faith, with evil intent. It is the opposite of *bona fides*. Something that is opposed to good faith. *The fraudulent deception of another person; the intentional or malicious refusal to perform some duty or contractual obligation.*Bad faith is not the same as prior judgment or Negligence. One can make an honest mistake about one's own rights and duties, but whenthe rights of someone else are intentionally or maliciously infringed upon, such conduct demonstrates bad faith.

MALUM IN SE (plural MALA IN SE) 'wrong in itself'. It is a term used to describe something that is inherently immoral, regardless of whether it is defined by law as illegal. Crimes such as larceny, rape and murder are considered malum in se. this concept was used to develop the various common-law crimes. t is distinguished from malum prohibitum or wrongs that are only wrong by statute, such as parking violations. For example, the murder of human beings is universally agreed to be a wrong regardless of whether a law exists making it a crime. Therefore, it is malum in se. On the other hand violation of driving laws are malum prohibitum law because the act is not inherently bad, but is forbidden by policy, set forth by the policy-makers of the jurisdiction. They are acts morally wrong; offenses against conscience. In criminal law, crimes are categorized as either mala in se or mala prohibita, a term that describes conduct that is specifically forbidden bylaws. Although the distinction between the two classifications is not always clear, crimes mala in se are usually common law crimes or those dangerous to life or limb. *Che Su Binti Shafie v. Superintendent of Prisons,Pulau Jerejak,Penang [1974] 2 MLJ 194 Pg.194; Appoo S/O Krishnan v. Ellamah D/O Ramasamy [1974] 2 MLJ 201 Pg.205; Khan Kam Chee v. Loke Wan Yat Realty Sdn Bhd [1974] 1 MLJ 206 Pg.207, Frank Merrels & Others v. Wee Chin Koon [1940] 9 MLJ 212 at Pg. 213; In Re W.J.D. Hogg, Decd; Anderson v. The Commissioner of Estate Duties [1939] 8 MLJ 112 at Pg. 116, 120; Gan Khuan v. Tan Jin Luan [1939] 8 MLJ 220 at Pg. 221; Ramamoorthy v. Mentri Besar of Selangor & Amor. 98; Karam Singh v. Menteri Hal Ehwal Dalam Negeri, Malaysia [1969] 2 MLJ 129; Thambipillai v. The Government of Malaysia [1969] 2 MLJ 207*

MALUM IN SE (plural MALA IN SE) 'wrong in itself'. It is a term used to describe something that is inherently immoral, regardless of whether it is defined by law as illegal. Crimes such as larceny, rape and murder are considered *malum in se*. This concept was used to develop the various common-law crimes. It is distinguished from *malum prohibitum* or wrongs that are only wrong by statute, such as parking violations. For example, the murder of human beings is universally agreed to be a wrong regardless of whether a law exists making it a crime. Therefore, it is *malum in se*. On the other hand violation of driving laws are *malum prohibitum* law because the act is not inherently bad, but is forbidden by policy, set forth by the policy-makers of the jurisdiction. They are acts morally wrong; offenses against conscience. In criminal law, crimes are categorized as either mala in se or mala prohibita, a term that describes conduct that is specifically forbidden bylaws. Although the distinction between the two classifications is not always clear, crimes mala in se are usually common law crimes or those dangerous to life or limb. *Kang Yeow Hool & Ors V. Public Prosecutor [1954] 20 MLJ at Pg. 235; Kee Ah Low v. The Public Prosecutor [1940] 9 MLJ 256 at Pg. 257; Tiong Chi Seng & Anor v. Public Prosecutor [1973] 2 MLJ106 Pg.107*

MALUM PROHIBITUM 'prohibited wrong'. Something wrong or illegal by virtue of it being expressly prohibited, that might not otherwise be so.

MANDAMUS 'to order, command'. An extraordinary writ or order issued from one court to another court, or to a public official, or to a corporation or person, compelling performance of a ministerial act that the law recognizes as an absolute duty. The writ is used to correct abuses of judicial and administrativ.e power and to compel action. The prerogative writ of mandamus i.e. in its form, a command issuing in the king's name, anti directed to any person, corporation, or inferior court of judicature, requiring them· to do some particular thing which appertains to their office and dnty. In its application, it may be considered as confined to cases where relief is required in respect of the infringement of some *public* right or duty, and where no effectual relief can be obtained in the ordinary course of an action. For the rules of procedure. *In Re Tan Eng Seong of Chop Thye Eng Seong v. The Rubber Supervision Licensing Board For The District of Bentong, Pahang [1950] 16 MLJ at Pg. 228; Tok Jwee Kee v. Tay Ah Hock & Son Ltd. & Town Council, Johore Bahru [1969] 1 MLJ 199; Ee Kim Kin v. The Collector Of Land Revenue, Alor Gajah [1967] 2 MLJ 89 Pg.89; C. v. Comptroller of Income Tax [1967] 2 MLJ 137 Pg.137; Ex Parte Tan Swee Eng [1941] MLJ 161, Leong Yuet Heng v. Chan Thai & Ors [1973] 1 MLJ 62 Pg.62, Re Application By Sreedharan[1974] 1 MLJ 118 Pg.118*

MANDAMUS an action or judicial proceeding of a civil nature extraordinary in the sense that it can be maintained only when there is no other adequate remedy, prerogative in its character to the extent that the issue is discretionary, to enforce only clear legal rights and to compel Courts to take jurisdiction or proceed in the exercise of their jurisdiction or to compel corporations, public and private and public boards, commissions or officers, to exercise their jurisdiction or discretion and to perform ministerial duties, which duties result from an office, trust or station and are clearly and peremptorily enjoined by law as absolute an official. It also means an order issued by a court to compel a public official to exercise a power in accordance with his or her public duty. Mandamus may be ordered to compel the performance of a duty generally (such as to exercise statutory discretion) but not to compel performance in a particular manner. Mandamus does not lie to enforce a civil liability arising out of a breach of contract or to enforce rights based on contract. A civil suit for damages or for the enforcement of the civil liability may be the only proper remedy in such a case. Similarly mandamus does not issue to enforce a civil liability arising under torts. Ther are four prerequisites essential to the issue of an order under section 44 or of a mandamus:- (1) Whether the applicant has a clear and specific legal right to the relief sought; (2)Whether there is a duty imposed by law on the respondent ;(3) Whether such duty is of an imperative ministerial character involving no judgement or discretion on the part of the respondent; (4) Whether the applicant has any remedy, other than by way of mandamus, for the enforcement of the right which has been denied to him. These are the questions, but only some of the questions, which are necessary to be answered in every application for mandamus. The applicant must show not only that he has a legal a legal right to have the act performed but that the right is doubtful, or is qualified one or where it depends upon an issue of fact to be determned by the respondent. *Koon Hoi Chow v Pretam Singh [1972] 1 MLJ 108 at 182 Per Sharma J*

MANDANS the employing party in a contract of mandate.

MANDATUM contract of mandate.

MANSUETAE NATURAE 'animals which are generally domestic, presumed gentle and readily tamed'. For example, dogs, cats, cows and horses. Animals mansuetae naturae, that is, the class of domesticated animals, are regarded as inherently non-offensiv.e, and not being of a risk to human beings, and ev.ery man has the right to keep and harbor animals mansuetae naturae. *Periasamy v. Suppiah [1967] 1 MLJ 19 Pg.20, Mariyayee & Anor v. Nadarajan [1975] 2 MLJ267 Pg. 270*

MANSUETAE NATURAE tame by nature. The term is used to denote tamed or domesticated animals in which a person may ac-quire special property. Tamed and domesticated animals. A distinction has been made between two species of animals, tame animals or animals mansuetae nature as they are called eg a dog or horse and ferocious animals. Tame by nature. A phrase used to categories animals. A domesticated animal (domitae naturae) was distinguished from a wild animal (ferae nature). The distinction was significant in applying the scienter rule, under which keepers of mansuetae naturae were not liable for damage caused by their animals un-less the keeper was negligent or aware of the animal's peculiarly mischievous or vicious disposition. Mansuetae naturae encompasses such animals as cats, dogs, cows, goats and kangaroos. If an animal mansuetae naturae manifests a vicious tendency, the scienter rule applies to it as if it were ferae naturae. The law has often been put in that way, for example, by Lord Wright, in Knott v Lon-don County Council [1934] 1 KB 126 at 139. How is the principle applied? Suppose that a large dog collides with a child and knocks him down, that is an accident and not a manifestation of a vicious pro-pensity and the scienter rule does not apply at all: if the dog bites a child, it becomes ferae naturae and the strict rule thereafter applies. It would, however, seem to be unreasonable that the strict rule should require the dog to be kept under complete restraint. Suppose that its keeper muzzles it and that while muzzled the dog playfully or accidentally knocks a child down, ought the keeper to be liable? There is a good deal of authority, referred to by Professor Glanville Williams, to show that the keeper is not liable; and the learned author considers that the damage must have in some way been intended by the animal, that its benevolence or its mens rea is relevant and that, at least in the case of harmless animals, the rule is that the injury must be the result of a vicious propensity.

MANUS hand; marital power.

MARE CLAUSUM 'Closed Sea'. A body of water under the jurisdiction of a state or nation, to which access is not permitted, or is tightly regulated.

MARE LIBERUM 'Open sea'. A body of water open to all. Typically a synonym for International Waters, or in other legal parlance, the "High Seas".

MARITUS husband.

MAXIM 'large'. A basic or general truth. a statement expressing a concept accepted by all. a principle tested and accepted ov.er time. An established principle or proposition. a principle of law univ. ersally admitted, as being just and consonant with reason. maxims in law are somewhat like axioms in geometry. they are principles and authorities, and part of the general customs or common law of the land; and are of the same strength as acts of parliament, when the judges hav.e determined what is a maxim; which belongs to the judges and not the jury. maxims of the law are holden for law, and all other cases that may be applied to them shall be taken for granted. the application of the maxim to the case before the court, is generally the only difficulty. the true method of making the application is to ascertain bow the maxim arose, and to consider whether the case to which it is applied is of the same character, or whether it is an exception to an apparently general rule. the alterations of any of the maxims of the common law are dangerous. *T. Chelliah v. Laxman Singh & Anor* [1954] 20 MLJ at Pg. 211; *Chye Ah San v. Regina* [1954] 20 MLJ at Pg. 220; *Yeo Ah Seng v. Public Prosecutor* [1967] 1 MLJ 231 Pg.234

MEMO DEBET BIS VEXARI *Syed Ismail v. Public Prosecutor* [1967] 2 MLJ 123 Pg.128

MENS REA literally mean s 'a litigant, defendant, a person accused'. A guilty mind; a criminal or wrongful purpose. An essential element of most crimes. The mental state accompanying or inducing an unlawful act. The defendant's guilty state of mind, as an element in prov. ing the crime with which he or she is charged. *Goh Yoke v. Public Prosecutor [1970] MLJ 1 63, at 65; Mahesan v. Public Prosecutor [1970] 1 MLJ 255, at 258; Public Prosecutor v. Teck guan co. Ltd [1970] 2 MLJ 141, at 141, 142; Wolfgang Pzetzhold v. Public Prosecutor [1970] 2 MLJ 195, at 196, 197; Ng Chwee Poh v. Public Prosecutor [1977] 2 MLJ 230 Pg. 237; Tham Kai Yau & Ors v. Public Prosecutor [1977] 1 MLJ 174 Pg. 176; Public Prosecutor v. Datuk Haji Harun Bin Haji Idris & Ors [1977] 1 MLJ 180 Pg. 180, Public Prosecutor v. Osman Bin Abdul Hamid & Anor [1978] 2 MLJ 38 Pg. 38; Public Prosecutor v. Kedah & Perlis Ferry Services Sdn Bhd [1978] 2 MLJ 221 Pg. 221; Khoo Cheh Yew & Anor v. Public Prosecutor [1978] 1 MLJ 141 Pg. 142; Sak & Anor v. Public Prosecutor [1978] 1 MLJ 181 Pg. 183*

MESNE 'occupying a middle, intermediate position. The middle between two extremes, that part between the commencement and the end, as it relates to time. Hence the profits wbich a man receiv.es between disseisin and recov. ery of lands are called mesne profits. Process which is issued in a suit between the original and final process, is called mesne process. *Koh Lan Eng & Anor. v. Tee Choon Yong [1970] 1 MLJ 153, at 158 B. H Oon & Ors. v. The Government of The State Of Penang & Ors. [1970] 1 MLJ 244, at 245; Kian Hin & Co. Ltd. v. Kan Yeow Weng [1970] 1 MLJ 273, at 274; Pi. Ararunasalan Chettiar & Ors. v. Pi. Palaniappa [1969] 1 MLJ; Syed Ahmad Al-Juneid & Ors. v. Reshty [1965] 1 MLJ 77 Pg. 78, 80, 81*

MESNE PROFITS 'torts, remedies'. the value of the premises, recov.ered in ejectment, during the time that the lessor of the plaintiff has been illegally kept out of the possession of his estate by the defendant; such are properly recov.ered by an action of trespass, quare clausum fregit, after a recov. ery in ejectment. as a general rule, the plaintiff is entitled to recov.er for such time as be can prov.e the defendant to hav.e been in possession, prov.ided he does not go back beyond six years, for in that case, the defendant may plead the statute of limitations. the value of improv.ements made by the defendant, may be set off against a claim for mesne profits, but profits before the demise laid, should be first deducted from the value of the improv.ement's. The profit receiv.ed from an estate by a tenant in wrongful possession. mesne profit is often calculated when there is a claim to recov.er the accruals from a property illegitimately held by a person. it is the profit that has accrued while there was a dispute ov.er land ownership. if a party using a particular parcel of land did not hav.e legal ownership, the true owner can sue for some or all of the profit that the person made during the period of illegal tenancy. Mary Ng v. Singapore Improvement Trust [1954] 20 MLJ at Pg. 32; Re Tan Tye Deceasedd [1969] 2 MLJ 201 Reshty v. Syed Ahmed

Al-Junied & Ors [1966] 2 MLJ 121 at Pg. 123, 124, Re Tan Tye Deceased [1969] 2 MLJ 201

MOBILIA movables; movable things otherwise called 'res mobilia.' Furnitures that may be moved about and do not become permanent fixture of the demised premises. Movables are items such furnitures that may be moved about and do not become permanent fixture of the demised premises. Movables includes inanimate things as well as livestock.

MODUS manner; means.

MODUS OPERANDI 'the mode of operation." the way in which a thing is done. Measure, method, manner to work, labor. The manner of operation; a term used by the police to describe the characteristic methods used by a suspect in performing his crimes. Patterns of activity so unique to a particular criminal that he can be identified by them. *Datuk Haji Harun Bin Haji Idris & Ors V. Public Prosecutor [1978] 1 MLJ 240 Pg.248, Gan Leong & Anor v. Public Prosecutor [1969] 2 MLJ 79*

MONETA money.

MORA ACCIPIENDI 'Delay of creditor'. Delay in payment or performance in the part of the creditor or obligor

MORA SOLVENDI 'delay of debtor'. Delay in payment or performance in the part of the debtor or the obligee

MORTIS CAUSA (DONATIO MORTIS CAUSA) 'a gift made in apprehension of death'. a death-bed disposition of property, when a person deliv.ers his personal goods to another to keep, in case of his decease. gift in prospect of death. when a person in sickness, apprehend ing his dissolution near, deliv.ers, or causes to be deliv.ered to another, the possession of any personal goods, to keep as his own, in case of the donor's decease the civ.il law defines it to be a gift under apprehension of death; as, when any thing is given upon condition that if the donor dies, the donee shall possess it absolutely, or return it if the donor should surv.iv.e, or should repent of hav.ing made the gift, or if the donee should die before the donor. donations mortis causa, are now reduced, as far as possible, to the similitude of legacies. with respect to the nature of a donatio mortis causa, this kind of gift so far resembles a legacy, that it is ambulatory and incomplete during the donor's life; it is, therefore, rev.ocable by him and subject to his debts upon a deficiency of assets. but in the following particulars it differs from a legacy: it does riot fall within an administration, nor require any act in the executors to perfect a title in the donee.

MOS PRO LEGE 'custom for law', that which is the usual custom has the force of law.

MOTION IN LIMINE 'motion at the start'. motions offered at the start of a trial, often to suppress or pre-allow certain evidence or testimony.

MUTATIS MUTANDIS 'changing what should be changed'. a. warrant made out against b will do for e, mutatis mutandis i. e. changing one name for the other. The necessary changes. This is a phrase of frequent practical occurrence, meaning that matters or things are generally the same, but to be altered, when necessary, as to names, offices, and the like. *Datuk Haji Harun Bin Haji Idris v. Public Prosecutor [1977]* *2 MLJ 155 Pg.158, Re Cheong Yuk Sim (f) Ex Parte, Cheong Mook Lim [1954] 20 MLJ at Pg. 130; Diana Ellis v. Khoo Ek Neo and Anor [1950] 16 MLJ at Pg. 169; K.A.R.S.T. Arunasalam Chettiar v. S. Abdul Raman Bin Suleiman & Anor. [1933] 2 MLJ 48 Pg. 50; Baju Ria v. Liau Kim Lian [1965] 1 MLJ 128 Pg. 130; Re Monteiro R.A. [1949] 15 MLJ 185 Pg.186*

N

NE BIS IN IDEM 'Not twice in the same'. It is for the prohibition against double jeopardy. It simply means that a legal action cannot be brought twice for the same act or offense.

NE EXEAT 'Let him not exit [the republic]'. Shortened version of ne exeat repiblica: "let him not exit the republic". It is a form of a writ to prevent one party to a dispute from leaving (or being taken) from the court's jurisdiction.

NEC VI, NEC CLAM, NEC PRECARIO 'without force, without secrecy, without permission'. It is the principle by which rights may be built up over time, principally public rights of way in the United Kingdom. *Yong Joo Lin & Ors v. Fung Pol Fong [1941] MLJ 60*

NECESSITAS need, exigency, unavoidability.

NEGOTORIUM GESTIO 'management of estate'. Obligation arising from good works affecting other people, obliging the creditor to pay for the reimbursement of the cost that was used in doing good works.

NEMO AUDITUR PROPRIAM TURPITUDINEM ALLEGANS 'no one can be heard, who invokes his own guilt'. Nobody can bring a case that stems from their own illegal act.

NEMO DAT QUOD NON HABET 'no one can give what he does not hav.e'. For intance, the purchase of a possession from someone who has no ownership right to it also denies the purchaser any ownership title. this rule aims to protect bonafide purchasers and usually stays v.alid ev.en if the purchaser does not know that the seller has no right to claim ownership of the subject matter assuming that the purchaser is a bona fide purchaser. there are numerous exceptions to the nemo dat rule. this is particularly true in the case of negotiable instruments, such as checks. if a thief a steals a check from b and sells it to innocent c, c is entitled to deal with the check, and a cannot claim it back from c. *T. Chelliah v. Laxman Singh & Anor [1954] 20 MLJ at Pg. 211; Chanan Singh v. Thiyagalechumi [1965] 2 MLJ 158 Pg. 160*

NEMO DEBET BIS PUNIRI PRO UNO DELICTO No one ought to be punished twice for the same offense. *Yau Tin Kwong v. Public Prosecutor [1970] 1 MLJ 159, at 162*

NEMO DEBET ESSE JUDEX IN PROPRIA CAUSA no one can be a judge in his own cause. As the defendant is acting here in a quasi-judicial capacity, the rules of natural justice apply the common law rule applicable to the disciplinary inquiry is that of nemo debet esse judex in propria causa, which is that a judge may not have a personal or pecuniary interest or involvement in a case which he tries. He concedes that in the instant case the defendant is personally involved in at least three of the five charges but to take his client outside the ambit of the common law rule, he relies on what is known as the rule of necessity, which according to Flick of Natural Justice (1979 Edn) 'Is perhaps the greatest single common law exception to the general rule that an adjudicator who appears to be biased or prejudiced must disqualify himself from participating in a proceeding. The rule is firmly established in both English and Commonwealth jurisdictions and in American jurisdictions and it is to the effect that disqualification of an adjudicator will not be permitted to destroy the only tribunal with power to act. Anwar Siraj v Tang I Fang [1982] 1 MLJ 308 at 310 Per Rajah J. Cheak Yoke Thong v Public Prosecutor [1984] 2 MLJ 119 at 121 Per Salleh Abas LP

NEMO EST HAERES V.IV.ENTIS no one is the heir of a liv.ing person. a person becomes an actual, complete heir of another only when the ancestor dies. before a person can be an heir, his/her ancestor or person from who s/he inherits must be dead. in accordance with the maxim, nemo est haeres v.iv.entis, the liv.ing children are only heirs expectant, and hence no one can take an estate under that designation while the ancestor is living. *Rahimaboo Binte Mohamed Salleh Angullia v. Mohamed Ahmad Angullia & Others [1940] 9 MLJ 265 at Pg.268*

NEMO EST HAERES VIRENTIS no one is an heir to the living'. No one is heir of the living. By law no inheritance could vest, nor could any person be the actual complete heir of another, till the ancestor was dead; before the happening of this event he was called the heir-apparent or heir presumptive and his claim, which could only be to an estate remaining in the ancestor at the time of his death and of which he had made to testamentary disposition, might be defeated by the superior title of an alienee in the ancestor's lifetime, or of a devisee under his will. The doctrine that 'Equity considers that as done, which should have been done' cannot be applied to a case of a spes successionis, ie such as the interests of a reversioner. There is no such character in law as the heir of a living person or his statutory next of kin. Posibilities coupled with an interest, such as contingent interests may be called contingent interest and a bare possibility such as a hope of inheritance, mere expectancies inasmuch as a possibility coupled with an interest is more than a possibility and is a present devisable interest. It is said on the one hand that you cannot have an heir except at your death, nemo est haeres virentis, and that therefore the use of the word 'heir' must pre-suppose that at the death of the wife the testator is already dead so that he can have an heir-at-law in the strict sense of the term.

NEMO no one, nobody.

NEMO PLUS JURIS AD ALIUM TRANSFERRE POTEST QUAM IPSE HABET 'no one can transfer a greater right than he himself has'. The purchaser of a stolen good from a thief will not acquire a title to that property. The person purchasing from such a person has no right ov.er the property, when compared with the real owner. purchaser will not acquire title because s/he purchased the property from a person who has no title to the property. however, persons who hav.e obtained property lawfully can prov.ide better title than himself to the purchaser. in such cases, the possessor's title will be of an agent. T. *Chelliah v. Laxman Singh & Anor [1954] 20 MLJ at Pg. 211*

NEMO POTEST ESSE TENENS ET DOMINUS 'no one can at the same time be a tenant and a landlord. (of the same tenement). *Goodland Ltd v. Lim ban toon [1966] 2 MLJ 198 at Pg. 200, Chew Khan v. Limweng Yoon & Anor [1965] 2 MLJ 136 Pg. 137, 140*

NEMO TENETUR SEIPSUM ACCUSARE 'no one shall be compelled to bear witness against himself. No one is bound to accuse himself. *Chua Beow Huat v. Public Prosecutor [1970] 2 MLJ 29, at 34; Abu Bakar Bin Nazmeer v. Public Prosecutor [1970] 2 MLJ 216, 217, Chye Ah San v. Regina [1954] 20 MLJ at Pg. 219; Chye Ah San v. Regina [1954] 20 MLJ at Pg. 220; Goh Yin Guan v. Public Prosecutor [1967] 1 MLJ 114*

NEXUS 'to bind, fasten together, join'.a link, a causal connection, a chain of related objects. the connection between a corporation and a state in which it does business. whether a business has sufficient *nexus* with a state to be taxed by it depends on an analysis of its activ.ities within that state. *The Sultan of Johore v. Tungku Abubakar & Ors. [1950] 16 MLJ at Pg. 25; Tan Boon Teek*

v. Public Prosecutor [1950] 16 MLJ at Pg. 45

NIHIL DICIT 'he says nothing'. It is a judgement rendered in the absence of a plea, or in the event one party refuses to cooperate in the proceedings.

NISI 'if not, unless'.used before or after a word such as *decree, order, judgment,* or *rule,* to indicate that an adjudication is conditional and not absolute, but that it will become final and absolute *unless* the party who is the subject of the decree or order takes steps to cure a defect, i.e., that he appear, show cause, appeal, etc., before a specified date or ev.ent. this word is frequently used in legal proceedings to denote that something has been done, which is to be v.alid unless something else shall be done within a certain time to defeat it. for example, an order may be made that if on the day appointed to show cause, none be shown, an injunction will be dissolv.ed of course, on motion, and production of an affidav.it of serv.ice of the order. This is called an order nisi. Under the compulsory arbitration law of pennsylv.ania, on the filing of the award, judgment nisi is to be entered: which judgment is to be as v.alid as if it had been rendered on the verdict of a jury, unless an appeal be entered within the time required by the law. *In Re An Advocate and Solicitor [1950] 16 MLJ at Pg. 114; Re Makhanlall & Co. Ltd [1969] 1 MLJ 36; Ho Hong Bank Ltd v.S. Ho Kai Neo & Another [1932] 1 MLJ 76 Pg.76, 80; The Straits Steamship Co. Ltd v. S. Lieut J.H. Owen [1932] 1 MLJ 167 Pg.171; Megat Ibrahim v.S. The British*

Resident Of Perak & Anor. [1933] 2 MLJ 154 Pg. 154; Mohamed Bin Haji Omar v. S. Zainab Binte Mohamed Syed [1934] 3 MLJ 71 at Pg. 71; Wah Tat Bank Ltd & Ors v. Chan Cheng Kum & Ors [1967] 2 MLJ 263 Pg.264

NISI unless the word 'nisi' is often affixed, as a kind of elliptical expression, to the words, 'rule', 'order', 'decree', 'judgment' or 'confirmation', to indicate that the adjudication spoken of is one which is to stand as valid and operative unless the party affected by it shall appear and show cause against it, or take some other appropriate step to avoid it or procure its revocation. A decree or judgment Nisi, is one that is conditional and requires something more to be done to make it absolute.

NISI PRIUS 'the first', 'the former'. a trial before a single judge or a judge and jury, as distinguished from a proceeding before an appellate court. the phrase dates to practice in the early english common law courts. Now used to distinguish a trial court from an appellate court. These words, which signify 'unless before,' are the name of a court. The name originated as follows: formerly, an action was triable only in the court where it was brought. But, it was prov.ided by magna charta, in ease of the subject, that assises of novel disseisin and mort d'ancestor (then the most usual remedies,) should thenceforward instead of being tried at westminster, in the superior court, be taken in their proper counties; and for this purpose justices were to be sent into ev.ery county once a year, to take these assises there. 1 reev.es, 246; 2 inst. 422, 3, 4. these local trials being found convenient, were applied not only to assises, but to other actions; for, by the statute of 13 edw. i. c. 30, it is prov.ided as the general course of proceeding, that writs of venire for summoning juries in the superior courts, shall be in the following form. praecipimus tibi quod v.eneri facias coram justiciariis nostris apud westm. in octabis seti michaelis, nisi talis et talis tali, die et loco ad partes illas v.enerint, duodecim, &c. thus the trial was to be had at westminster, only in the ev.ent of its not prev.iously taking place in the county, before the justices appointed to take tlie assises. it is this prov.ision of the statute of nisi prius, enforeed by the subsequent statute of 14 ed. iii. c. 16, which authorizes, in england, a trial before the justices of assises, in lieu of the superior court, and gives it the name of a trial by nisi prius. *Theory of Precedent [1940] 9 MLJ v.i at Pg. ix*

NOLLE PROSEQUI 'To be unwilling to prosecute'. An acknowledgment by the plaintiff that he will not proceed any further with his suit. A statement to the court by the plaintiff in a civ.il action and, more frequently, by the prosecutor in a criminal action that he does not wish to proceed, i.e., that the action is dropped and discontinued. The statement is made part of the record and results in dismissal of the action. *Ey Yee Hua v. Public Porsecutor [1969] 2 MLJ 128, Yeap Hock Seng v. Minister For Home Affairs, Malaysia [1975] 2 MLJ 279 Pg. 285*

NOLO CONTENDERE 'I do not wish to dispute'. A type of plea whereby the defendant neither admits nor denies the charge. Commonly interpreted as "No contest."

NOMINATIM appointment; a resolution submitted to the electors that the party named is a nominating; the act, process or an instrument of nominating; an act or right of designating for an office or duty. 'Nominations' is equivalent to the word 'appointments' when used by a mayor in an instrument executed for the purpose of appointing certain persons to office.

NON ADIMPLETI CONTRACTUS 'Of a non-completed contract'. In the case where a contract imposes specific obligations on both parties, one side cannot sue the other for failure to meet their obligations, if the plaintiff has not themselv.es met their own.

NON COMPOS MENTIS 'not in possession of [one's] mind'. not having mental capacity to perform some legal act

NON CONSTAT 'it is not certain'. Refers to information given by one who is not supposed to give testimony, such as an attorney bringing up new information that did not come from a witness. Such information is typically nullified.

NON EST FACTUM 'It was not done'. The general issue m an action on bond or other deed, whereby the defendant denies that to be his deed on which he is impleaded. to make, do. Literally, it was not done (by me). A plea at common law by which the defendant denied that the instrument sued upon was executed by him or that he knew the nature of the instrument when he signed it. (it is not his deed). The plea of the general issue in an action on a deed, denying the/ act of the deed having been executed. *Sheikh Abdullah Bin Sheikh Mohamed v. Kang Kok Seng & Ors [1974] 1 MLJ 174 Pg.175, Sithambaran Chettyar v. Chong Fatt [1939] 8 MLJ 230 at Pg. 230; Yeap Lean Seng & 4 Ors v. Kok Ho Teik & Anor [1951] 17 MLJ at Pg. 237; Webster Automatic Packeting Factory Ltd. v. S. Chop Kim Leong Thye [1933] 2 MLJ 61 Pg. 66; Awang Bin Omar V. Haji Omar Bin Ismail & Anor [1949] 15 MLJ 96 Pg.96, Public Prosecutor v. Datuk Haji Harun Bin Haji Idris & Ors [1977] 1 MLJ 180 Pg. 182*

NON EST INVENTUS 'He is not found'. Reported by a sheriff on writ when the defendant cannot be found in his county or jurisdiction.

NON FACIAT MALUM, UT INDE VENIAT BONUM 'not to do evil that good may come'. Performing some illegal action is not excused by the fact that a positiv.e result came therefrom. Often used to argue that some forms of expression, such as graffiti or pornographic films, cannot be given the protection of law (e.g. copyright) as they are or may be considered illegal or morally reprehensible.

NON LIQUET 'it is not clear'. A type of v.erdict where positiv.e guilt or innocence cannot be determined. Also called "not proven" in legal systems with such verdicts.

NON OBSTANTE VERDICTO 'notwithstanding the verdict'. A circumstance where the judge may override the jury v.erdict and reverse or modify the decision.

NON SEQUITUR 'it does not follow'. an expression used in argument to indicate that the premises do not warrant the inference drawn from them. an assumption or inference that does not follow from a prior statement; a response that is not logical in the light of a statement previously made. *Rex v. Lee Hoey [1939] 8 MLJ 37 at Pg. 38; Chandu Revenue Ordinance, Yue Sang Cheong Sdn Bhd v. Public Prosecutor [1973] 2 MLJ 80 Pg.81*

NOSCITUR A SOCIIS 'to know, be acquainted with, joint, common, associated with; a partner or companion'. To be known by his or its associates. One is known by the company he keeps. A rule of construction which dictates that the meaning of a word in a statute or other text will be determined by the meaning of the words which surround it. A rule of interpretation that states that the meaning of unclear language in a contract or other legal document should be construed in light of the language surrounding it. *Ipoh Garden Sdn Bhd v. Ismail Mahyuddin Enterprise Sdn Bhd [1975] 2 MLJ 241 Pg. 243, S.V.R.Y. Somasundaram v. S. Ong Yeo Seng Alias Wong Yee Seng & Ors [1932] 1 MLJ 113 Pg.115*

NOSCITUR A SOCIIS 'it is known by friends'. An ambiguous word or term can be clarified by considering the whole context in which it is used, without hav.ing to define the term itself.

NOSCITUR A SOCIIS the meaning of a doubtful word may be ascertained by reference to the meaning of the words associated with it. It also means one is known by his companions; the meaning of a word or expression is to be gathered from the surrounding words, that is, from the context. It is known by its associates. It is rule laid down by Lord Bacon that the coupling of words together shows that they are to be understood in the same sense. And where the meaning of a particular word is doubtful or obscure, or where a particular expression when taken singly is inoperative, the intention of a party who used it may frequently be ascertained by looking at adjoining words, or at expressions occurring in other part of the same instrument. One provision of an instrument must be construed by the bearing it will have upon another. Kesultanan Pahang v Sathask Realty Sdn Bhd [1998] 2 MLJ 513 at 553 Per Peh Swee Chin FCJ, Sykt Perniagaan United Acess Sdn Bhd v Majlis Perbandaran Petaling Jaya [1997] 1 MLJ 394 at 401 Per Wan Yahya FJC. When two or more words which are susceptible of 'analogous meanings are coupled together noscitur a sociis. They are understood to be used in their cognate sense. They take, as it were, their colour from other, that is, the more general is restricted to a sense analogous to the less general.The effect of the principle is that a word or phrase appearing in a statute must fall to be judge by the company in which it is to be found. The expression 'order of committal' therefore takes its colour from the expression 'writ of attachment' to which it is joined by the conjunction 'or'.The suggestion by the respondent that the words 'order of committal' should be widely construed so as to include a conjunction cuts across well settled principles of construction and does violence to the language used by Parliament. We have, therefore, no hesitation whatsoever in rejecting it. DP Vijandran v Majlis Peguam [1994] 3 MLJ 576 at 590 Per Gopal Sri Ram JCA

NOSCITUR A SOCIIS OR EJUSDEM GENERIS *Nadimuthu v. Public Prosecutor [1974] 1 MLJ 20 Pg.20*

NOTA BENE 'note well'. A term used to direct the reader to cautionary or qualifying statements for the main text.

NOV.US ACTUS INTERV.ENIENS 'to set in motion, to come between, to interv.ene'. A new and interv.ening act. In tort law, an act or cause that comes into play following the act constituting the defendant's negligence and that contributes to the damage or injury complained of by the plaintiff. *Guan Soon Tin Mining Co. v. Wong Fook Kum [1969] 1 MLJ 101, Sri Jaya Transport Co. (P.T.M) Bhd v. Ang Chai Hai & Ors [1974] 2 MLJ 92 Pg.93; Ang Chai Ha v. Sri Jaya Transportation Co (P.T.M) Bhd [1974] 1 MLJ 87 Pg.87*

NOVA CONSTITUTIO FUTURIS FORMAM IMPONERE DEBET, NON PRAETERITIS a new enactment ought to impose form upon what is to come, not upon what is past. It also means a new law ought to be prospective, not retrospective, in its operation. Or a new law ought to impose form on what is to follow, not on the past. It is a general principle than no statute shall be construed so as to have a retrospective operation, unless its language is such as plainly to require that construction; and this involves the subordinate rule that a statute is not to be construed so as to have a greater retrospective operation than its language renders necessary. Except in special cases, a new Act ought to be construed so as to interfere as little as possible with vested rights; and where the words admit of another construction, they should not be so construed as to impose disabilities not existing at the passing of the Act.

NOVUS ACTUS INTERVENIENS AND VOLENTI NON FIT INJURIA to deny the defendants' proposition does not mean that a master can enter ports that are obviously un-safe and then charge the charterers with damage done. The damages for any breach of warranty are always limited to the natural and probable consequences. The point then becomes one of remoteness of damage; or, if it is thought better to put it in latin, the expressions novus actus interveniens and volenti non fit injuria are ready to hand. There is also the rule that an aggrieved party must act reasonably and try to minimise his damage.

NUDUM PACTUM 'a naked agreement'. a bare promise, made in words only, and not confirmed by a written contract. A voluntary promise made without consideration, usually as an act of affection or good will. *Tiun Eng Jin v. Wong Sie Kong [1975] 2 MLJ 34 Pg. 37, Yokohama Specie Bank Ltd. v. Lee Kwock Jou & Ors [1933] 2 MLJ 122 Pg. 123*

NULLA BONA 'no goods'. Notation made when a defendant has no tangible property av.ailable to be seized in order to comply with a judgement.

NULLA POENA SINE LEGE 'no penalty without a law'. One cannot be prosecuted for doing something that is not prohibited by law.

NULLUM CRIMEN, NULLA POENA SINE PRAEVIA LEGE POENALI 'no crime, no punishment without a previous penal law'. One cannot be prosecuted for doing something that was not prohibited by law at the time and place it was committed, notwithstanding laws made since that time. A form of prohibition on retroactive laws.

NULLUM TEMPUS OCCURIT REGI 'no time runs against the king'. Sometimes abbrev.iated *nullum tempus*, is a common law doctrine originally expressed by bracton in his *de legibus et consuetudinibus angliae* in the 1250s.

it states that the crown is not subject to statute of limitations.[1] this means that the crown can proceed with actions that would be barred if brought by an indiv. idual due to the passage of time. the doctrine is still in force in common law systems today. *Philip Hoalim v. Collector of Land Revenue, Singapore [1975] 1 MLJ 231 Pg. 234*

NUNC now, at the present time, soon, at this time.

NUNC PRO TUNC 'Now for then' When courts take some action nunc pro tunc, that action has retroactive legal effect, as though it had been performed ata particular, earlier date. The most common use of nunc pro tunc is to correct past clerical errors, or omissions made by the court, that may hinder the efficientoperation of the legal system. For example, if the written record of a trial court›s judgment failed to correctly recite the judgment as the courtrendered it, the court has the inherent power to change the record at a later date to reflect what happened at trial. The decision, as corrected,would be given legal force from the time of the initial decision so that neither party is prejudiced, or harmed, by the error. The purpose of nuncpro tunc is to correct errors or omissions to achiev.e the results intended by the court at the earlier time. *S. Muthucumaru v.S. Alkaff & Co. [1933] 2 MLJ 27 Pg. 27*

O

OBITER 'in passing, by the way, incidentally'. Collaterally, incidentally, as an aside or afterthought. *Amerco Timbers Pte Ltd v. Chatsworth Timber Corporation Pte Ltd [1977] 2 MLJ 181Pg. 184*

OBITER DICTA 'By the way'. A passing statement reached in a court opinion that is irrelevant to the outcome of the case. *The "Permina 108" [1977] 1 MLJ 43 Pg. 45*

OBITER DICTUM 'a thing said incidentally or 'by the way'. Parenthetically. *Navaradnam v. Suppiah Chettiar [1973] 1MLJ 173 Pg. 179, Re Chai Kai Wooi [1970] 1 MLJ 34, at 36 (Advocates and Solicitors); Nagapushani v. Nesaratnam & Anor. [1970] 2 MLJ 8, at 10 (Hindu), The Halcyon Isle [1978] 1 MLJ 189 Pg. 190*

OBITER DICTUM *Murugappa Chettiar v. S. Seeniv.Asagam [1940] 9 MLJ 217 at Pg. 228, 229, 232, 239; Official Assignee v. Leong Cheong Wai [1939] 8 MLJ 148 at Pg. 150, 156; Official Administrator, K.L. V. China Insurance Co. Ltd [1955] 21 MLJ at Pg. 139; In Re Abraham Penhas, Deceased [1950] 16 MLJ at Pg. 109*

OBITER by the way, in passing, incidentally, collaterally. *Edgar Joseph Jr FCJ in Co-operative Central Bank Ltd (In receivership) v Feyen Development Sdn Bhd [1997] 2 MLJ 829 at 836A, Datuk Tan Leng Teck v Sarjana Sdn Bhd & Ors [1997] 4 MLJ 329, where at 347 Augustine Paul JC*

OBLIGATIO a legal bond which obliges the performance of something in accordance with the law of the land.

OBREPTIO the obtaining of a thing by fraud or surprise.

OFFICINA workshop, factor.

OMNIA PRAESUMUNTUR RITE ESSE ACTA 'All things are presumed to be done in due form'. *Rangasamy Pillai v. Comptroller of Income Tax [1970] 1 MLJ 233, at 236 (Bankcrupcy), Ho Hong Bank Ltd v.S. Ho Kai Neo & Another [1932] 1 MLJ 76 Pg.82, Public Prosecutor v. Thum Soo Chye (1954) 20 MLJ at Pg. 98; (Evidence Ordinance 1950- Criminal Procedure Code); Sochalingam Chettiar v. Samasundaram Chettiar [1941] MLJ 90*

OMNIA PRAESUMUNTUR RITE ET SOLEMNITER ESSE ACTA 'All acts are presumed to have been done rightly and regularly'. *Sim Tiew Bee v. Public Prosecutor [1973] 2 MLJ 200 Pg. 202,*

OMNIBUS for all; containing two or more independent matters.

ONUS 'weight, burden'. Burden of proof. Responsibility to come forward, proceed or perform. Unpleasant duty. Also, blame. *Ahmad bin hussin v. Hajjah Mek [1973] 1MLJ 18 Pg. 23; Harbans Singh Sidhu v. Public*

Prosecutor [1973] 1MLJ 41 Pg. 41,42, Chi Liung & Son Sdn Bhd v. Chong Fah & Son Sdn Bhd& Anor [1974] 2 MLJ 211 Pg.212; Re Hume Industries (F.E) LTD[1974] 2 MLJ 167 Pg.168, Chow Yew Hon & Ors v. Oon Kim Meng [1975] 2 MLJ 19 Pg. 19; Chew Chee Sun v. Public Prosecutor[1975] 2 MLJ 58 Pg. 58; Port Swettenham Authority v. T.W. Wu & Co (M) Sdn Bhd [1975] 2 MLJ 73 Pg. 75; T.W Wu & Co(M) Sdn Bhd v. Sanko Asia Line Ltd[1975] 1 MLJ 15 Pg.16; Zainun Binti Abdul Ghani & Anor v. Chong Ah Seng & Anor [1975] 1 MLJ 33 Pg. 35

ONUS a burden or load; a weight. Burden of responsibility or proof.

ONUS PROBANDI 'the burden of proving'. a responsibility which by our law lies on the person making the charge. The burden of proof. this is a highly complex concept which governs the balance of proof in civ.il and criminal trials. the burden is really two burdens: the burden of production and the burden of persuasion. under the first, the party asserting a position must offer some evidence to support it. under the second, the party asserting a position must offer sufficient evidence to satisfy a standard of proof defined by the rules of the court in particular cases (*preponderance of the evidence* in civil cases; *beyond a reasonable doubt* in criminal cases). *Selvaduray v. Chenniah [1939] 8 MLJ 195 at Pg. 197;* (Evidence)

OPTIMA EST LEX, QUAE MINIMUM RELINQUIT ARBITRIO JUDICIS

'That is the best system of law which confides as little as possible to the discretion ofthe judge'. *Chiu Nang Hong v. Public Prosecutor [1965] 1MLJ 40 Pg. 43*

OPTIO option; Choice; freedom to choose between alternatives; as, to offer options for settling a claim.

OPUS deed, labour.

ORDINATUM EST it is ordered. Rules of court when entered in Latin.

OTIOSE WORDS at leisure. Otiose means functionless, indolent or futile: Oxford Dict. Otiose words are words which are not required or serving no useful or practical purpose. The wording of the regulation is not easy to construe, and there are two possible views as to its proper construction. The first view is this. The general intention of the definition appears to be directed to temporary structures, and the words 'and includes any working platform, gangway, run, ladder or step-ladder' intend to refer only to such working platforms (etc) as are temporary. Admittedly the words would then be otiose, since temporary working platforms (etc) have been already covered by the earlier part of the definition, vis, any temporary structure on or from which persons perform work ... And any temporary structutre which enables persons to obtain access. But the otiose words, it is said, are inserted ex abundanti cautela, and the words in brackets, '(other than an independent ladder or step-ladder which does not form part of such structure)', by referring back to a temporary structure show that the whole of the definition is concerned with such structures. This view would make the whole definition more or less accord with the natural meaning of 'scaffold'.

P

PACARE to pay.

PACTA SUNT SERVANDA 'agreements must be kept'. A fundamental principle of law

PACTUM DE RETROVENDENDO Wong See Leng v. C. Saraswathy Ammal [1954] 20 MLJ at Pg. 143; (Land Law)

PACTUM agreement, contract, covenant, pact, treaty.

PAR DELICTUM 'equal fault'. It is used when both parties to a dispute are at fault.

PARENS PATRIAE 'Parent of his or her country'. The state, in its role of prov. ider of protection to people unable to care for themselv.es; a doctrine giv. ing the Government standing to sue on behalf of a citizen who is unable to pursue an action due to a legal disability. The role of the state or central government as sovereign guardian of persons who require special protection because of a legal disability or infirmity. For example, the interest of the state in protecting the rights of minors and the insane. In early England, the King had the prerogative to step in to protect the rights of infants. In the U.S., the right to intercede to protect others belongs to the states and is exercised by such state officers as the Attorneys General. These officers will intercede in cases of child abuse or in custody cases. *Syed Salih Bin Ali Bin Sallay Al Hamid v. Syed Aidroos Bin Ali Bin Sallay Al Hamid and Others [1934] 3 MLJ at Pg.3*

PARI DELICTO 'In a similar offence or crime; equal in guilt. A person who is in pari delicto with another, differs from a particeps criminis in this, that the former always includes the latter but the latter does not always include the former. *Ahmad Bin Udoh & Anor v. Ng Aik Chong [1969] 2 MLJ 117 (Contract), Ahmad Bin Udoh & Anor v. Ng Aik Chong [1969] 2 MLJ 117 (Contract), Ng Siew San v. Menaka [1973] 2 MLJ 154 Pg.157; Menaka v. Ng siew san [1973] 1MLJ 50 Pg. 53*

PARI MATERIA 'Of equal matter', on the same subject. Of the same matter; on the same subject; as, laws pari materia must be construed with reference to each other. *Anthony Gomez v. Ketua Polis Daerah Kuantan[1977] 2 MLJ 24 Pg. 25; Goh Hooi Yin v. Lim Teong Ghee & Ors [1977] 2 MLJ 26 Pg. 28; Yew Lean Finance Development (M) Sdn Bhd v. Director of Lands and Mines,Penang [1977] 2 MLJ 45 Pg. 47; Tan Thean Choo v. Cheah Kah Seong & Anor [1977] 2 MLJ 107 Pg. 107; The "Permina 108" [1977] 1 MLJ 49 Pg. 51; Choo Fah Fatt & Anor v. Che Rus Bin Othman & Ors [1977] 1 MLJ 230 Pg. 231; Michael Chong Ngian Fong v. Syarikat Fong Sam Timber & Anor [1977] 1 MLJ 263 Pg. 264, In Re G.G Ponnambalam [1969] 2 MLJ 264 (Advocate and Solicitors), Peter Lai Khee-Chin & Anor v. Collector Of Stamp Duties[1973] 2 MLJ 33 Pg.34;*

Rajalachmi v. Sinniah [1973] 2 MLJ 133 Pg.134; Isman Bin Osman v. Government of Malaysia[1973] 2 MLJ143 Pg. 145; Re Kathiravelu Deed[1973] 2 MLJ 165 Pg. 166; Lebai Taib v. Abdul Ghani & Anor[1973] 1 MLJ 109 Pg. 111, Public Prosecuter v. Nazarid Fernandez [1954] 20 MLJ at Pg. 6, 7; (Criminal Procedure Code); In Re G.G Ponnambalam [1969] 2 MLJ 264 (Advocate and Solicitors); Official Assignee, States of Malaya v. Tat Fatt Shirts Manufacturers [1969] 1MLJ 3 (Contract); X., Trustee of The Estate of Y. Deceased v. Comptroller of Income Tax, States Of Malaya [1969] 1 MLJ 158 (Trust); In Re XY & Co [1966] 2 MLJ 11 at Pg. 14.

PARI PASSU 'with equal steps'. neck and neck. Equally, upon the same terms. In bankruptcy, creditors of the same class share *pari passu* in the assets of the debtor. In contracts, prov.ision may be made to pay some parties *pari passu*, i.e., in equal shares from a common fund. *In Re W.J.D. Hogg, Decd; Anderson v. The Commissioner of Estate Duties [1939] 8 MLJ 112 at Pg. 113, 118; (Estate Duty, Shares); Re P. K. Kassim Serang [1939] 8 MLJ 139 at Pg. 139; (Bankruptcy)*

PARIMUTUEL 'mutual betting'. a system of betting on races in which those backing the winners div.ide, in proportion to their wagers, the total amount bet, minus a percentage for the track operators, taxes, etc. *Rex v. Li Kim Poat & Another [1933] 2 MLJ 164 Pg. 168*

PARRICIDE the criminal act of murdering one's father; also parricidium.

PARRICIDIUM the murder of a parent.

PARS a party (to an action, deed, proceedings).

PARTICEPS CRIMINIS 'one who has a share in a crime' or 'an accomplice in a crime'. *Mohamed Adat & Ors. v. Public Prosecutor [1967] 2 MLJ 50 Pg.5*

PARTICEPS a participant; partaker, partner, sharer, comrade.

PATER FAMILIAS 'father of the family'. The head of household, for purposes of considering the rights and responsibilities thereof.

PATIT MAL 'A form of epilepsy with v.ery brief, unannounced lapses in consciousness. A petit mal seizure involves a brief loss of awareness, which can be accompanied by blinking or mouth twitching. Petit mal seizures have a very characteristic appearance on an electroencephalogram (EEG). *Lim Kim Chai & Anor. v. Foo See Fatt; Gan Chin Baw & Anor. v. Foo See Fatt [1970] 2 MLJ 207, at 208*

PECUNIA it has a wider meaning than 'money'. It also include every thing which constituted the private property of an individual, or which was a part of his fortune.

PENDENTE LITE 'The strife still pending'. The trial not being concluded. Suspended while the lawsuit lasts. Awaiting the outcome of the action. Pending the lawsuit. A matter *pendente lite* is contingent on the outcome of litigation. The appointment of a guardian *pendente lite* is an appointment which lasts during, and terminates upon the end of, a law suit. *Government of Malaysia v. Iznan bin osman [1977] 2 MLJ 1 Pg. 4; Government Of Malaysia v. Zainal Bin Hashim [1977] 2 MLJ 254 Pg. 255, Damodaran v. V.Esudevan [1975] 2 MLJ 231 Pg. 232, Hoi Yin v. Sim Sie Hau [1969] 2 MLJ 3 (Succession)*

PER ALIAM VIAM *Chai Sau Yin v. Kok Seng Fatt [1966] 2 MLJ 54 at Pg. 58, Chai Sau Yin v. Kok Seng Fatt [1966] 2 MLJ 54 at Pg. 58*

PER ALLUV.IONEM 'By alluvion, or the gradual and imperceptible increase arising from deposit by water. Per alluv.ionem id v.idetur adjici qnod ita paulatim adjicitnr nt intelligere non possnmns quantum quoquo momento temporis adjiciatur. That is said to be added by alluvion which is so added little by little that we cannot tell how much is added at any one moment of time. *B. H Oon & Ors. v. The Government of The State of Penang & Ors. [1970] 1 MLJ 244, at 248*

PER ANNUM 'by the year'. Yearly. over the course of a year; annually, as in *interest per annum.* Jayal Singh v. Leong Yung Kwok [1954] 20 MLJ at Pg. 92; (Money Lenders Ordinance 1951); Tengku Zahara Binti Tengku Chik v. Che Yusoff Bin Che Mat [1951] 17 MLJ at Pg. 4

PER AUTRE DROIT Hendrik Christiaan V.an Hoogstraten v. Low Lum Seng [1940] 9 MLJ 138 at Pg 140, 142, 147

PER CAPITA 'By the head'. Through or by the head, top or summit. Counted or calculated by the number of heads (i.e., persons) inv.olv.ed. The div.ision and distribution of an estate in equal shares, the number of which is determined by counting and div.iding equally among all liv.ing persons descended from the decedent, regardless of the shares which would hav.e been taken by the ancestors of those persons. Example: A dies leav.ing one liv.ing son, B; two liv.ing grandsons, C and D, the sons of deceased son X; and three greatgrandchildren, E, F and G, the descendants of deceased son Y. A's estate will be div.ided into six equal shares, one each for B, C, D, E, F and G. Most states apply *per capita* distribution only when all takers are of the same generation. Distribution *per capita* is distinguished from distribution *per stirpes.* Also, by each individual in the population, as a *per capita* tax. Cha Hock Seng v. Thor Keng Hong & Ors. [1970] 2 MLJ 12, at 12, 13f (Construction of Will), *In Re The Estate of T.M.R.M. V.Engadasalam Chettiar Deceased [1940] 9 MLJ 155 at Pg. 162; (Customary Law); Meyappa Chettiar v. Federated Malay States [1941] MLJ 115*

PER CENTUM 'By the hundred'. Used in the abbrev.iated form *percent.* Measured by the number of parts in a hundred; of each hundred. A whole div.ided into 100 parts. Hin Seng & Co. V. Seac Co. [1966] 1 MLJ 235 at Pg. 236, Public Prosecutor v. Ong Chang Sow [1954] 20 MLJ at Pg. 82; *Ban Kok Hotel v. Low Phek Choon 1950] 16 MLJ at Pg. 251; (Land Law); Syed Ahmad Al-Junied & Ors. v. Reshty [1969] 1 MLJ 88*

(Tenancy); Hin Seng & Co. V. Seac Co. [1966] 1 MLJ 235 at Pg. 236

PER CONTRA 'on the contrary' or 'by way of contrast'. *In Re Settlement of Shaik Salleh Bin Obeid Bin Abdat & Anor [1954] 20 MLJ at Pg. 10; (Trust); Re Kana Moona Syed Abubakar Deceased. Khatijah Nachiar v. Sultan Alauddin and The Assistant Official Assignee, Penang & Others [1940] 9 MLJ 4 at Pg. 7; (Contract); Dharmaratna v. Dharmaratna [1939] 8 MLJ 238 at Pg. 241; (Land); Quah Ooi Keat & Anor v. Yew Phaik Hoon [1966] 2 MLJ 208 at Pg. 213; K. Ismail Ganey Rowther & Co. V.S. M.A. Abdul Kader Etc. [1933] 2 MLJ 98 Pg. 99, Quah Ooi Keat & Anor v. Yew Phaik Hoon [1966] 2 MLJ 208 at Pg. 213*

PER CURIAM 'meeting place of the Roman Senate; courthouse; Court'. An opinion which is joined in by an entire appellate court, as opposed to one which is written for the court by a single judge. Also, a short statement of the disposition of an appeal without a formal opinion or explanatory discussion. *Island & Peninsular Development Ltd & Anor v. Registrar of Titles, Kedah[1973] 2 MLJ 69 Pg. 69, Johannes Koplan v. Aw Chen [1970] 1 MLJ 220, at 220 (Third Party Insurance); Chua Beow Huat v. Public Prosecutor [1970] 2 MLJ 29, at 29 (Law of Evidence); Re Herbert Victor Morais [1970] 2 MLJ 88, at 88 (Admission of Advocate and Solicitors); Abu Bakar Bin Nazmeer v. Public Prosecutor [1970] 2 MLJ 216, 217; Tan Chwee Geok & Anor v. Khaw Yen-Yen & Anor [1975] 2 MLJ*

188 Pg. 188, Herchun Singh & Anor v. Public Prosecutor [1969] 2 MLJ 209

PER INCURIAM 'through lack of care'. A court decision made per incuriam is one which ignores a contradictory statute or binding authority, and is therefore wrongly decided and of no force. A judgment that's found to hav.e been decided per incuriam does not then hav.e to be followed as precedent by a lower court.In criminal cases a decision made per incuriam will usually result in the conv.iction being ov.erturned. A judgment of a court which has been decided without reference to a statutory prov.ision or earlier judgment which would hav.e been relev.ant. The significance of a judgment hav.ing been decided *per incuriam* is that it does not then hav.e to be followed as precedent by a lower court. Ordinarily, in the common law, the *rationes* of a judgment must be followed thereafter by lower courts hearing similar cases. A lower court is free, howev.er, to depart from an earlier judgment of a superior court where that earlier judgment was decided *per incuriam*. *Abdul Bin Palaga v. Public Prosecutor [1973] 2 MLJ177 Pg. 177; Government of Malaysia v. Rosalind Oh Lee Pek Inn [1973] 1 MLJ222 Pg. 225, Helen Ho Quee v. Lim Pui Heng [1974] 2 MLJ 51 Pg.53; Yeoh Tat Thong v. Government of Malaysia & Anor[1974] 2 MLJ 119 Pg.120; Public Prosecutor v. Teoh Hock Hai[1974] 2 MLJ 119 Pg.122, Ng Kay Thong v. Chan Shon Shong [1966] 2 MLJ 305 at Pg. 306*

PER 'Through, along, over (for space or distance)'. Throughout, during (for time); also, by means of, because of. *Rex v. Singapore British Malay Football Club [1934] 3 MLJ at Pg. 4; Lee Mion Alias Lee Miow v. Public Prosecutor of Johore [1934] 3 MLJ 124 at Pg. 125; Tan Joo Hern and Anor. V.S. The Sze Hai Tong Banking Insurance Co. Ltd. and Ors. [1934] 3 MLJ 127 at Pg. 133; (Trust – Trustees's Power)*

PER by, through, by means of; for.

PER MENSEM 'ev.ery month or by the month'. *Re Karthigasu Arumugam Exparte J.K.R. Leonard [1940] 9 MLJ 71 at Pg. 73; (Bankruptcy); Ban Kok Hotel v. Low Phek Choon [1950] 16 MLJ at Pg. 251.252; (Land Law); Re Othman Bin Abu Bakar, Ex Parte Official Assignee [1954] 20 MLJ at Pg. 76; Fatimah v. Moideen Kutty [1969] 1 MLJ 73 (Land Law); Employees Provident Fund Board v. R. R. Chelliah Bros. [1969] 1 MLJ 166 (Legislative);Koh v. Koh [1965] 1 MLJ 99 Pg. 99, 100, 101; OV.Erses Chinese Banking Corporation Ltd v. Tan Cheng [1967] 1 MLJ 98 –Pg. 99*

PER MINAS 'through threats'. Used as a defense, when illegal acts were performed under duress

PER QUOD 'by which'. Used in legal documents in the same sense as "whereby". A per quod statement is typically used to show that specific acts had consequences which form the basis for the legal action

PER REM JUDICATAM *Lee Sock Goh v. Straits Cabaret (1963) Ltd. [1965] 1 MLJ 98 Pg. 98, Lee Sock Goh v. Straits Cabaret (1953) Ltd. [1965] 2 MLJ 3 Pg. 5, 6*

PER SE 'By itself', or, 'For its own sake'." 'No man likes mustard per se. Through itself; by means of itself. In and of itself, intrinsically; inherently. Established without extrinsic proof. Inherent in the act itself. A *per se* violation in antitrust law is an act so clearly inimical to competition and fair trade as to require no further inquiry by the court into whether it has actually resulted in injury to the public. In tort law, an action which clearly violates the terms of a statute or rule may constitute *negligence per se*, whether or not there is any other evidence of fault by the defendant. *Chop Seng Heng v. Thevannasan & Ors [1975] 2 MLJ 3 Pg. 6; Workers' Party v. Tay Boon Too & Anor [1975] 2 MLJ 124 Pg. 127; Mak Sik Kwong v. Minister of Home Affairs,Malaysia [1975] 2 MLJ168 Pg. 169; Zainun Binti Abdul Ghani & Anor v. Chong Ah Seng & Anor [1975] 1 MLJ 33 Pg. 35; Worker's Party v. Tay Boon Too [1975] 1 MLJ 47 Pg. 47, L.K.C v. Comptoller-General of Inland Revenue [1973] 2 MLJ 17 Pg. 19; Syed Husin Ali v. Sharikat Penchetakan Utusan Melayu Berhad & Anor [1973] 2 MLJ 56 Pg. 59; Harbans Singh Sidhu v. Public Prosecutor [1973] 1MLJ 41 Pg. 41; Muniandy & Anor v. Public Prosecutor [1973] 1 MLJ 179 Pg. 183, Lim Ah Toh v. Ang Yau Chee & Anor. [1969] 2 MLJ*

PER STIRPES 'According to the original stock'. It means through or from the roots. The division and distribution of an estate into shares determined by the *right of representation*, i.e., each liv.ing descendant entitled to a share takes all or a portion of the share his or her ancestor would hav.e taken. Nearly all the states apply *per stirpes* distribution when all the surv.iv.ors are not of the same generation. Example: A dies leav.ing one liv.ing son, B; two liv.ing grandsons, C and D, the sons of deceased son X; and three greatgrandchildren, E, F and G, the descendants of deceased son Y. The estate will be div.ided into three equal parts. B will get one whole part, or onethird; C and D will div.ide one part between them, resulting in one-sixth for each; and E, F and G will div.ide one part among them, leav.ing one-ninth for each. Distinguished from *per capita* distribution, in which B, C, D, E, F and G would each take an equal one-sixth interest. *Cha Hock Seng v. Thor Keng Hong & Ors. [1970] 2 MLJ 12, at 12 (Construction of Will), In Re The Estate of T.M.R.M. v.Engadasalam Chettiar Deceased [1940] 9 MLJ 155 at Pg. 162; (Customary Law); Tan Joo Hern and Anor. v.S. The Sze Hai Tong Banking Insurance Co. Ltd. and Ors. [1934] 3 MLJ 127 at Pg. 130; (Trust – Trustees's Power); Meyappa Chettiar v. Federated Malay States [1941] MLJ 115*

PER STIRPES By the number of families. A distribution of property 'per stirpes and not per capita' means that all the beneficiaries will not, necessarily or probably, take equal shares but, that the property is to be divided into as many parts as there are stocks and each stock will have one and only one, of such parts though such stock may consist of many persons whilst another may only consist of one person. (Stroud) By stocks in inheritance the chil-dren of each descendant dividing only the share that would have been their parents. By root, stock or branch. In Roman law, division of an inheritance through descendants in a straight line. Refers to the method of division and distribution of a deceased estate based on the stocks of the family or branches of descent; a distribution method by representation or substitution of a person's children or remoter issue where that person entitled under intestacy rules dies before the intestate. Under per stirpes, no child can take concurrently with its parent. For example, if X dies intestate leaving children A, B and C, the children would share the estate in equal thirds as there are three stocks or stirps; however, if child B predeceased X leaving issue B1 and B2 and C has grandchildren C1 and C2, then by per stripes division, X's surviving children A and C would still take one-third, B's issue B1 and B2 would take one-sixth each (sharing equally B's one-third entitlement) and C's grandchildren C1 and C2 would receive nothing as their grandparent C survived X. There is a statutory preference for per stirpes distribution on intestacy: for example (NSW) Wills, Probate and Administration Act 1898 s 61c. To be contrasted with per capita, a distribution by which each beneficiary receives an equal share of the property in his or her own right, based on a beneficiary as a unit, not as a member of a generation.

PER STIRPITAL *Cha Hock Seng v. Thor Keng Hong & Ors. [1970] 2 MLJ 12, at 12*

PER VERBA DE PRAESENTI 'by words of the present tense'. sometimes used refering to marriage by means of words of present assent. marriage per v.erba de praesenti is a common-law marriage entered into by the parties by their joint consent, without the interposition of any person authorized to solemnize the marriage and without formal solemnization. Sometimes known as commonlaw marriages, were an agreement to marry, rather than a marriage. The Marriage Act of 1753 also did not apply to Britain's ov.erseas colonies of the time, so common law marriages continued to be recognized in the future United States and Canada. *In Re Abraham Penhas, Deceased [1949] 15 MLJ at Pg. 105*

PERCUTIO to strike hard, pierce, transfix or shock. If a man by a grasp of the hand infect another with small-pox it is impossible to trace out in detail the connection between the act and the disease, and it would, I think, be an unnatural use of language to say that a man by such an act 'inflicted' small-pox on another. It would be wrong in interpreting an Act of Parliament to lay much stress on etymology, but I may just observe that 'inflict' is derived from 'infligo', to which in Facciolati's Lexicon three Italian and three Latin equivalents are given, all meaning 'to strike', viz, dare, ferire and percuotere in Italian, and impigno, and percutio in Latin.

PERICULUM IN MORA 'danger in delay'. A condition given to support requests for urgent action, such as a protective order or restraining order.

PERIMO to slay.

PERJURO to break an oath.

PERSONA character in virtue of which certain rights belong to a man and certain duties are imposed upon him. The word 'persona' in its primitive sense, was applied to the mask's worn by the actors in the dramatic performance of Rome and Greece, which masks were made to represent the character which the actor performed; and in the same sense it was subsequently employed in jurisprudence to signify the role or status which a man fills in the social organisation. Thus the same man may at different times and even at the same time, represent different persons or roles, as, in his youth he represents the person of a minor and after his maturity, that of a major, each having different qualities, rights and obligations.

PERSONA NON GRATA 'unwelcome person'. A person who is officially considered unwelcome by a host country in which they are residing in a diplomatic capacity. The person is typically expelled to their home country.

PETITIO PRINCIPII 'laying claim to a principle', or 'postulation of the beginning, begging the question'. a logical fallacy in which a premise is assumed to be true without warrant or in which what is to be prov.ed is implicitly taken for granted. *In Re the Estate of T.M.R.M. v.Engadasalam*

Chettiar Deceased [1940] 9 MLJ 155 at Pg. 161

PIED-A-TERRE literally means 'foot on the ground'. Atemporary or second lodginga flat, house, or other lodging for secondary or occasional use. *Thong Seong Poh & Anor v. Thong Meng Tee [1967] 2 MLJ 153 pg. 153, Pok Kew Chai v. Yeoh Thian Seng & Anor [1975] 1 MLJ 220 Pg. 222, Pok Kew Chai v. Yeoh Thian Seng [1975] 1 MLJ 220 Pg. 221*

PIGNUS pledge, gage, collateral, surety, pawn.

POSSE COMITATUS 'power of the county'. A body of armed citizens pressed into serv.ice by legal authority, to keep the peace or pursue a fugitive.

POSSIM *Hendrik Christiaan v. An Hoogstraten v. Low Lum Seng [1940] 9 MLJ 138 at Pg. 145*

POST DIEM 'day, daytime'. For instance, after the designated date. a payment which is made after the maturity date is a payment *post diem*. After the day; as a plea of payment post diem, after the, day when the money became due. *Suchait Singh v. Sher Ali Khan [1939] 8 MLJ 23 at Pg. 24*

POST HOC, ERGO PROPTER HOC 'after this', therefore because of this". It is used to describe a fallacy in thinking that one ev.ent causes another simply because the supposed cause occurred before the proposed effect. For example, such reasoning might occur when a person becomes sick after shaking hands with a person who is ill. Without more proof of a causal connection, such reasoning may be said to be post hoc ergo propter hoc. The logical fallacy of believing that temporal succession implies a causal relation. *Government of Malaysia & Anor v. Chin Keow [1965] 2 MLJ 91 Pg. 94*

POST MORTEM 'after death'. Refers to an autopsy, or as a qualification as to when some ev.ent occurred.

POST MORTEM AUCTORIS 'after the author's death'. Used in reference to intellectual property rights, which usually are based around the author's lifetime.

POTESTAS power; authority, domination.

PRAECIPE (PRECIPE) 'to take before', 'to obtain in adv.ance'. A document or writ directing a court officer or clerk to perform a ministerial act in furtherance of an order or decision of the court, e.g., an order directing the clerk to issue execution after judgment. Also, an order directing a person to commit some act or to refrain from committing it. An application for the issuance of a summons by the court clerk. Also, an application to a judge similar to a motion. practice. The name of the written instructions given by an attorney or plaintiff to the clerk or prothonotary of a; court, whose duty it is to make out the writ, for the making of the same. *Ratna Ammal v. Tan Chow Soo [1966] 2 MLJ 294 at Pg. 297, Ratna Ammal v. Tan Chow Soo [1966] 2 MLJ 294 at Pg. 297, Nayar v. Gian Singh &*

co. Ltd [1970] 1 MLJ 176, at 176, 178 (Amended Statement of Claim); Civil District Courts Singapore [1970] 1 MLJ v.ii, at v.iii

PRAEPOSITUS the person in charge.

PRAESENTIA presence, presence of mind, effect, power.

PRAESUMPTIO presumption.

PRAETEREA besides, moreover, as indeed it is.

PRAETOR PEREGRINUS 'magistrate of foreigners'. The Roman Praetor (magistrate) responsible for matters inv. olv.ing non-Romans.

PRAXIS the practice of the judges is the interpreter of the laws.

PRIMA FACIE 'face, form, figure; at first v.iew, on its face'. On first appearance. A fact presumed to be true in the absence of a showing to the contrary. The first v.iew or appearance of the business; as, the holder of a bill of exchange, indorsed in blank, is prima facie its owner. *Director-General of inland Revenue v. A.L.B. Co. Sdn Bhd [1975] 2 MLJ 27 Pg. 27, Port Swettenham Authority v. T.W. Wu & Co. (M) Sdn Bhd [1975] 2 MLJ 73 Pg. 76; Public Prosecutor v. Ku Hang Chua[1975] 2 MLJ 99 Pg. 101; Wah Loong (Jelapang) Tin Mine Sdn Bhd v. Chia Ngen Yiok[1975] 2 MLJ 109 Pg. 110; Gah Hay Chong v. Siow Kian Yuh & Anor [1975] 2 MLJ 129 Pg. 130, Lim Su Sang v. Teck Guan Construction & Development Co. Ltd [1966] 2 MLJ* 29 at Pg. 30; *Lim Ko & Anor v. Board of Architects [1966] 2 MLJ 80 at Pg. 92, 94; Bata Shoe Co. Ltd v. Singapore Manual & Mercantile Workers' Union [1966] 2 MLJ 104 at Pg. 105; Hoon Wee Thim v. Pacific Tin Consolidated Corporation [1966] 2 MLJ 240 at Pg. 250; Gnanasundram v. Public Services Commission [1966] 1 MLJ 157 at Pg.158; Victoria Hotel v. Ho See Teck [1966] 1 MLJ 29 at Pg. 32, Public Prosecutor v. Tang Chew Weng [1969] 2 MLJ 17 (Criminal); Re Gan Kim Chong Deed. [1969] 2 MLJ 67 (Sucession); Lim Chin Poh v. Public Prosecutor [1969] 2 MLJ 161 (Negligence); Lim Ah Toh v. Ang Yau Chee & Anor. [1969] 2 MLJ 194 (Negligence); Shaaban & Ors v. Chong Fook Kam & Anor [1969] 2 MLJ 219 (False Imprisonment); Wong See Kui v. Hong Hing Tin Mining Co. [1969] 2 MLJ 236 (Nuisance); Public Prosecutor v. Chen Kee Nan [1969] 2 MLJ 238 (Cheating)*

PRIOR TEMPORE POTIOR IURE 'earlier in time, stronger in law'. A legal principle that older laws take precedent over newer ones. Another name for this principle is lex posterior.

PRIORI (A PRIORI) 'From what is before'. Deductiv.e reasoning or the ascertaining of truth by proceeding from an assumption to its logical conclusion rather than by actual experience or observ.ation. For example, one who walks by a store when its alarm is sounding and sees that its window is broken can deduce that a burglary has occurred without hav.ing watched the burglars commit the actual crime.

'from the cause to the effect'. A priori is a term of logic used to denote that when one generally accepted truth is shown to be a cause, another particular effect must necessarily follow. This phrase refers to a type of reasoning that examines given general principles to discov.er what particular facts or real-life observ.ations can be deriv.ed from them. Another name for this method is deductiv.e reasoning. Howev.er, modern usage has dev.iated significantly from the Latin. An a priori conclusion or judgment is one that is necessarily true, that is neither prov.ed by nor capable of being disprov.ed by experience, and that is known to be true by a process of reasoning independent of all factual evidence. The term is commonly used to indicate a judgment that is widely believ.ed to be certain or that is introduced presumptiv.ely, without analysis or inv.estigation. Thus to accuse someone of hav.ing assumed a fact or conclusion a priori is often to disparage him or her for hav.ing failed to support a judgment through evidence or analysis. *Tengku Mariam Binte Tengku Sri Wa Raja & Anor v. Comminssioner For Religious Affairs, Terengganu & Ors. [1969] 1 MLJ 111 (Islamic Succession); He Nestle & Anglo-Swiss Condensed Milk Co. v.S. The East Asiatic Co. Ltd. [1933] 2 MLJ 30 Pg. 32; Collector of Land Revenue, Klang v. Tan Toh and Yong Wee Chai [1934] 3 MLJ 12 at Pg. 13*

PRIUS QUAM EXAUDIAS NE IUDICES 'before you hear, do not judge'.

PRIVATA DELICTA *Mr. Abdul Hasanat, J.P., Super Intendent of Police, Naokhali, Bengal, India; [1939] 8 MLJ ii-v.ii at Pg. iv*

PRIVATUM private.

PRO BONO 'For good'. Professional work done for free.

PRO BONO PUBLICO 'For the public good'.

PRO FORMA 'as a matter of form' or things done as formalities.

PRO FORMA to form, shape, fashion] For the sake of form; as a matter of form. Done as a mere formality or perfunctorily. Also, a document which assumes certain facts and then utilizes them to estimate or project future activities or results. A *pro forma* statement is a financial statement forecasting the results of business operations or of a particular business transaction. Done as a formality, rather than because of conviction, in order to make possible further proceedings. 2 In accounting procedures, done in adv.ance to provide a what-if statement, predict results, or to conv.ince. For example, a balance sheet showing combined figures of two companies in case of a merger. *Daiman Development Sdn Bhd v. Mat Hew Lui Chin Teck [1978] 2 MLJ 239 Pg. 240, Public Prosecutor v. Raman I, Raman Ii & Ayappan [1940] 9 MLJ 163 at Pg. 167; (Criminal Procedure Code); Public Prosecutor v. Bahadar Khan [1940] 9 MLJ 180 at Pg. 180; (Criminal)*

PRO HAC VICE 'For this one purpose or occasion'. The allowing of something not usually allowed, usually referring to an attorney who normally could not practice in a certain jurisdiction, but is allowed to just for one case. The phrase usually refers to an out-of-state lawyer who has been granted special permission to participate in a particular case, ev.en though the lawyer is not licensed to practice in the state where the case is being tried. *Chang Fah Lin v. United Engineers (M) Sdn Bhd [1978] 2 MLJ 260 Pg. 265; Karuppan Bhoomidas v. Port of Singapore Authority [1978] 1 MLJ 49 Pg. 50*

PRO PER (Abbreviation of PROPRIA PERSONA) meaning "one's own person" Representing oneself, without counsel. Also known as pro se representation.

PRO RATA 'to think, judge, fix'. Calculated by or according to a proportional measure. To div.ide, fix or assess proportionately. To div.ide or allocate in proportion to some measure of time, space or value. A corporation will pay a div.idend to its common stockholders *pro rata*, i.e., according to the percentage each owns of the common stock. According to the rate, proportion or allowance. A creditor of an insolvent estate is to be paid pro rata with creditors of the same class. *K.P Kunchi Raman v. Goh bros sdn bhd [1978] 1 MLJ 89 Pg. 90, Official Assignee v. Leong Cheong Wai [1939] 8 MLJ 148 at Pg. 156; (Bankruptcy); H.G. Warren v. Tay Say Geok & Ors. [1965] 1 MLJ 44 Pg. 45*

PRO SE 'for himself'. Representing oneself, without counsel. Also known as pro per representation.

PRO TANTO 'so much, to such extent; that's as far as it goes; so much and no more'. Used to indicate that only a part of an obligation has been satisfied, or that only part of an event has occurred. Examples: if a testator pays a part of a bequest to a beneficiary before death, he may intend a *pro tanto* ademption. If a defendant has performed only part of his obligations, the plaintiff may recov.er *pro tanto*. A municipality may make a *pro tanto* payment to a landowner in an eminent domain proceeding while the landowner pursues her claim for a larger amount. For so much, or so far as it will go ; as if a tenant for life make a lease for 100 years, the lease is good *pro tanto*, that is, for such an estate or interest as the tenant for life may lawfully convey. *Johnson Tan Han Seng v. Public Prosecutor [1977] 2 MLJ 66 Pg. 75, Meenachi Sundram & Anor v. Kunjan Pillai [1955] 21 MLJ at Pg. 129; (Landlord and Tenant); Leong Hoi Kow v. Chan Ho Yat [1951] 17 MLJ at Pg. 67; (Landlord and Tenant); John Puddicombe Wilkins & 2 Others v. John Patrick Kenelm Wilkins & Another [1951] 17 MLJ at Pg. 80; (Civil Procedure); Pakala Narayana Swami v. King-Emperor [1939] 8 MLJ 48 at Pg. 51; (Evidence Ordinance); Boota Singh v. P.P. [1933] 2 MLJ 195 Pg.196; YONG JOO LIN & ORS V. FUNG POL FONG [1941] MLJ 56, T. Mahesan v. Malaysia Government Officer's Cooperative Housing Society [1978] 1 MLJ 149 Pg. 152*

PRO TANTO ULTRA V.IRES *The Batu Pahat Bank v. The Official Assignee of the PropertY of Tan Keng Tin [1933] 2 MLJ 237 Pg. 238*

PRO TEMPORE (PRO TEM) 'a div. ision; time, a period of time'. For the time being. Temporarily, provisionally. Used to indicate that some office or right is being held temporarily, e.g., "she is serv.ing as chairperson *pro tem*", or, "Mr. Clark is dean *pro tem.*" A position or office held until the person elected or appointed to fill it permanently can assume it. "For the time being." A temporary position or appointment. *R.M.N.L. Letchumanan Chettiar v. A.V.L. Alagappa Chettiar, Etc. [1934] 3 MLJ 50 at Pg.51, 54, 56*

PRO TEMPORE 'for the time being'. Something, such as an office held, that is temporary.

PROBATIO VINCIT PRAESUMPTIONEM 'proof overcomes presumption'.

PROCURATIO management, administration, direction, supervision.

PROCURATIONEM procuration, that is by the action of another. In the ordinary way, when a formal document is required to be 'signed' by a person, it can only be done by that person himself writing his own name on it, or affixing his own signature on it, with his own hand

PROPOSITUS the immediate person.

PROPRIA PERSONA 'proper person'. Refers to one reperesenting themselves without the services of a lawyer. CAlso known as pro per representation.

PROPRIO MOTU 'by one's own motion'. *B.A Rao & Ors v. Sapuran Kaur & Anor [1978] 2 MLJ 146 Pg. 150*

PROSEQUI to follow up or pursue; to sue or prosecute.

PROUT PATET PER RECORDUM 'as appears in the record'. Used to cite something that has already been admitted into the record.

Prov.incial judicature *In Re Abraham Penhas, Deceased [1950] 16 MLJ at Pg. 110*

PROVISO 'to look forward'. a condition, stipulation or limitation. a clause in a contract, deed, statute, or other legal document, which expresses or contains a condition or restriction. these clauses usually begin with such words as "upon condition that", "prov.ided that", "with the understanding that." the name of a clause inserted in an act of the legislature, a deed, a written agreement, or other instrument, which generally contains a condition that a certain thing shall or shall not be done, in order that an agreement contained in another clause shall take effect. It always implies a condition, unless subsequent words change it to a cov.enant; but when a prov.iso contains the mutual words of the parties to a deed, it amounts to a cov.enant. a prov.iso differs from an exception. an exception exempts, absolutely, from the operation of an engagement or an enactment; a prov.iso defeats their operation, conditionally. An exception takes out of an engagement or enactment, something which would otherwise be part of the subject-matter of it; a prov.iso av.oids them by way of defeasance or excuse. *Re Karthigasu Arumugam Exparte J.K.R. Leonard [1940] 9 MLJ 71 at Pg. 73; (Bankruptcy); Ang Khye Pang v. Chop Ban Aik [1939] 8 MLJ 217 at Pg. 219; (Trust); Chelliah v. Public Prosecutor [1941] MLJ 16*

PROVISO a clause in a deed or section of a statute which limits or qualifies the principal clause. The proviso may provide for an exception or qualification not inconsistent with what is expressed in the earlier part of the section.

PUBLIC JUDICIAL *Criminal Law and Crime; Mr. Abdul Hasanat, J.P., Superintendent of Police, Naokhali, Bengal, India; [1939] 8 MLJ ii-v.ii at Pg. iv, Public Prosecutor v. Lee Kee Chang [1974] 2 MLJ 15 Pg. 15,16; King Hock Ching v. Ung Siew Ping [1974] 2 MLJ 16 Pg.17; Ho Kean v. Kong Lai Soo[1974] 2 MLJ 63 Pg.64; Re Chen Sing Chew [1974] 2 MLJ 69 Pg.69, Public Prosecutor v. Ong Chang Sow [1954] 20 MLJ at Pg. 82; (Dangerous Drugs Ordinance 1952); Jayal Singh v. Leong Yung Kwok [1954] 20 MLJ at Pg. 92; (Moneylenders Ordinance 1951); 3.Successors of Moine & Co. Ltd v. East Asiatic Co. Ltd & Singapore Harbour Board [1954] 20 MLJ at Pg. 114; (Estoppel); Moh Yee Chong*

(f) & Anor v. Public Prosecutor [1955] 21 MLJ at Pg. 115; (Criminal Law and Procedure);Public Prosecutor v. Looi Yew Chun & Two Others [1951] 17 MLJ at Pg. 30; (Custom Enactment); Khoo Soo Jin & Anor v. Lye Yew Song [1951] 17 MLJ at Pg. 232

PUBLICI JURIS 'right or law'. A right or privilege av.ailable to all; a public or common right. The rights to light, air and water are all *publici juris*. A right of a public. When a right belongs to the public it is called publici juris. Publici juris refers to common resources. For example, roads and bridges regulated by a state for general public benefit relates to publici juris. States can grant franchise to priv.ate parties to maintain such general resources. Howev.er, these grants remain under state superv.ision to preserv.e public right access. Now, publici juris is used in intellectual property rights cases. In some cases patent rights are not granted to certain inv.ention on the basis of publici juris. This means that there was no nov.elty in the inv.ention and it had always belonged to the public. *The Nestle & Anglo-Swiss Condensed Milk Co. v.S. The East Asiatic Co. Ltd. [1933] 2 MLJ 30 Pg. 32*

PUNCTUM TEMPORIS 'A point of time; an indivisible period of time; the shortest space of time. *Ho Tong Cheong & Ors. v. Oversea Chinese Banking Corporation Limited [1969] 1 MLJ 131*

Q

QUA considered as; in so far as; in the character or capacity of. For example 'the trustee qua trustee (that is in his character as trustee) is not liable. It means in the capacity of; as being: shareholders qua members may be under obligations to the company. Lee See Chian v. The Public Prosecutor [1940] 9 MLJ 148 at Pg. 148; Muthiah Chetty v. Arokiamariammal & Anor [1939] 8 MLJ 66 at Pg. 67; A.Sahib Bin Ali v. Rex [1939] 8 MLJ 216 at Pg. 217; (Lottery); Pi. AR.Arunasalan Chettiar & Ors. v. PI. Palaniappa [1969] 1 MLJ 5; Tan Ah Lek v. Rex [1941] MLJ 48

QUAERE 'to seek, to want to know, to inquire'. an inquiry, a question, the search for an answer. In a legal article or text, the use of this word indicates that the writer is introducing an inquiry into some issue or question. Example: *"quaere: what do we mean by the term proximate cause?"*. A word frequently used to denote that an inquiry ought to be made of a doubtful thing. To query or inquire. Used in law textbooks to indicate that a point was dubious or questionable. *Rex v. Lim Soon Gong & Ors [1939] 8 MLJ 8 at Pg. 8; (Criminal), Harun v. Public Prosecutor [1966] 2 MLJ 166 at Pg. 167, Harun v. Public Prosecutor [1966] 2 MLJ 166 at Pg. 167; Webster Automatic Packeting Factory Ltd. v.S. Chop Kim Leong Thye [1933] 2 MLJ 61 Pg. 69; S.V.S. Muthuraman Chettiar v.S. EE Kong Guan and Another [1934]*

3 MLJ 32 at Pg. 31; (Trust – Fraudulent Breach of Trust); Malayan Trading Co. v. Lee Pak Yin [1941] MLJ 171

QUANTUM as much it is worth.

QUANTUM MERUIT 'As much as he deserv.ed'. An action grounded on a promise, actual or implied that the defendant should pay to the plaintiff for his serv.ices as much as he should reasonably deserv.e. Originally, this described an inquiry by the equity courts into the value of a plaintiff's goods and serv.ices whenever fairness required that a contract between the parties be implied. The requirements for recov.ery were the rendering of goods or serv.ices by the plaintiff to the defendant, the acceptance and use of the goods or serv.ices by the defendant, the reasonable expectation of the plaintiff that he would be paid for the goods or serv.ices, and the refusal of the defendant to pay. A contract created by implication under the doctrine of *quantum meruit* is called an *implied contract* or a *quasi-contract*. *Quantum meruit* applies also to cases in which part performance under an express contract is given and accepted. *Ban Hong Joo Mines Ltd v. Chen & Yap Ltd. [1969] 2 MLJ 83 (Contract), Kui Ti Eng Ors. v. Singapore Fishery Ltd. [1955] 21 MLJ at Pg. 141; Ban Hong Joo Mines Ltd v. Chen & Yap Ltd. [1969] 2 MLJ 83 (Contract); Lim Su Sang v. Teck Guan Construction & Development Co. Ltd [1966] 2 MLJ 29 at Pg. 32; Yong Mok Hin v. United Malay States Sugar [1966] 2 MLJ 286 at Pg. 289; Liew Yu Fatt v. Teck Guan & Co. Ltd [1966] 1 MLJ 87 at Pg. 90; Yong Mok Hin v. United*

Malay States Suhar Industries Ltd [1967] 2 MLJ 9 Pg.14; Ho Ah Loke Abraham v. William Manson-Hing [1949] 15 MLJ 37 Pg.38

QUANTUM VALEBANT 'as much as they were worth'. Under Common Law, it is a remedy to compute reasonable damages when a contract has been breached—the implied promise of payment of a reasonable price for goods. In contract law, for requirements of consideration, reasonable worth for goods delivered. Usage: quantum meruit has replaced quantum valebant in consideration; in the case of contract remedy, *quantum valebant* is being used less, and could be considered to be obsolete.

QUARE CLAUSUM FREGIT 'why did he break (into) the closed area'. why did he v.iolate the enclosure? An early form of common law trespass for wrongful entry upon another's land. Wherefore he broke the close. In actions of trespass to real estate the defendant is charged with breaking the close of the plain-tiff. Formerly the original writ in such a case was a writ of trespass quare clausum fregit, now the charge of breaking the close is laid in the declaration. Goh Suat Neo (w) v. Roberts & Ors [1950] 16 MLJ at Pg. 289; (Land); Government of Malaysia & Anor v. Kong EE KI [1965] 1 MLJ 81 Pg. 83

QUAREITUR 'it is sought'. The question is raised. Used to declare that a question is being asked in the following verbiage.

QUASI 'as if, just as, almost as, sort of, approximating, so to speak; about, nearly, almost, like'. In the law, *quasi* is used before other words to suggest that those words are limited and qualified in some respect. the resulting phrase conv. eys the sense of approximate but inexact similarity. examples: a *quasi admission* is an admission which is implied from prior inconsistent statements made by a witness, including statements made extra-judicially. a *quasi-judicial* proceeding is one which has all the elements of a trial — submission of evidence, trying the facts, applying the law, etc., — but is conducted by an administrativ.e agency or officer and not by a court. a *quasi in rem* claim is one in which the plaintiff seeks to recov.er damages against a party who is unreachable for personal jurisdiction, by attaching some of his property. It marks the resemblance, and supposes a little difference between two objects.

QUASI CONTRACTUAL (QUASI CONTRACT) 'A legal agreement created by the courts between two parties who did not hav.e a prev.ious obligation to each other. A normal contract requires two parties to consent to mutually agreeable terms. a binding obligation that is imposed by the courts to av.oid injustice or unjust enrichment. An implied-in-law contract imposed by the courts to prev.ent injustice. A special form of contract that lacks mutual assent of the parties but which is imposed on the parties by the courts to av.oid injustice. A situation in which there is an obligation as if there was a contract, although the technical requirements of a contract hav.e not been fulfilled. *Liew Yu Fatt v. Teck Guan & Co. Ltd [1966] 1 MLJ 87 at Pg. 90*

QUASI EX CONTRACTUS 'from, out of to bring together, to unite'. A right or obligation growing out of a contract which is implied by the law in order to av.oid the unjust enrichment of one party at the expense of another. *Anthony Lucas v.S. The Malayan Cultures Co. Ltd. [1933] 2 MLJ 21 Pg. 22*

QUASI JUDICIAL '*the action taken and discretion exercised by public administrativ.e agencies or bodies that are obliged to inv.estigate or ascertain facts anddraw conclusions from them as the foundation for official action's. Lim Ko & Anor v. Board of Architects [1966] 2 MLJ 80 at Pg. 82*

QUASI as if; apparently but not really; a kind of. It also means As if; as it were analogous to; seemingly not really. This term is used in legal phraseology to indicate that one subject resembles another, with which it is compared, in certain characteristics, but that there are also intrinsic differences between them. The word 'quasi' marks the resemblance and supposes a little difference, between two objects.

QUASI-ADOPTEES *Official Administrator, As Administrator of The Estate Of Chua Swee Sim Neo, Decd v. State of Selangor & Ors [1939] 8 MLJ 175 at Pg. 176*

QUERENS a plaintiff; complainant; inquirer.

QUI FACIT PER ALIUM, FACIT PER SE ' "he who acts through another, acts himself". It is regarded as a fundamental premise of agency law. In Colonial Secur., Inc. v. Merrill Lynch, Pierce, Fenner & Smith, Inc., 461 F. Supp. 1159 (S.D.N.Y. 1978), it is stated that "the common law maxim qui facit per alium facit per se, he who acts through another acts himself operates to make the acts of an agent within the scope of his authority, in legal effect, the acts of his principal." Qui facit per alium facit per se is the authorized act of an agent and is equated to the principal's acts. A principal's tort liability is based not on an agency but on the relationship of master and serv.ant expressed in the maxim "respondent superior". Howev. er, both rules and maxims are founded upon the principle that a duty rests upon ev.ery man in managing his/ her own affairs, either by himself/herself or by his/her agents or serv.ants. But if another person gets injured as a result of the acts, the principal is liable for the damage. Karthiyayani & Anor v. Lee Leong Sin & Anor [1975] 1 MLJ 119 Pg.122, Dan Sin Wah v. Chan Hai Swee [1951] 17 MLJ at Pg. 193

QUI SAUVE LE VAUTOUR EST REPONSABLE DE SA GRIFFE

QUI SENTIT COMMODUM DEBET SENTIRE ET ONUS 'He who deriv. es a benefit ought also to bear a burden. *David v. Chettiappan [1967] 2 MLJ 207&211*

QUI TAM (abbreviation of QUI TAM PRO DOMINO REGE QUAM

PRO SE IPSO IN HAC PARTE SEQUITUR) - meaning 'who pursues in this action as much for the king as himself'. In a *qui tam* action, one who assists the prosecution of a case is entitled to a proportion of any fines or penalties assessed.

QUIA because.

QUIA TIMET 'to fear, dread'. Because he fears. A bill in equity submitted by anyone who feared that the threatened action of another would cause him or his property injury or damage. The relief, after a showing of imminent harm, was by injunction or restraint. According to Lord Coke, "there be six writs of law that may be maintained quia timet, before any molestation, distress, or impleading; as. 1. A man may hav.e his writ or mesne, before he be distrained. 2. A warrantia chartae, before he be impleaded. 3. A monstrav.erunt, before any distress or vexation. 4. An audita querela, before any execution sued. 5. A curia claudenda, before any default of inclosure. 6. A ne injuste vexes, before any distress or molestation. And those are called brev.ia anticipantia, writs of prevention. *Haji Ismail Bin Che Cik v. State Commisioner,Penang [1975] 1 MLJ 271 Pg. 272, The United Kingdom Tobacco (1929) Ltd. v.S. The Malayan Tobacco Distributors Ltd. [1933] 2 MLJ 1 Pg. 9; The Pahang Consolidated Co. Ltd. v. The State Of Pahang [1933] 2 MLJ 247 Pg. 248*

QUICQUID whoever, whatever, whatsoever, anything at all.

QUICQUID PLANTATUR SOLO SOLO CEDIT 'Whatever is affixed to the soil belongs to it'. In Roman law, the maxim was applied mostly to determine that trees and crops were sold with, and formed part of the land. According to the maxim, loose bricks are chattels or mov.able or personal property. Loose bricks do not form part of the land. Howev.er, if loose bricks are cemented together and used to erect a house, the bricks become part of the land and get conv.erted to real property. Chattels which gets conv.erted to real property by operation of the maxim are called fixtures. Quicquid Plantatur Solo, Solo Cedit is of great significance in tenancy laws. Any improv.ement made by a tenant, that gets conv.erted to real property, by operation of the maxim becomes part of landlord's property. The improv.ement cannot be reclaimed by the tenant at the end of the lease. *Mohamed Yusoof v. Murugappa Chettiar [1941] MLJ 202*

QUICQUID PLANTATUR SOLO, SOLO CEDIT whatever is affixed to the soil becomes part of the soil (and is therefore owned by the owner of the soil). From this maxim flows the law of fixtures, establishing whether or not ownership of an item remains in the person who brought it onto the land or runs with the ownership of the land. It also means whatever that is fixed to the land belongs to the soil. 'the English law as embodied in (this) maxim ... applied; that it was based on the presumption that annexation of the chattels to the land was intended to be permanent;' see Chua Sai Ngoh v Beh Ai Meng [1955]

MLJ 167. ' ... whether underground tanks are land within the definition of land: see The Shell Company of the Fed. of Malaya Ltd v Comm of the Fed Capital of Kuala Lumpur [1964] MLJ 302. - 'tank' may not be a 'building' within the definition contained in the Enactment, its attachment to the soil nevertheless makes it in law part of the land: quicquid plantatur solo, solo cedit ... the fact that the tanks retain identity as such below ground is entirely immaterial because oak trees, rubber trees and oil palms are no less part of the land although they are growing things and not earth ...' per Ong J. The general principle of the English law is embodied in the maxim of Gaius 'quicquid plantatur solo, solo cedit', although the rigour of that maxim has been mitigated in favour of trade fixtures and later in the case of agricultural fixtures. It is based on the presumption that annexation of the chattels to the land is intended to be permanent. As was pointed out by Sproule CJC, in Goh Chang Hin's 5 FMSLR 86 case, supra, 'if the nature, degree, and object of the annexation be such as to show that the intention was to annex the chattels to the land only temporarily, then the general rule will not apply' and His Lordship later went on to point out that by reason of the decision in the case of Wake v Hall (1882-1883), 8 App Cas 195 'proved custom, then, by itself can displace the presumption of intention of permanent [or at Page 169] annexation.' It is no doubt by reason of this exception in favour of 'proved custom' that the Courts in this country have exempted from the rigour of the rule Malay houses on stilts as in Kiah's (1953) MLJ 82 case, supra. Chua Sai Ngoh (f) v Beh Ai Meng [1955] MLJ 167 at 168 Per Thomson J, Gebrueder Buehler Ag. v Peter Chi Man Kwong & Ors [1987] 1 MLJ 356 at 358 Per Thean J ... the learned judge first considered the issue whether, for the purposes of the retention of title clause, the equipment had become so 'integrated' with the plant such that it was no longer 'identifiable', thus defeating the retention of title clause. His conclusion on this issue was that 'the equipment, though they formed a part of the entire processing plant, remained unaltered and are clearly identifiable'. This part of his judgment -- which is adverse to the respondents -- is not under appeal. The learned judge then went on to consider -- and it is his conclusion on this issue which is under appeal -- whether (as counsel for the respondents had argued before him) the equipment, when installed in the factory, had been so 'permanently fixed to the land or the building and become part of the land: quicquid plantatur solo, solo cedit (whatever is affixed to the soil belongs to the soil)' and that 'the equipment had ceased to be chattels and passed with the land to the chargee, the bank'. On this issue, he held that the equipment had become so affixed and that the appellants had lost their title to it.

QUID PRO QUO 'this for that'. An equal exchange of goods or services, or of money (or other consideration of equal value) for some goods or services.

QUO ANIMO 'the spiritual; the soul; the heart'. By what intention or motive? What did he intend to do? What motiv. ated him? An inquiry into the defendant's motives. (with what intention). A phrase often used in criminal trials. Where there is question of certain ov.ert acts having been committed by the accused and the only question is with what intention they were done. *Reshty v. Syed Ahmed Al-Junied & Ors [1966] 2 MLJ 121 at Pg. 123, Reshty v. Syed Ahmed Al-Junied & ors [1966] 2 MLJ 121 at Pg. 123; Then Thaw En & Anor v. Wong Juat Eng [1965] 2 MLJ 103 Pg. 105; Ho Wee Cheong v. Ho Poi Yuen [1967] 2 MLJ 150 Pg.152*

QUO ANTE The condition or state, which existed before the present condition. On an application by one party to rescind a contract, the court may order rescission and restore the parties to the *status quo ante*, i.e., the condition which existed for each of them before the contract was executed *Menaka v. Ng Siew San [1973] 1MLJ 50 Pg.53*

QUO denotes the end or terminal point.

QUO WARRANTO'by what right or authority'. At common law, a writ emanating from the right of the King to inquire into the right of an official to perform an act or of an indiv.idual to exercise a license or franchise. A writ which enabled a court to determine whether an official who presumed to exercise some authority was entitled to do so under the law. The writ was intended to prev.ent the unlawful and unauthorized usurpation of power or authority by public officers. In the law of corporations, *quo warranto* proceedings test whether a corporation was properly formed or has a v.alid existence, and also whether it has a power it claims for itself. The state in which a corporation doing business may bring a *quo warranto action* to attack the corporate status of the business. Defacto corporations and corporations by estoppel are subject to attack by the state in these proceedings, as are corporations which exceed their powers. *Munusamy v. Subramaniam & Ors. [1969] 2 MLJ 108, Munusamy v. Subramaniam & Ors. [1969] 2 MLJ 108*

QUOAD HOC 'as to this'. Used to mean "with respect to" some named thing, such as when stating what the law is in regards to that named thing.

QUOD EST NECESSARIUM EST LICITUM 'What is necessary is lawful.

QUOD the better; the faster; and, but, now, since, as far as, to the extent that; whereas, the point that, the fact that.

QUOD PRINCIPI PLACUIT,

QUONDAM *Lim Ker v. Chew Seok Tee [1967] 2 MLJ 253 Pg.254*

QUORUM a majority of the entire body; 'Quorum' in Latin means 'of which or whom.' The specified minimum number of members whose presence is necessary to validate the transactions of a meeting of members of a body. The quorum is composed by those actually present at a time and place when all should and might be present as opposed to an ad hoc meeting. This word was anciently used in commission of justices of the peace. Thus a commission issued to certain persons, authorising them to hold court, & c of whom (quorum) such and such particular person are always to be one. The persons so specified are called justices of the quorum.The term quorum is al-so used for a sufficient number to proceed to business. The number of the members of an organised body of persons (as a legislative body or board of directions) that when duly assembled is legally competent to transact business in the absence of other members [s 17(2), Industrial Finance Corporation Act and Art 100(3), Const]. Quorum denotes the minimum number of members of any body of persons whose presence is necessary in order to enable that body to transact its business validly, so that its acts may be lawful'. Quorum denotes minimum number of member of any body of persons whose presence is necessary to enable that body to transact its business validly, so that its act may be lawful. It is generally left to committees themselves to fix the quorum for their meetings. The minimum number of directors constituting a quorum would be stipulated in the articles. Logically the minimum number would be two directors. A 'one man' directors' meeting is invalid. *United In-vestment & Finance Ltd v Tee Chin Yong Ors [1967] 1 MLJ 31*. Lack of quorum is a procedural irregularity, *Sum Hong Kum v Li Pin Furniture Industries Pte Ltd [1996] 2 SLR 488*. In *Tan Guan Eng v BH Low Holdings Sdn Bhd & Ors & Anor [1992] MLJ 105*, Wan Adnan J held that a meeting is not invalid if a member leaves the meeting and renders the quorum in ad-equate. In Re Salvage Engineers Limited [1962] MLJ 438 it was held that a meeting where the only per-son present holds a proxy from another member of the company is invalid. In the appeal, the main issue for determination concerned the interpretation of the word 'quorum' in the statutory provisions of the Land Titles (Strata) Act (Cap 158) (the Act). As a postscript, I would add that since my decision the Act has been amended with regard to the provi-sion relating to 'quorum'. It is now provided in para 3 of the Third Schedule to the 1988 Edition of the Act as follows: (1) No business shall be transacted at any general meeting of a management corporation un-less a quorum of members is present. (2) For the purposes of this paragraph, the number of subsidiary proprietors present at the meeting either in person or by proxy who own not less than one half of share values for all the lots shown on the strata title plan shall form a quorum. *Lee Tat Property Management Pte Ltd v Management Corp Strata Title No 360 [1991] 1 MLJ 390 at 392 Per Sinnathuray J*. On the first question, the argument of the plaintiffs is that you cannot have a meeting with only one per-son. The plaintiffs' counsel cited to me, inter alia, the following: (i) Shackleton on The Law & Practice of Meetings (8th Ed) at 44: 'In general, two persons is the minimum number for a meeting to be properly constituted, since the term 'meeting' prima facie means a coming together of more than one person.'(ii) Walter Woon on Company Law at 138:

'The general rule is that there must be at least two members personally present to constitute a meeting', where the author relies on Sharp v Dawes, 1 Re Salvage Engineers Ltd 2 and United Investment & Finance Ltd v Tee Chin Yong & Ors 3 in support of that statement. (iii) Pennington's Company Law (5th Ed) at 709: '... one person alone cannot constitute a meeting.'To my mind, there is no doubt that as a general rule you need at least two persons to constitute a meeting. The leading case on this point appears to be Sharp v Dawes [1876] 2 QB 26. In that case only one shareholder was present at a general meeting of a mining company, although the secretary was also in attendance. That shareholder took the chair and made a number of decisions, including a resolution to make a call. The secretary sought to enforce the call. The Court of Appeal held that as only one person was present at the meeting, he could not constitute a meeting and the resolution making the call was therefore invalid. Lord Coleridge CJ said (at 29 of the report) that the word 'meeting' prima facie meant coming together of more than one person. But he also went on to say that 'it is, of course, possible to show that the word 'meeting' has a meaning different from the ordinary meaning, but there is nothing here to show this to be the case.' Shackleton also recognises (at 45) that there may be circumstances where the general rule will not apply, such as 'where one person holds all of a class of shares, where one creditor attends a creditors' meeting in an insolvency, where there is a committee of one, or where the articles of a company provide for a quorum of one director at the board meetings...'

R

RAISON D 'ETRE.'reason for existence'. It is the main or primary purpose of a thing or person. *Chu Chee Peng v. Public Prosecutor [1973] 2 MLJ 35 Pg.36; Navaradnam v. Suppiah Chettiar [1973] 1MLJ 173 Pg.175, Mak Sik Kwong v. Minister Of Home Affairs,Malaysia [1975] 2 MLJ168 Pg. 171*

RATIO DECIDENDI 'the reason for the decision'. ratio decidendi refers to the legal, moral, political and social principles on which a court's decision rests. it is the rationale for reaching the decision of a case. it is binding on lower courts through the principle of stare decisis. ratio decidendi is a helpful tool for a lawyer. ratio is a ruling on a point of law and the decision on a point of law depends on facts of a case. culling out ratio from a judgment is difficult. a thorough reading of an entire judgment is required to identify a ratio. Ratio decidendi can be determined or identified in the following ways: by distinguishing material facts from unimportant facts. by discov.ering the precedents applied to identify the court's approach. by restricting analysis to the majority opinions. by reading out subsequent decisions and considering it at several levels. *Public Prosecutor v. Ong Chang Sow [1954] 20 MLJ at Pg. 82; Official Administrator, K.L. v. China insurance co. Ltd [1955] 21 MLJ at Pg.139; Seet Soon Guan V. Public Prosecutor [1955] 21 MLJ at Pg.225;*

Lim Su Sang v. Teck Guan Construction & Development Co. Ltd [1966] 2 MLJ 29 at Pg. 31; Re Tan Teng Trading Etc v. Re Chop Hoe Seng [1932] 1 MLJ 159 Pg.161, Cheam See Loo Brothers v. Kong Yoon Choy & Anor [1973] 2 MLJ 13 Pg.14; Lee Sum Soh v. Low Ngah [1973] 1 MLJ 97 Pg.99; Muthuraku v. Kuala Lumpur Municipality Workers Trade Union [1973] 1MLJ 206 Pg.207; Public Prosecutor v. Khoo Kay Jin [1973] 1 MLJ 259 Pg.260

RATIO SCRIPTA'written reason'. The popular opinion of Roman law, held by those in the mediev.al period.

RATIONAE SOLI 'by reason of the soil'. certain rights may arise by virtue of ownership of the soil upon which wild animals are found.

REBUS SIC STANTIBUS 'things thus standing'. A qualification in a treaty or contract, that allows for nullification in the ev.ent fundamental circumstances change.

RECLAMARE reclamation, restoration to a useful condition; as, the reclamation of barren, unproductive land.

RECTITUDO right or justice.

REDDENDO rendering; the formal word by which in old conveyancing a rent was reserved to the grantor.

REDDENDO   SINGULA SINGULIS'referring solely to the last'. The canon of construction that in a list of items containing a qualifying phrase at the end, the qualifier refers only to the last item in the list.

REDUCTIO AD ABSURDUM 'A reduction to an absurdity'. Or 'to draw back, lead back'. To reason or argue in such a way that an absurd conclusion is inev.itable. To carry something to an absurd extreme. To disprov.e a theory or proposition by showing that if followed logically it will lead to an absurd result. A phrase used in logical or mathematical reasoning, when the adv.ersary is reduced to submission by prov.ing the ahsurdity of his position. *R. Sambasivam v. Public Services Commosion & Anor. [1970] 1 MLJ 61, at 62*

REPATRIARE to return to the country of origin; as, to repatriate refugees, 'to go back to one's country'.

RERBATIM ET LITERATEM *Marian Rebello & P.A. Peries v. Harbans Singh [1933] 2 MLJ 279*

RES COMMUNIS 'common to all'. Property constructs like airspace and water rights are said to be res communis - that is, a thing common to all, and that could not be the subject of ownership. With airspace, the difficulty has been to identify where the fee simple holder's rights to the heav.ens end. Water is a bit more defined — it is common until captured.

RES DERELICTA 'to abandon, forsesake, leav.e behind'. Any property, which has been abandoned by its owner. *Hans L.*

Simon v. Geoffrey John Taylor & Ors [1975] 1 MLJ 236 Pg. 236

RES GESTAE 'to carry, bear, perform'. All those matters, facts, statements, acts and ev.ents which tend to explain or clarify a point or fact at issue in a litigation. those matters which are inherent in or essential to an occurrence or ev.ent. a *res gestae* witness is a witness who has experienced an ev.ent or act at issue by his own senses and can help the factfinder to find the truth by his testimony. *res gestae* refers to any spontaneousdeclaration or statement made at the same time as, or immediately after, an ev.ent, by a v.ictim or a witness, under circumstances which support truth and reliability; these statements, which are now generally referred to as *spontaneous declarations*, are admissible into evidence as an exception to the hearsay rule. things done. either the ev.ents at issue or other things, such as utterances, that are contemporaneous with the res gestae; spontaneous statements or exclamations made by the participants, perpetrators, v.ictims, or onlookers at or immediately following the ev.ent, be it criminal or the subject of litigation. as present-sense impressions, they are excluded from the hearsay rule. *Sheikh Hassan Bin Sheikh Ibrahim v. Public Prosecutor [1940] 9 MLJ 69 at Pg.71; Pakala Narayana Swami v. King-Emperor [1939] 8 MLJ 48 at Pg.50; Tan Geok Kwang v. Public Prosecutor [1949] 15 MLJ 203 Pg.203*

RES INTEGRA 'to complete, make whole'. Anything new and novel. In legal writing, the phrase refers to a nov.el issue, an undecided question, a case of first impression. An affair not broached or meddled with; one on which no action had been taken, or deliberation had. *East Asiatic Co. Ltd v. Othman [1966] 2 MLJ 38 at Pg. 39, In Re Zainab Binte Mat Diah, Deed (1951) 17 MLJ at Pg. 145; East Asiatic Co. Ltd v. Othman [1966] 2 MLJ 38 at Pg. 39; Ch'ng Joo Tuan Neoh & Anor v.S. Khoo Tek & Other [1932] 1 MLJ 141 Pg.148; The United Kingdom Tobacco (1929) Ltd. v.S. The Malayan Tobacco Distributors Ltd. [1933] 2 MLJ 1 Pg. 5*

RES INTER ALIOS ACTA 'between, among, to set in motion, driv.e'. Anything inv.olv.ing another place, person or thing than the relev.ant one; not related or relev.ant; concerning other matters. In the law of evidence, the doctrine which makes irrelev.ant and therefore inadmissible, evidence relating to a person extraneous to the action, or to a place other than the place at issue, or to a time not relev.ant to the acts inv.olv.ed in the litigation. This is a technical phrase which signifies acts of others, or transactions between others. Neither the declarations nor any other acts of those who are mere stran-gers, or, as it is usually termed, any res inter alios ada, are admissible in evidence against any one when the party against whom such acts are offered in evidence, was priv.y to the act, the objection ceases; it is no longer res inter alios. *Malayan Banking Ltd. v. Raffles Hotel Ltd [1966] 1 MLJ 206 at Pg. 208*

RES IPSA LOQUITUR 'the thing itself speaks'. Is a doctrine that states that the elements of duty of care and breach can sometimes be inferred from the v.ery nature of an accident or other outcome, ev.en without direct evidence of how any defendant behaved. Although modern formulations differ by jurisdiction, the common law originally stated that the accident must satisfy the necessary conditions of negligence. It is a doctrine of law that one is presumed to be negligent if he/she/it had exclusiv.e control of whatev.er caused the injury ev.en though there is no specific evidence of an act of negligence, and the accident would not hav.e happened without negligence. The traditional elements needed to prov.e negligence through the doctrine of res ipsa loquitur include; The harm would not ordinarily hav.e occurred without someone's negligence, The instrumentality of the harm was under the exclusiv.e control of the defendant at the time of the likely negligent act, The plaintiff did not contribute to the harm by his own negligence. There has been some change in the modern application of the abov.e elements. The "exclusiv.e control" element has been softened in modern cases to a less strict standard, where the plaintiff must prove that other responsible causes, including the conduct of the plaintiff and third persons, are sufficiently eliminated by the evidence. The last element has also softened to a more comparativ.e standard, so that if plaintiff was only 5% negligent in contributing to the accident, the minimal contributory negligence of the plaintiff won't bar a recovery. *Hiap Lee (Cheog Leong & Sons) Brickmakers Ltd. v. Weng Lok Mining Co. Ltd. [1974] 2 MLJ 1 Pg. 2, Tan Kia*

Chee & Ors. v. Chan Kian Wah & Anor. [1970] 1 MLJ 205, Pg. 207; Elizabeth Choo v. Government of Malaysia & Anor.[1970] 2 MLJ 171, at Pg.172; M.A Clyde v. Wong Ah Mei & Anor. [1970] 2 MLJ 183, at 183, 185, 188, 189, 190; Lim Kim Chai & Anor. v. Foo See Fatt; Gan Chin Baw & Anor. v. Foo See Fatt [1970] 2 MLJ 207, at Pg. 207; K.M.A Abdul Rahim & Anor v. Owners Of "Lexa Maersk" & Ors [1973] 2 MLJ 121 Pg.123 Guan Soon Tin Mining Co. v. Ampang Estate Ltd [1973] 1 MLJ 25 Pg.26; Palaniayee & Anor v. Toh Whye Teck Realty Ltd & Anor [1973] 1 MLJ 34 Pg.34

RES JUDICATA 'to judge, decide'. the thing has been decided; the matter has been adjudged. A doctrine which dictates that matters litigated between the parties in one action or proceeding may not be litigated again between the same parties; i.e., once a final judgment on the merits has been rendered by a court of competent jurisdiction, it is conclusiv.e as to the parties inv.olv. ed and the matters litigated. A thing decided. A doctrine whereby the court's decision is binding upon the parties in any and all subsequent litigation concerning the same case. In effect, it bars the litigants from seeking to take the same case to another court in hopes of a different outcome, or of raising new issues that were not raised at the first trial. *Chu Chee Peng V. Public Prosecutor [1973] 2 MLJ 35 Pg.35; Government of Malaysia v. Dato Chong Kok Lim [1973] 2 MLJ 74 Pg.75; Tio Chee Hing v. Tractors Malaysia Bhd [1973] 1 MLJ 66 Pg.67, Chung Guat Hooi (m.w) v. G.H.Goh*

[1954] 20 MLJ at Pg. 132,133,134; Kesarmal & Anor v. Valliappa Chettiar & Anor [1954] 20 MLJ at Pg. 180; Chen Chi Wei v. Khoh Keng Chong. [1951] 17 MLJ at Pg.204, 206; Kok Hong Leong Kongsi & 5 Others v. Seow Kah Cheng & Another [1950] 16 MLJ at Pg.88; In Re Xy & Co. [1966] 2 MLJ 11 at Pg. 13,15; District Council Central, Province Wellesley v. Yegappan [1966] 2 MLJ 177 at Pg. 181; PP v. Lee Siew Ngock [1966] 2 MLJ 225 at Pg. 225, 228; Andavan v. Thong Nyik Lin [1966] 1MLJ 57 at Pg. 57; Public Prosecutor v. Lee Siew Ngock [1966] 1 MLJ 225 at Pg. 229

RES JUDICATA PRO VERITATE ACCIPITUR 'a thing adjudged must be taken for truth' **or** a matter which has been tried and adjudicated should be accepted as true. *Sambasivam v. The Public Prosecuter, Federation of Malaya [1950] 16 MLJ at Pg.151; Syed Ismail v. Public Prosecutor [1967] 2 MLJ 123 Pg.127, Yau Tin Kwong v. Public Prosecutor [1970] 1 MLJ 159, at Pg. 162*

RES 'thing, matter, issue, affair'.

RES a thing; a matter; the entire property of an individual, an issue or dispute between parties to litigation; the subject matter of a real contract.

RES NULLIUS 'A thing which has no owner'. A thing which has been abandoned by its owner is as much res nullius as if it had never belonged to any one. The first possessor of such a thing becomes the owner, res nullius fit primi occupantis. *Hans L. Simon v. Geoffrey*

John Taylor & Ors [1975] 1 MLJ 236
Pg.239

RES PUBLICA CHRISTIANA 'Christian public affair'. All things of concern to the worldwide body of Christianity

RES PUBLICA 'public affair' or all things subject to concern by the citizenry. This is the root of the word republic.

RESPONDEAT SUPERIOR 'to match, agree with, answer, reply,standing abov.e'. Let the one in higher position or authority reply; let the master respond. A doctrine of agency law, which assigns responsibility and liability to the employer or principal for the acts of her employee or agent, including negligence, prov.ided the employee or agent is acting within the scope of his employment or agency. Because the doctrine is based on agency, the employer is not liable when the employee's act is beyond the scope of his employment. Let the superior be held responsible.) In pursuance of this maxim, a principal is liable in damages for the act of his agent, and a master for the act of his serv.ant: prov.ided that in each case the act of the inferior, whether specifically authorised or not, was within the scope of the duties imposed by the superior. *Public Prosecutor v. Chuan Keat Chan Ltd [1973] 1 MLJ 249 Pg.250, Swamy v. Matthews & Anor [1967] 1 MLJ 142*

RESTITUTIO IN INTEGRUM 'to replace, restore, to complete, make whole'. Restoration of a party to his condition or position before the injury or wrong complained of. The principle that a court ordering rescission of a contract should restore the parties as closely as possible to their state or condition before the contract was executed. The restoration of a thing to its original state or in its entirety. In Admiralty Law, the doctrine which prov.ides for full and complete compension to the owner of a v.essel after a loss or damage, to enable him to restore the v.essel to its original condition. *Chng Hen Tiu & Anor v. Sime Darby Holdings Ltd [1978] 2 MLJ 83 Pg.83, Senanayake v. Annie Yeo [1965] 2 MLJ 241 Pg. 241, 244, 245, 246, 247, v. Aynar Suppiah & Sons v. K.M.A. Abdul Rahim & Anor [1974] 2 MLJ 183 Pg.188*

REX the king regarded as the party prosecuting in a criminal actions; as in the form of entitling such actions.

RIPA the bank of a river; 'rivers'.

S

SACRAMENTUM oath, sacraments, sacred rites.

SALLE DE PAS PERDUS *Opening of the New Supreme Court Building; [1939] 8 MLJ xlii-xliv at Pg. xlii*

SALUS POPULI SUPREMA LEX 'The health of the people should be the supreme law'. Welfare of the people shall be the supreme law. The maxim tends to imply the information that law exists to serv.e common good. In the U.S., public health is considered as a common good and therefore, laws are framed keeping public health a central issue. *Government of Malaysia v. Mahan Singh [1975] 2 MLJ 155 Pg.165*

SCANDALUM MAGNATUM 'scandal of the magnates'. Defamation against a peer in British law. Now repealed as a specific offense.

SCIENTER 'knowingly'. Used when offenses or torts were committed with the full awareness of the one so committing.

SCIRE FACIAS 'let them know'. It is a writ directing local officials to officially inform a party of official proceedings concerning them.

SCIRE FECI 'I have made known'. The official response of the official serving a writ of scire facias, informing the court that the writ has been properly delivered.

SE DEFENDENDO 'self-defense'. The act of defending one's own person or property, or the well-being or property of another.

SECUS otherwise; to the contrary, to the contrary effect.

SEMBLE 'it appears'. This term is used in discussing a court judgment where there is some uncertainty about what the court intended. It is commonly used before the statement of a point of law which has not been directlysettled; but about which the court hav.e expressed an opinion, and intimated what it is. *Chew Cheng Swee v. Chan Chye Neo [1932] 1 MLJ 5 Pg. 5; Michi (F) and Anoyu (F) v. Rex [1934] 3 MLJ 11 at Pg. 11*

SEMPER INTENDIT QUOD CONVENIT RATIONI Re Ang Teck Say [1934] 3 MLJ 25 at Pg. 26

SEQUELAE 'a pathological condition resulting from a disease'. injury, or other trauma. It can also be secondary consequence or result. For example, paralysis is one of the sequela of poliomyelitis. The following is an example of a case law defining Sequela: The word "sequela" is to be treated as a term of art that carries a "precise and special meaning." The Court defined the term as referring to "somatic conditions or ev.ents recognizable as the pathological sequence or result of an existing disease or disorder or as an independent accompaniment of such a disease or disorder." *J.K.R. Leonard v. Karumugam [1934] 3 MLJ 93 at Pg. 94; Leong Luen Kiew & Anor v. The New Zealand Insurance Co. Ltd. [1939] 8 MLJ 136 at Pg.139*

SERIATIM 'to join together, place in a row'. In regular order, successiv.ely, one by one, separately, as in "the court will consider the parties' motions *seriatim.*" In sequence. Successiv.ely; in successiv.e order, one by one; in due order; sequentially, one at a time. *Muniandy & Ors V. Public Prosecutor [1966] 1 MLJ 257 at Pg. 258, Ramalingam Naykav. Adiar V. Ganapathy Pillay [1941] MLJ 96; Braga V. Braga [1949] 15 MLJ 162, The Quality Of Judgment [1970] 2 MLJ xlv., at xlix*

SERIATIM one by one; in succession; one after the other.

SIC UTERE TUO UT ALIENUM NON LAEDAS 'use your property in such a fashion so as to not disturb others'. "The maxim sic utere tuo ut alienum non laedas does not mean that one must never use his own property in such a way as to do any injury to his neighbor. It means only that one must use his property so as not to injure the lawful rights of another. Under this maxim, it is well settled that a property owner may put his own property to any reasonable and lawful use, so long as he does not thereby depriv.e the adjoining landowner of any right of enjoyment of his property which is recognized and protected by law, and so long as his use is not such a one as the law will pronounce a nuisance. *Lim Kar Bee V. Abdul Latif Bin Ismail [1978] 1 MLJ 109 Pg. 111*

SIGNUM a seal is placed on a document to render its contents inaccessible and to protect against forgery. It also means a seal, a sign, a mark, a species of proof; a sign; a mark; a seal. The seal of an instrument.

SILENTIO to keep silent, to silence.

SIMPLICITER 'simply, without artfulness'. In a simple way. Without fanfare. Directly, summarily, immediately. Simply, without ceremony; in a summary manner. *Ey Yee Hua v. Public Prosecutor [1969] 2 MLJ; Public Prosecutor V. Balakrishnan [1967] 1 MLJ 181 —Pg.182, Sebastian v. Public prosecutor [1970] 2 MLJ 76, at 78*

SIMPLICITER of its owns force; without any addition.

SINE DAMNO 'damage, injury, penalty'. Without any injury or damage. *Shaik Sahib Bin Omar, Etc v. The Municipal Commissioners [1932] 1 MLJ 53 Pg. 55*

SINE DIE 'Without a day'. An assembly is adjourned sine die when no time is named for its reassembling for the consideration of the business for which it originally met. Without a day, without time; without setting a new date. A court or legislativ.e body adjourns *sine die* when it adjourns without appointing a day on which to sit or assemble again. *Comptroller Of Income Tax V. B.S Pte Ltd [1978] 2 MLJ 182 Pg. 183, In Re*

XY & Co. [1966] 2 MLJ 11 at Pg.12,
Sim Hong Boon v. Lois Joan Sim [1973]
1 MLJ 1 Pg.2

SINE QUA NON indispensable condition. An indispensable requisite. The word (from the Latin sine, without, cura, care) is popularly applied to any office carrying a revenue or salary to which no employment or duties are annexed. *Lam Shes Tong & Ors v Lam Kee Ying Sdn. Bhd [1973] 1 MLJ 203 at 206 Per Ong CJ*

SINE QUA NON 'Without which, not'. Anything indispensable, and without which another cannot exist. The essential thing upon, which another depends for its existence. *Ali Anberan v. Tunku Abdullah [1970] 2 MLJ 15, at 17; Liquidateor, Paramount Ltd. v. Comptroller-General of Inland Revenue [1970] 2 MLJ 193, at 193; Lam Shes Tong & Ors v. Lam Kee Ying Sdn Bhd [1973] 1 MLJ 203 Pg.206, Ponnodurai v. Jayatileka [1965] 1 MLJ 131 Pg. 132*

SINE QUA RES IPSA HABERI NON DEBET *Yong Joo Lin & Ors v. Fung Pol Fong [1941] MLJ 56*

SITUS 'the place'. Used to refer to laws specific to the location where specific property exists, or where an offense or tort was committed.

***SOI-DISANT** 'calling oneself, thus; self-styled. Chua Sin Ghee & Ors v. Chua Tian Choon & Ors [1933] 2 MLJ 259 Pg. 259*

SOLATIUM (Valuation of Land Act, 1960 (Vic) s 26, as amended by the Valuation of Land (Appeals) Act, 1965 (Vic). 'Solatium' is an expression apt to describe an award of some amount to cover inconvenience and in a proper case, distress caused by compulsory taking. It is quite inapt to describe an amount awarded for provable loss to which the claimant is entitled per Barber J in March v City of Frankston (1969) VR 350. By analogy it was said that damages for pain and suffering being excluded by the law of Malta, with was a substantive right which was for the lex loci delicti and damages on this account could not be awarded by the court of the forum. It is true that in Scots law the Latin term solatium is used without dis-tinction both to indicate a claim for compensation for the grief and suffering sustained by the death of a near relative and also for the pain and suffering occasioned to an injured party. But in my view the term solatium may connote different rights. Solatium properly so called denotes a separate right of action given only to near relative whereas solatium for pain and suffering of an injured party--a term not known apparently to English law--connotes an element in the ascertainment of damages for the injuries suffered by a plaintiff. These consist of various elements, solatium for the pain and suffering, out-of-pocket expenses, actual loss of wages and future problematical patrimonial loss due to loss of earning capacity. These elements comprise the head of damages due to an injured person by English law. It would not be correct, in my view, to talk of compensation for pain and suffering as a head of damage apart from patrimonial loss. It is merely an element in the quantification of the total compensation.

SOLUTA *In Re Abraham Penhas, Deceased [1950] 16 MLJ at Pg.106;*

SOLUTIO INDEBITI 'solution for the undue'. It is an obligation arising from undue payment, obliging the debtor to return the undue payment.

SOLUTUS 'loosed; freed from confinement; set at liberty. In Re Abraham Penhas, Deceased (1950) 16 MLJ at Pg.106

SPECIALIA GENERALIBUS NON ABROGATION *K.A.R.S.T. Arunasalam Chettiar v. S. Abdul Raman Bin Suleiman & Anor. [1933] 2 MLJ 48 Pg. 51*

SPECIFICATIO making a new thing out of other materials. In Roman law, the word denoted the process by which own-ership is acquired of property made from the materials of another.

SPOLIUM a thing violently or unlawfully taken from another.

STARE DECISIS ET NON QUIETA MOVERE to stand by decided cases; to uphold precedents; to maintain former adjudications. To stand by things decided;to abide by precedents where the same points come again in litigation. It is a general maxim that when a point of law has been settled by deci-sion, it forms a precedent which is not afterwards to be departed from. The Rule as stated is 'to abide by former precedents (stare decisis), where the same points come again in litigation as well to keep the scale of justice even and steady and not liable to waver with every new judge's opinion, as also because the law in that case being solemnly declared and determined, what before was uncertain and perhaps indifferent, is now become a permanent rule, which it is not in the breast of any subsequent judge to alter or swerve from according to his private sentiments; he being sworn to determine not according to his own private judgment, but according to the known; laws and customs of the land, not delegated to pronounce a new law, but to maintain and expound the old one jusdicere et non jus dare.The doctrine under which a court is bound to follow previous decisions, unless they are inconsistent with a higher court's decision or wrong in law. Stare decisis operates to secure certainty in the law. *Re Golden Palace Masical Hall Sdn. Bhd [1988] 2 MLJ 634, In Yeop Kia Heng v Pendakya Raya (1992) 1 MLJ 327, Mah Kah Yew v Public Prosecutor [1971] 1 MLJ 1 at 2 Per Wee Chong Jin CJ PARALLEL CITATION: [1969-1971] SLR 441, Lee Lee Cheng v Seow Peng Kwang [1960] MLJ 1 CA, Khoo Hean Kee v Chop Wong Soon Co [1964] MLJ 19 at 19, Lew Voon Kong & Anor v Mustaffa bin Kamis [1978] 1 MLJ 217 at 218 Per Chang Min Tat FJ, Periasamy s/o Sinnappan v Public Prosecutor [1996] 2 MLJ 557 at 582 Per Gopal Sri Ram JCA, Dalip Bhagwan Singh v Public Prosecutor [1998] 1 MLJ 1 at 12 Per Peh Swee Chin*

FCJ, *Chiu Wing Wa & Ors v Ong Beng Cheng [1994] 1 MLJ 89 at 96, Mohd Azmi SCJ, Paari a/l Perumal v Abdul Majid Hj Nazardin & Ors [2000] 6 MLJ 602 at 613 Per Faiza Tamby Chik J, Mah Kah Yew v Public Prosecutor [1971] 1 MLJ 1 at 2 Per Wee Choong Jin CJ PARALLEL CITATION: [1969-1971] SLR 441*

STARE DECISIS 'to stand, to cut short; to settle or arrange'. To stand by that, which was decided. One of the fundamental principles of British and American jurisprudence, *stare decisis* stands for the rule that once an issue is decided or settled by a court of appellate jurisdiction which has considered all the elements of that issue, that decision should be followed by all courts of equal or lower jurisdiction in subsequent cases, whether or not they inv.olv.e the same parties. The doctrine prov.ides for stability and consistency in the administration of justice. It is a rule which encourages adherence to judicial precedent. The rule applies only within the limits of one state and does not bind the courts of another state. To abide or adhere to decided cases. It is a general maxim that when a point has been settled by decision, it forms a precedent which is not afterwards to be departed from. The doctrine of stare decisis is not always to be relied upon, for the courts find it necessary to ov.errule cases which hav.e been hastily decided, or contrary to principle. Many hundreds of such ov.erruled cases may be found in the American and English books of reports. *Lew v.Oon Kong & Anor v. Mustaffa Bin Kamis [1978] 1 MLJ 217 Pg. 218*

STATUS QUO ANTE 'the condition or state which existed before the present condition. On an application by one party to rescind a contract, the court may order rescission and restore the parties to the *status quo ante*, i.e., the condition which existed for each of them before the contract was executed'. The situation as it existed before. As things were before whatev.er happened or is being discussed took place. For example, status quo ante bellum is the situation as it existed before the war. *Ahmad Bin Udon & Anor v. Ng Aik Chong [1970] 1MLJ 82, at Pg. 84; Ng Siew San v. Menaka [1973] 2 MLJ 154 Pg.157*

STATUS QUO 'The situation as it currently exists'. It is the existing condition or state of affairs. The posture or position which the parties are occupying or hav.e just occupied. The condition of the parties before any action is taken to change that condition; the existing condition can be preserv.ed by the court through a restraining order or temporary injunction. *Federal Transport Service Co Ltd & Ors v. Abdul Malik & Ors [1973] 1 MLJ 216 Pg.218; Lim Siew Leong & Anor v. Vallipuram [1973] 1 MLJ 241 Pg. 244, Hong Kong Vegetable Oil Company Ltd v. Malin Sirinaga Wicker & Ors [1978] 2 MLJ 13 Pg. 15; Chip Chong Sawmill Co. Sdn Bhd v. Chai Khiun Fui [1978] 2 MLJ 24 Pg. 26; Tengku Haji Jaafar & Anor v. Government of Pahang [1978] 2 MLJ 105 Pg.106; Sim Siok Eng v. Government of Malaysia [1978] 1 MLJ 15 Pg.23; Mohamed Zainuddin Bin Puteh v. Yap Chee Seng [1978] 1 MLJ*

40 Pg. 40, *Murugappa Chettiar v. S. Seenivasagam [1940] 9 MLJ 217 at Pg.235; John Puddicombe Wilkins & 2 Others v. John Patrick Kenelm Wilkins & Another [1951] 17 MLJ at Pg. 80; Hock Yew Co. v. Fraser & Neave (M) Ltd. & Ors. [1965] 2 MLJ 254 Pg. 251*

STRATUM 'a covering, from neuter past participle of sternere, to spread'. In property law, condominiums has said to occupy stratum many stories about the ground.2) Stratum can also be a societial lev.el made up of indiv.iduals with similar status of social, cultural or economic nature. 3) Stratum can refer to classification in an organized system along the lines of layers, lev.els, div.isions, or similar grouping.

STRATUM a layer, especially one of several superimposed one on another. A part of land consisting of a space or layer below, on or above the surface of the land or partly below and partly above the surface of the land, whether some of the dimensions of the space or layer are unlimited or whether all the dimensions are limited, but refers only to a stratum rateable or taxable under any Act.

STRICTO SENSU 'in the restricted sense'. *District Council Central, Province Wellesley V. Yegappan [1966] 2 MLJ 177 at Pg. 181, Kesatuan Pekerja2 Kenderaan Sri Jaya v. Industrial Court [1969] 2 MLJ Pg.28*

SUA SPONTE 'of its own accord'. Some action taken by the court or another official body, without the prompting of another party.

SUB JUDICE 'to judge'. Under authority of a court; before a court or judge for consideration. Under a judge. A case that is before the bar for determination, rather than one being settled out of court. *Fan Yew Teng V. Setia Usaha, Dewan Rakyat & Ors [1975] 2 MLJ 40 Pg. 42, RM. P RM. P. v. Palaniappan v. NPI STM V. Ramananathan [1977] 2 MLJ 34 Pg. 35 T.O. Thomas v. Asia Fishing Industry Pte Ltd [1977] 1 MLJ 151 Pg.152*

SUB JUDICE 'under the judge'. Refers to a matter currently being considered by the court.

SUB MODO 'subject to modification'. Term in contract law that allows limited modifications to a contract after the original form has been agreed to by all parties.

SUB NOMINE 'under the name'. Abbreviated sub nom.; used in case citations to indicate that the official name of a case changed during the proceedings, usually after appeal (e.g., rev.'d sub nom. and aff'd sub nom.

SUB SILENTIO 'under silence'. A ruling, order, or other court action made without specifically stating the ruling, order, or action. The effect of the ruling or action is implied by related and subsequent actions, but not specifically stated.

SUBPOENA AD TESTIFICANDUM A more technical name for a subpeona. An order compelling attendance by a witness for the purpose of giv.ing testimony. The most common type of subpoena, ordering a witness to testify. *Pit Stop Auto Accessories v. Tan Kok Siang; The Minister of Communications [1974] 2 MLJ 79 Pg.79, 82, Tan Siew Sin v. Hasnul Bin Abdul Hadi [1967] 2 MLJ 191 Pg.191*

SUBPOENA DUCES TECUM 'bring with you under penalty'. An order compelling an entity to produce physical evidence or witness in a legal matter.

SUBPOENA 'Under a penalty." The title of a writ issued for summoning witnesses. 'Money paid in atonement; punishment, penalty'. A document which compels attendance by a witness or the production of evidence. The writ issued under authority of a court to compel the appearance of a witness or the production of evidence at a judicial proceeding. *Abdul Rahman Talib v. Seenivasagam & Anor [1965] 1 MLJ 142 Pg. 164*

SUBPOENA under a penalty; a judicial writ commanding appearance of a person under a penalty. A judicial writ commanding appearance of a person (generally a witness) under a penalty. See s 174 ill(a) IPC. The sole office of a writ subpoena is to bring the defendant into Court, in order that the Court may acquire jurisdiction over his person. Bouvier defines 'subpoena' as a 'process to cause a witness to appear and give testimony, commanding him to lay aside all pretences and excuses, and appear before a Court or Magistrate therein named at a time therein mentioned to testify for the party named under a penalty therein mentioned. The purpose of a subpoena is to place the witness under the order of the Court, and a writ which does not effect this is not subpoena within the meaning of the law. 'Subpoena' also meansna court order issued in court proceedings requesting the person to whom it is directed to attend a court at a specified place and time for the purpose of giving evidence, producing documents or both. Failure to comply attendance is contempt. In Ismail v Hasnul; Abdul Ghafar v Hasnul [1968] 1 MLJ 108 Raja Azlan Shah J, Pit Stop Auto Accessories v Tan Kock Siang; The Minister of Communications [1974] 2 MLJ 79. The court has inherent power to set aside a subpoena.

SUGGESTIO FALSI 'false suggestion'. A false statement made in the negotiation of a contract.

SUI GENERIS 'of its own kind'. Of its own genus or class, as distinguished from any other. *Chen Chi Ya v. K. Nagappan [1949] 15 MLJ 271 Pg.169, T. Mahesan V. Malaysia Government Officer's Cooperative Housing Society [1978] 1 MLJ 149 Pg. 152*

SUI JURIS 'of his own right'. Not dependent on the will or control of another. Of his own right; a term used to describe one who is no longer dependent upon others, e.g., one who has reached the age of majority. possessing the legal capacity to act in one's own behalf. enjoying all the rights of citizens, including the right to vote. In Re Maria Huberdina Hertogh; Adrianus Petrus

Hertogh and Anor v. Amina Binte Mohamed and Ors [1951] 17 MLJ at Pg.15; Shanti Rupchand Binwani Alias Shanti v. Udharam Dayaram Binwani [1951] 17 MLJ at Pg. 31; In The Matter of Maria Huberdina Hertogh, An Infant; Amina Binte Mohamed v. The Consul-General for The Netherland [1950] 16 MLJ at Pg.215; Tan Joo Hern and Anor. v. S. The Sze Hai Tong Banking Insurance Co. Ltd. and Ors. [1934] 3 MLJ 127 at Pg. 128

SUO MOTU 'on its own motion". It is used in situations where a Government or court official acts of its own initiative. *Public Prosecutor v. Datuk Haji Harun Bin Haji Idris & Ors [1977] 1 MLJ 180 Pg. 189, Superintendant of Lands and Surveys Sarawak v. Aik Hoe & co. Ltd [1966] 1 MLJ 243 at Pg. 251*

SUPERSEDEAS 'refrain from'. A bond tendered by an appellant as surety to the court, requesting a delay of payment for awards or damages granted, pending the outcome of the appeal.

SUPPRESSIO VERI 'suppression of the truth'. Willful concealment of the truth when bound to rev.eal it, such as withholding details of damage from an auto accident from a prospectiv.e buyer of the car in that accident.

SUPRA 'abov.e, ov.er, on top of'. Abov.e. In a written work, the word refers the reader from one reference or citation to a preceding section, phrase or citation. *Heng Yik Fang v. Public Prosecutor [1973] 1MLJ 193 Pg.194, Kersah La'usin v. Sikin Menan [1966] 2 MLJ 20 at Pg. 22; Public Prosecutor v. Lee Siew Ngock [1966] 1 MLJ 225 at Pg. 229, Lee Ah Low v. Cheong Lep Keen & Anor. [1970] 1 MLJ 7, at 10; Re Chai Kai Wooi [1970] 1 MLJ 34, at 36; Board of Governors of Sekolah Menengah St. Gabreal v. Ranjit Singh [1970] 1 MLJ 38, at 40; Mahadevan v. Anandarajan & Ors. [1970] 1 MLJ 50, at 54; Goh Yew & Anor v. Soh Kian Tee [1970] 1 MLJ 138, at 142; Yap Hong Thin & Anor v. Seenevasam [1970] 1 MLJ 143; B. H Oon & Ors. v. The Government of The State of Penang & Ors. [1970] 1 MLJ 244, at 245*

SUPRA above; the word or phrase having appeared in a previous part of the article or book.

T

TABULA RASA 'a smoothed' or 'planed tablet'. this expression is used by metaphysicians to indicate the state of the human mind before it has receiv. ed any impressions. the ancients used tablets cov.ered with wax, on which they wrote with an iron instrument called a stylus, one end of which was broad and flat, for obliterating what had been written by smoothing the wax. hence the expression. *In The Estate of Choo Kim Kiew (Deceased) [1949] 15 MLJ 144 Pg.145*

TALES DE CIRCUMSTANTIBUS 'practice. Such persons as are standing round. Whenever the panel of the jury is exhausted the court order that the jurors wanted shall be selected from among the bystanders which order bears the name of tales d circumstantibus. *Notes [1932] 1 MLJ 151 Pg.152, Tan Chye Choo & Ors v. Chong Kew Moi [1966] 2 MLJ 4 at Pg.7, Tan Hua Lam v. Public Prosecutor [1966] 1 MLJ 147 at Pg. 150, Tengku Besar Zabaidah v. Kong Cheng Whum [1969] 2 MLJ 228*

TERMINUS a boundary mark, limit, end, border.

TERRA FIRMA a 'solid land. *Liew yu fatt v. Teck Guan & Co. Ltd [1966] 1 MLJ 87 at Pg. 88*

TERRA earth; soil; arable land.

TERRA NULLIUS 'no one's land'. Land that has never been part of a sov.ereign state, or land which a sovereign state has relinquished claim to.

TESTAMENTUM a testament; a will, or last will.

Testatrix (testator) 'to bear witness'. It is the male and female forms of the word describing a person who dies leav.ing a v.alid will. one who makes a will, especially one who dies and leav.es a will. because testator has come to be applied to both sexes, the use of the feminine testatrix has become obsolete. Lim Eow Thoon & Anor v. Tan Peng Neoh [1950] 16 MLJ at Pg. 262

TESTIFICANDUM 'to give evidence, bear witness to'. literally "for testifying". Used to describe the process by which witnesses are compelled to testify; e.g., by a *subpoena ad testificandum. Phang Moh Shin v. Commissioner of Police & Ors [1967] 2 MLJ 186 Pg.187*

TESTIMONIA PONDERANDA SUNT NON NUMERANDA Section 134 of the Evidence Act 1950 follows the moxim, testimonia ponderanda sunt non numeranda, that testimony is to be weighed and not counted. 'More regard is to be paid to the character of the evidence adduced in support of case than to the number merely of the witness who gave it, for the evidence of two respectable and witnesses is to more value than of a dozen witnesses of notoriously abandoned nad profligate character. The court is concerned with the quality and not quality of evidence'

(Shankar at 1958). The weight to be attributed to evidence, testibus non testimoniis credendum est, depends upon the character and credibilty of a witness more than upon the probability or improbability of his statements. The value of the evidence given is to commensurate with the honesty and truthfulness of the witness; evidence as to an improbable fact spoken to by a witness above all suspicion deserves and receives more weight than the evidence of a doubtful or incredible witness regarding a fact itself very probable. *Khaw Cheng Bok v Khaw Cheng Poon [1998] 3 MLJ 457 at 584 Per Jeffrey Tan J*

TESTIMONIO an authentic copy of a deed or other instrument.

TESTIMONIUM proof, evidence, witness, indication; the clause at the end of the will certifying that the testator has signed in the presence of the witness.

That which is accorded to some and denied to others is not justice

THAVANAI LETTER *The Firm of Tarct. V. The Firm of S.N.Sarn. [1954] 20 MLJ at Pg. 72*

TOTO all together, completely towards.

TOUT COMPRENDrE, C'EST TOUT PARDONNER *Crime and Society; [1939] 8 MLJ v.iii- v.iv. at Pg. v.iii*

TRANSIT IN REM JUDICATAM 'The cause of action is changed into matter of record, which is of a higher nature, and the inferior remedy is merged in the higher'. It says that when the cause of action is changed into matter of record, which is of a higher nature, the inferior remedy is merged in the higher.' This principle does not apply where the judgment is foreign, since a foreign judgment is not considered to be of a higher nature than a domestic cause of action. The principle of transit in rem judicatam relates only to the particular cause of action in which the judgment is recov.ered, operating as a change of remedy from its being of a higher nature than before, *Syed Ismail v. Public Prosecutor [1967] 2 MLJ 123 Pg.128*

TRANSITU passage from one place to another.

TRIAL DE NOVO 'trial anew'. A completely new trial of a matter prev. iously judged. it specifically refers to a replacement trial for the previous one, and not an appeal of the previous decision.

TRINODA NECESSITAS 'three-knotted need'. It refers to a threefold tax levied on anglo-saxon citizens to cover roads, buildings, and the military.

TSIP *Chia Teck Leong & ors v. Estate & Trust Agencies (1927) Ltd [1939] 8 MLJ 96 at Pg.99; Limitation Ordinance*

TURPIS base; mean; vile; disgraceful; infamous; unlawful.

U

UBERRIMA FIDES 'abundant good faith'. Mostly, the term is used in insurance contracts. The term is used in the concept that both the parties to the contract should express all the material facts in an insurance contract in good faith. The insured should disclose all relev.ant facts to the insurer. *Abu Bakar v. Oriental Fire & General Insurance Co Ltd [1974] 1 MLJ 150 Pg.150, Ong Eng Chai v. China insurance co. Ltd [1974] 1 MLJ 82 Pg.82*

UBERRIMA FIDES 'rich, abundant; fully, completely, trust or confidence'. It means the the utmost good faith, such as the responsibility owed by an agent to his principal or by an attorney to his client. This phrase is used to express that a contract must be made in perfect good faith, concealing nothing; as in the case of insurance, the insured must observ.e the most perfect good faith towards the insurer. *National Insurance Co Ltd v. S. Joseph [1973] 2 MLJ 195 Pg.197*

UBI SUPRA 'above, over', where (stated or written) or above where cited. Above ordinarily shortened to the one word *supra*, the term refers to a prev.ious place in a text at which the same matter, case, v.olume and page, etc., is cited. *Yim Yip Kae & Anor V. Kwong Hock Cheong Sawmill & Co. Ltd. (1954) 20 MLJ at Pg.28; Toh Ah Moh v. Tungku Abdullah [1939] 8 MLJ 91 at Pg.92; Sunny Tay,*

Etc. v. Seow See Neo and Anor. [1934] 3 MLJ 83 at Pg. 89

ULTIMO in the last month.

ULTRA POSSE NEMO OBLIGATUR 'no one is obligated (to do) more than he can'. specifies that one should do what he can to support the community, but since everyone has different levels of ability, it cannot be expected that all will perform the same.

ULTRA VIRES 'beyond, power, strength'. Any act performed without authority. Acts by a corporation beyond the powers granted in its charter or articles of incorporation. Generally, acts performed by a corporation which are not permitted under the laws of the state of incorporation or the state(s) in which the corporation does business, or which, if they are permitted, are performed in an unlawful or irregular way. An *ultra vires* act, e.g., an *ultra vires* contract, is unenforceable. That which is beyond a corporation's or an agency's authorized power. A corporation's ultra vires activity may lead to its forfeiting its charter of incorporation. *Assa Singh v. Mentri Besar, Johore [1969] 2 MLJ 31; Karam Singh v. Menteri Hal Ehwal Dalam Negeri, Malaysia [1969] 2 MLJ 130, Arumugam Pillai v. Government of Malaysia [1975] 2 MLJ 29 Pg. 29; Selangor Pilot Association (1946) v. Government of Malaysia & ANOR [1975] 2 MLJ 66 Pg.68; Kee Peng Kwan v. Colonel v. N. Stevenson & Ors [1975] 2 MLJ 139 Pg.139; Sarawak Electricity Supply Corpn v. WangTeck Chai [1975] 2 MLJ 144 Pg.145; Government of*

Malaysia v. Mahan Singh [1975] 2 MLJ 155 Pg.157, B. v. Comptroller of Inland Revenue [1974] 2 MLJ 110 Pg.111; Yeoh Tat Thong v. Government of Malaysia & Anor [1974] 2 MLJ 119 Pg.119; Selangor Pilot Association v. Government of Malaysia & ANOR[1974] 2 MLJ 123 Pg.124; S. Nadarajah Pillay & Anor v. Hindu Development Board [1974] 2 MLJ 147 Pg.147; Public Prosecutor v. Lee Chin Chai [1974] 2 MLJ 174 Pg.175

UNIVERSUM universe; the world; universum jus means the whole world.

UNO FLATU 'in one breath'. It is used to criticize inconsistencies in speech or testimony, as in: one says one thing, and in the same breath, says another contradictory thing.

URATORES SUNT JUDICES FACTI 'jurors are the judges of fact' or juries are the judges of fact. In a trial by jury, while a judge decides questions of law and instructs the jury on matters of law, the facts in issue are solely within the province of the jury.

UT RES MAGIS V.ALEAT QUAM PEREAT'It is better for a thing to hav.e effect than to be made v.oid. A legal concept that stands for trying to coonstrue a law in a way to make sense, rather than v.oid it. The law should be given effect rather than be destroyed. *Stephen Kalong Ningkan v. Tun Abang Haji Openg and Tawi Sli [1966] 2 MLJ 187 at Pg. 191, Devi v. Francis [1969] 2 MLJ 171; Employees Provident Fund Board v. R. R. Chelliah Bros. [1969] 1 MLJ 165; New Zealand Insurance Co. Ltd v. Sinnadorai [1969] 1 MLJ 185; Stephen Kalong Ningkan v. Tun Abang Haji Openg and Tawi Sli [1966] 2 MLJ 187 at Pg. 191*

UT SIT FINIS LITIUM there should be finality of judgments.

UTI POSSIDETIS 'as you possess'. Ancient concept regarding conflicts, wherein all property possessed by the parties at the conclusion of the conflict shall remain owned by those parties unless treaties to the contrary are enacted.

UXOR 'wife'. It is used in documents in place of the wife's name. Usually abbreviated as '*et ux*'.

V

V.IRTUTE OFFICII 'By v.irtue of his office'. A sheriff, a constable, and some other officers may, v.irtute officii, apprehend a man who has been guilty of a crime in their presence. *Lim Ko & Anor v. Board Of Architects [1966] 2 MLJ 80 at Pg. 83*

VACATUR let it be vacated.

VADIUM pawn or pledge; bailment of goods when they are delivered to another as pawn to be security for money borrowed of him by the bailor.

VALENS strong, powerful, healthy, able, worthwhile.

VEL NON 'Whether or not. An inquiry into the existence or lack of existence of a issue or fact. The term is defined as summary of alternativ.es, ie. "this action turns upon whether the claimant was the deceased's grandson v.el non." Vel non is a term used by the courts in reference to the existence or nonexistence of an issue for determination; for example: "We come to the merits v.el non of this appeal," means "we come to the merits, or not, of this appeal," and refers to the possibility that the appeal lacks merit. *Mohamed adat & Ors. v. Public Prosecutor [1967] 2 MLJ 52*

VENIRE FACIAS DE NOVO A calling of a new jury panel for the purpose of holding a second trial, in cases where a first trial has failed to render a v.erdict. a judicial order for a new trial after the first trial is declared a mistrial due some impropriety or irregularity in the original jury's return or v.erdict so that no judgment can be given on it. For example, when the jury has been improperly chosen, or an uncertain, ambiguous or defectiv.e v.erdict has been rendered. The result of a new v.enire is a new trial. In substance, the writ is a motion for new trial, but when the party objects to the v.erdict because of an error in the course of the proceeding the form of motion was traditionally for a venire facias de novo. *Plea Bargaining [1970] 2 MLJ ii, at iii*

VERA COPULA true sexual intercourse formerly required for the legal consummation of marriage. It also means conjunction of bodies; Sexual intercourse per se; sexual union. The question, therefore, is what is meant by this 'conjunction of bodies' or, to use the Latin phrase, vera copula. There is no question in this case, but that full entry and penetration has been achieved. It is submitted on behalf of the wife that there is no vera copula unless there is not only full entry and pene-tration, but also completion of the act within the body of the woman, whether with or without the use of mechanical contraceptives. On the other hand, it is contended that there is a complete conjunction of bodies, a vera copula - which means literally 'true conjunction' - as soon as full entry and penetration has been achieved. What follows goes merely to the likelihood or otherwise of conception.

VERBA DE PRAESENTI It is a marriage by means of words of present assent. Marriage per verba de praesenti is a common-law marriage entered into by the parties by their joint consent, without the interposition of any person authorized to solemnize the marriage and without formal solemnization. *In Re Abraham Penhas, Deceased [1950] 16 MLJ at Pg.106, 107; In the Estate Of Yeow Kian Kee (Deceased) [1949] 15 MLJ 171 Pg.172*

VERBA FORTIUS CARTARUM ACCIPIUNTUR CONTRA PROFERENTEM 'words must be construed against those who use them.' When the words of a contract are ambiguous, of two equally possible meanings, they should be interpreted against the author, drafter or writer of the contract and not against the other party. The words used are to be receiv.ed and accepted in the strongest sense against the party using them, according to the maxim v.erba fortius accipiuntur contra proferentem. *Thambipillai v. Borneo Motors (M) Ltd. [1970] 1 MLJ 70, at 72*

VERBA POSTERIORA PROPTER CERTITUDINEM ADDITA, AD PRIORA QUAE CER-TITUDINE INDIGENT SUNT REFERENDA subsequent words, added for the purpose of certainty, are to be referred to the preceding words in which certainty is wanting.

VERBATIM 'word'. using or following the exact words. a word-for-word rendition or transciption of something spoken. a

verbatim transcript is a word-for-word record of testimony by a witness. To cite or quote something in a manner that corresponds word for word. it refers to being in identical words, repeated exactly, written down, or copied word for word. Murugappa Chettiar v. Krishnappa Chettiar & Other [1940] 9 MLJ 200 at Pg.203; Lau Tai Thye, Etc. v. Leong Yin Khean and Ors. [1934] 3 MLJ 110 at Pg.118; Sungei Biak Tin Mines Ltd v. Saw Choo Theng & Anor. [1970] 1 MLJ 199, at 200

VERBATIM ET LITERATIM 'to the word and to the letter'. like the word seriatim, neither of these words is really latin, hav.ing been coined probably in the middle ages. the correct latin would be. ad verbum et ad litetiam. *Jackson & Co Ltd V. Seng Seng [1954] 20 MLJ at Pg. 229; Tong Swee King v. Pedang mining co. Ltd & Anor [1967] 2 MLJ 214 Pg.218*

VERITAS NIHIL VERITUR NISI ABSCONDI truth fears nothing but concealment.

VETO 'I forbid'. The power of an executiv.e to prev.ent an action, especially the enactment of legislation

VEXATA vexed; nothing added newly.

VIA by way of.

VICE VERSA 'The terms being rev.ersed." Or "rev.ersely." Or 'rev.erse position'. in the opposite way. E.g. The responsibilities of the employer towards the employees and vice versa.

Mak Sik Kwong v. Minister of Home Affairs,Malaysia [1975] 2 MLJ168 Pg. 171; Thanimalai & Government of Malaysia v. Lee Ngo Yew [1975] 1 MLJ 125 Pg.126; Tan Thang Sang v. Public Prosecutor [1975] 1 MLJ 204 Pg.206, Tan Ah Seah v. Teo Kai Min & Ors [1954] 20 MLJ at Pg.52; Re Cheong Yuk Sim (f) Ex Parte, Cheong Mook Lim [1954] 20 MLJ at Pg.130; Gurunathan Chettiar & Anor v. Public Prosecutor [1939] 8 MLJ 177 at Pg.177, 178; Wah Tat Bank Ltd & Ors v. Chan Cheng Kum & Ors [1967] 2 MLJ 263 Pg.264

VIDE'see.' It is a citation signal, and is found in some texts. Usually, it is seen in the abbrev.iated form. For example, q.v., denoting 'quod vide,' meaning 'which see.' Used to direct a reader's attention. *Assa Singh v. Mentri Besar, Johore [1969] 2 MLJ 31; Cheong Kong Enterprise Co. Sdn. Bhd. v. Foong Seong Mines Ltd. & Ors. [1969] 2 MLJ 247; Dobb & Co. Ltd v. Hecla [1973] 2 MLJ 128 Pg.129, Re Low Nai Bros. & Co. [1970] 1MLJ 238, at 239; Ang Siew Hock & Ors. v. Ang Choon Koay [1970] 2 MLJ 149, at 150; Mohamed Isa & Ors. v. Abdul Karim & Ors. [1970] 2 MLJ 165, at 167*

VIDELICET CONTRACTION OF VIDERE LICET 'it is permitted to see'. It is used in documents to mean "namely" or "that is". It is usually abbreviated '*viz*'.

VIDELICET to wit, that is to say, namely. Abbn for viz: namely; to wit; that is to say.

VIGILANTIBUS NON DORMIENTIBUS AEQUITAS SUBVENIT 'Equity aids the v.igilant, not the sleeping'. Concept that if an opposing party unreasonably delays bringing an action, that it is no longer considered just to hear their claim, due to fundamental changes in circumstance brought upon by their delay.

VINCULUM FIDEI *In Re Estate of Abraham Penhas (Deceased) [1949] 15 MLJ 223 Pg.227*

VINCULUM JURIS 'the chains of the law'. It is something, which is legally binding.

VIS MAJOR 'greater or superior force'. Events ov.er which no humans hav.e control, and so cannot be held responsible or an 'Act of God'. In law, the more common term is the French phrase 'Force majeure'.

VIS-À-VIS 'in relation to; regarding', 'face to face with; opposite', 'face to face; opposite, 'a person or thing that is situated opposite to another'. *Devi v. Francis – A Critique [1970] 1 MLJ x, at x, xi; Devi v. Francis – A Reply [1970] 1 MLJ xlv.i, Tengku Korish v. Mohamed Bin Jusoh & Anor, Abdul Raouf v. Ibrahim Bin Arshad & Anor, Mokhtar Bin Abdullah v. Mokhtar Bin Haji Daud & Anor. [1970] 1 MLJ 6, at 7; Hon Yan Meng v. Esah [1970] 1 MLJ 126, at 127; Devi v. Francis – A Critique [1970] 1 MLJ x, at x, xi, xii, Gan Hong Hoe v. Gan Kim Hee [1939] 8 MLJ 227 at Pg.227; In Re Lai Teng Fong Deceased; Yap Kwee Ying v. Lai Kim Foh [1950] 16*

MLJ at Pg.38; Re Yap E. Boon [1933] 2 MLJ 217 Pg. 220; Golden Hope Rubber Estate Ltd. v. Muniammah & Ors [1965] 1 MLJ 5 Pg. 15; Syed Ahmad Al-Juneid & Ors. v. Reshty [1965] 1 MLJ 77 Pg. 81; Wong Chop Saow v. Public Prosecutor [1965] 1 MLJ 247 Pg. 247

VISE-VERSA 'reverse position' or in the opposite way. E.g. The responsibilities of the employer towards the employees and vice versa *Macphail & Co (Ipoh) Ltd. v. Oam Parkash [1969] 2 MLJ 20*

VIVA VOCE 'By the living voice'. By oral testimony. The voice that lives. Word of mouth. Expressed orally. The testimony of a witness given orally before the trier of facts, instead of by deposition or transcript from a former record. *Re Chai Kai Wooi[1970] 1 MLJ 34, at 35; Re Onkar Shrian [1970] 1 MLJ 28, at 28; Si Toh Fok Tiak Trading As Chop Wing Loong v. Chop Swee Kee & Co [1954] 20 MLJ at Pg. 49,50; Public Prosecutor v. Raman I, Raman II & Ayappan [1940] 9 MLJ 163 at Pg.172; Ch'ng Joo Tuan Neoh & Anor v.S. Khoo tek & Other [1932] 1 MLJ 141 Pg.148; Marian Rebello & P.A. Peries v. Harbans Singh [1933] 2 MLJ 279 Pg. 280 ; Re Chop Kwong Fook Seng [1934] 3 MLJ 34 at Pg. 35; Re Lee Kim Soo, Deceased [1949] 15 MLJ 10; Abraham Ho Ah Loke v. William Manson-Hing [1949] 15 MLJ 43 Pg.43*

VIVA VOCE with living voice or word of mouth. In relation to evidence, it means oral evidence as opposed to written evidence such as affidavits. The general rule clearly is that all evidence at a trial must be given viva voce and the witnesses must be subject to cross-examination in the usual way before the trial Judge, and depositions are admissible only after proof that the parties who made them cannot themselves be produced. In the present case, the parties and their witnesses were before the President, and it is therefore manifest that the reception in evidence of their depositions in a former trial ought not to have been allowed. *Si Toh Fok Tiak Trading as Chop Wing Loong v Chop Swee Kee & Co [1954] MLJ 49 at 50 Per Bellamy J.* They admit that no written notice was given to any of them by the mortgages to sell, that the mortgages left the entire management of the mortgage securities in their hands, and that the statement that they would proceed instantly to advertise the property for sale was made solely because no means could be found whereby the interest due on the mortgages could be paid or secured. This last statement has been displayed by documentary evidence, and by the viva voce examination of the defendant Cox as to the moneys in the defendants' hands, received by the, in respect of a loan negotiated in July for the plaintiffs, and left incomplete for some reason incompatible with their duty to the plaintiffs, then their clients.

VIZ 'it is permitted to see'. It is used as synonyms for 'namely', "that is to say", and "as follows". It is used to elaborate on what has already been said in more particular or precise language. *Public prosecutor v. Tanga Muthu [1940] 9 MLJ 18 at Pg.18; Cheow Keok v. Public Prosecutor [1940] 9 MLJ 103 at Pg.106; Frank Merrels & Others v. Wee Chin Koon*

[1940] 9 MLJ 212 at Pg.213; Murugappa Chettiar v. S. Seenivasagam [1940] 9 MLJ 217 at Pg.229; S. Seethainayagee Ammal v. M.R.M. Ramasamy Chettiar [1940] 9 MLJ 289 at Pg.290; Lim Kee Butt v. Public Prosecuter [1954] 20 MLJ at Pg.36; Nanyang Manufacturing Co. v. The Collector of Land Revenue Johore [1954] 20 MLJ at Pg. 69

VOID AB INITIO 'to be treated as invalid from the outset' **or** invalid and a nullity from its very inception or void from the very beginning; never having existed in the eyes of the law. A contract is *void ab initio* if it is for an illegal purpose or if it offends public policy. On the other hand, a contract which is v.alid but which can be rescinded or av.oided by one of the parties because of a wrong by the other party is not v.oid, but voidable.

VOIRE DIRE 'to see or speak'. Voir dire is a legal procedure conducted before trial in which the attorneys and the judge question of prospective jurors to determine if any juror is biased and/or cannot deal with the issues fairly, or if there is cause not to allow a juror to serve. Some of the reasons a juror might not decide a case fairly include knowledge of the facts, acquaintanceship with parties, witnesses or attorneys, occupation which might lead to bias; prejudice against the death penalty, or prev.ious experiences such as hav.ing been sued in a similar case. The v.oir dire process allows an attorney to challenge a prospectiv.e juror "for cause" if that person says or otherwise expresses a bias against the attorney's case. Each

attorney can also exercise a limited number of "peremptory" challenges for which no reason is required. Those individuals who are accepted by both attorneys are impaneled and sworn in as the jury. Voir dire may be directed at the jury pool as a group, asking for a show of hands, or by questioning prospectiv.e jurors individually. Voire dire may also be conducted by he judge in some cases. *Lim Seng Chuan v. Public Prosecutor [1977] 1 MLJ*

VOLENS he is said to be willing who either expressly consents or tacitly makes no opposition. It also means wishing, willing, favorable, agreeing to be injured. *IB Drennan v RF Greer [1957] MLJ 77 at 80 Per Buhagiar J* for the word *volenti* The learned judge was referred to two English authorities, the first of which was Dann v Hamilton [1939] 1 All ER 59 ; [1939] 1 KB 509, in which Asquith J (as he then was) said: As a matter of strict pleading, it seems that the plea of volenti is a denial of any duty at all and, therefore, of any breach of duty, and an admission of negligence cannot strictly be combined with the plea. The plea of volenti differs in this respect from the plea of contributory negligence, which is not raised in this case. The learned judge went on to say: There was some discussion in academic circles as to the correctness of that decision and the matter was alluded to in Slater v Clay Cross Co Ltd [1956] 2 All ER 625; [1956] 2 QB 264. It was again a case where what was being discussed was the defence of volenti non fit injuria. It becomes relevant in a rather curious way, because Denning

LJ giving the first judgment, referred to a note which Lord Asquith had written for the Law Quarterly Review in which he referred to criticisms that had been made of his judgment in Dann v Hamilton and said: The criticisms were to the effect that even if the volenti doctrine did not apply, there was here a cast iron defence on the ground of contributory negligence. I have since had the pleadings and my notes exhumed, and they very clearly confirm my recollection that contributory negligence was not pleaded. Not merely so, but my notes show that I encouraged counsel for the defence to ask for leave to amend by adding this plea, but he would not be drawn: why, I have no idea. As the case has been a good deal canvassed on the opposite assumption, I hope you will not grudge the space for this not unimportant corrigendum.

VOLENTI NON FIT INJURIA 'injury is not done to the willing' or no injury is done to a consenting party'. It is the notion that a person cannot bring a claim against another for injury, if said person willingly placed themselves in a situation where they knew injury could result. This applies only to those who are by law considered responsible for their actions. A legal maxim standing for the principle that no legal wrong is done to a person who consents. In tort law, it refers to the fact that one cannot usually claim damages when he has consented to the activ.ity or nuisance that causes the damages. In commercial law, it sometimes precludes claims by parties who enter into agreements, which persons of ordinary prudence would not entertain. *Halijah v. Velaitham [1966] 1 MLJ 192 at Pg. 192, 195, Jackson's Malaya Berhad v. Penang Port Commision [1973] 2 MLJ 27 Pg.27, Manlio Vasta v. Inter-Ocean Salvage & Towage Ltd [1954] 20 MLJ at Pg. 261; Halijah v. Velaitham [1966] 1 MLJ 192 at Pg. 192, 195; Abdul Rahman Talib v. Seenivasagam & Anor [1965] 1 MLJ 142 Pg. 155*

VOX POPULI, VOX DES the voice of the people is the voice of God.